COMMUNICATING
SEQUENTIAL
PROCESSES

Prentice-Hall International
Series in Computer Science

C. A. R. Hoare, Series Editor

Published

BACKHOUSE, R. C., *Syntax of Programming Languages, Theory and Practice*
de BAKKER, J. W., *Mathematical Theory of Program Correctness*
BJORNER, D. and JONES, C., *Formal Specification and Software Development*
CLARK, K. L. and McCABE, F. G., *micro-PROLOG: Programming in Logic*
DROMEY, R. G., *How to Solve it by Computer*
DUNCAN, F., *Microprocessor Programming and Software Development*
ELDER, J., *Construction of Data Processing Software*
GOLDSCHLAGER, L. and LISTER, A., *Computer Science: A Modern Introduction*
HEHNER, E. C. R., *The Logic of Programming*
HENDERSON, P., *Functional Programming: Application and Implementation*
HOARE, C. A. R., *Communicating Sequential Processes*
HOARE, C. A. R., and SHEPHERDSON, J. C., (eds) *Mathematical Logic and Programming Languages*
INMOS, LTD., *The Occam Programming Manual*
JACKSON, M. A., *System Development*
JONES, C. B., *Software Development: A Rigorous Approach*
JOSEPH, M., PRASAD, V. R., and NATARAJAN, N., *A Multiprocessor Operating System*
LEW, A., *Computer Science: A Mathematical Introduction*
MacCALLUM, I., *Pascal for the Apple*
REYNOLDS, J. C., *The Craft of Programming*
TENNENT, R. D., *Principles of Programming Languages*
WELSH, J. and ELDER, J., *Introduction to Pascal, 2nd Edition*
WELSH, J., ELDER, J., and BUSTARD, D., *Sequential Program Structures*
WELSH, J. and McKEAG, M., *Structured System Programming*

COMMUNICATING

SEQUENTIAL PROCESSES

C.A.R. HOARE

Professor of Computation
Oxford University

Prentice/Hall International

ENGLEWOOD CLIFFS, NEW JERSEY   LONDON   MEXICO   NEW DELHI
RIO DE JANEIRO SINGAPORE SYDNEY TOKYO TORONTO WELLINGTON

DEDICATION

to the programming profession

Library of Congress Cataloging in Publication Data

HOARE, C.A.R. (Charles Antony Richard), 1934–
Communicating sequential processes

Bibliography: p.
Includes index
1. Electronic digital computers—Programming.
2. Parallel processing (Electronic computers).
I. Title.
QA76.6.H57   1985   001.64'2   84-22324
ISBN 0-13-153271-5

British Library Cataloguing in Publication Data

HOARE, C.A.R.
Communicating sequential processes.—(Prentice-Hall International series in computer science)

1. Parallel processing (Electronic computers)
2. Operating systems (Computers)
I. Title
001.64'25   QA76.6
ISBN 0-13-153271-5

© 1985 by PRENTICE-HALL INTERNATIONAL, UK, LTD.

ISBN 0-13-153271-5

PRENTICE-HALL, INC., *Englewood Cliffs, New Jersey*
PRENTICE-HALL INTERNATIONAL, UK, LTD., *London*
PRENTICE-HALL OF AUSTRALIA PTY., LTD., *Sydney*
PRENTICE-HALL CANADA, INC., *Toronto*
PRENTICE-HALL HISPANOAMERICANA, S.A., *Mexico*
PRENTICE-HALL OF INDIA PRIVATE LIMITED, *New Delhi*
PRENTICE-HALL OF JAPAN, INC., *Tokyo*
PRENTICE-HALL OF SOUTHEAST ASIA PTE., LTD., *Singapore*
PRENTICE-HALL DO BRASIL LTDA., *Rio de Janeiro*
WHITEHALL BOOKS LIMITED, *Wellington, New Zealand*

Typeset by HBM Typesetting Ltd., Chorley, Lancashire.
Printed in Great Britain by A. Wheaton & Co. Ltd, Exeter

10 9 8 7 6 5 4 3 2 1

CONTENTS

v

FOREWORD

For a variety of reasons, this is a book eagerly awaited by all who knew it was in the making; to say that their patience has been rewarded would be an understatement.

A simple reason was that it is Tony Hoare's first book. Many know him from the lectures he has untiringly given all over the world; many more know him as the articulate and careful author of a number of articles (of great variety!) that became classics almost before the printer's ink had dried. But a book is a different medium: here the author can express himself without the usually stringent limitations of time or space; it gives him the opportunity of revealing himself more intimately and of covering a topic of wider span, opportunities of which Tony Hoare has made the best use we could hope for.

A more solid reason was derived from the direct contents of the book. When concurrency confronted the computing community about a quarter of a century ago, it caused an endless confusion, partly by the technically very different circumstances in which it emerged, partly by the accident of history that it introduced non-determinism at the same time. The disentanglement of that confusion required the hard work of a mature and devoted scientist who, with luck, would clarify the situation. Tony Hoare has devoted a major part of his scientific endeavours to that challenge, and we have every reason to be grateful for that.

The most profound reason, however, was keenly felt by those who had seen earlier drafts of his manuscript, which shed with surprising clarity new light on what computing science could—or even should—be. To say or feel that the computing scientist's main challenge is not to get confused by the complexities of his own making is one thing; it is quite a different matter to discover and show how a strict adherence to the tangible and quite explicit elegance of a few mathematical laws can achieve this lofty goal. It is here that we, the grateful readers, reap to my taste the greatest benefits from the scientific wisdom, the notational intrepidity, and the manipulative agility of Charles Antony Richard Hoare.

Edsger W. Dijkstra

PREFACE

This is a book for the aspiring programmer, the programmer who aspires to greater understanding and skill in the practice of an intellectually demanding profession. It is designed to appeal first to a natural sense of curiosity, which is aroused by a new approach to a familiar topic. The approach is illustrated by a host of examples drawn from a wide range of applications, from vending machines through fairy stories and games to computer operating systems. The treatment is based on a mathematical theory, which is described by a systematic collection of algebraic laws. The ultimate objective of the book is to convey an insight which will enable the reader to see both current and future problems in a fresh light, in which they can be more efficiently and more reliably solved; and even better, they can sometimes be avoided.

The most obvious application of the new ideas is to the specification, design, and implementation of computer systems which continuously act and interact with their environment. The basic idea is that these systems can be readily decomposed into subsystems which operate concurrently and interact with each other as well as with their common environment. The parallel composition of subsystems is as simple as the sequential composition of lines or statements in a conventional programming language.

This insight brings practical benefits. Firstly, it avoids many of the traditional problems of parallelism in programming—interference, mutual exclusion, interrupts, multithreading, semaphores, etc. Secondly, it includes as special cases many of the advanced structuring ideas which have been explored in recent research into programming languages and programming methodology—the monitor, class, module, package, critical region, envelope, form, and even the humble subroutine. Finally, it provides a secure mathematical foundation for avoidance of errors such as divergence, deadlock and non-termination, and for achievement of provable correctness in the design and implementation of computer systems.

11

I have tried hard to present the ideas in a logically and psychologically well-ordered sequence, starting with the simple basic operators, and progressing towards their more elaborate applications. An assiduous reader may study the book from cover to cover. But many readers will start with greater interest in some topics than others; and for their benefit each chapter of the book has been structured to permit judicious selection.

1. Each new idea is introduced by an informal description and illuminated by a number of small examples, which will probably be helpful to all readers.

2. The algebraic laws which describe the essential properties of the various operations will be of interest to those with a taste for mathematical elegance. They will also be of benefit for those who wish to optimize their system designs by means of correctness-preserving transformations.

3. The proposed implementations are unusual in that they use a very simple purely functional subset of the well-known programming language LISP. This will afford additional excitement to those who have access to a LISP implementation on which to exercise and demonstrate their designs.

4. The definitions of traces and specifications will be of interest to systems analysts, who need to specify a client's requirements before undertaking an implementation. They will also be of interest to senior programmers, who need to design a system by splitting it into subsystems with clearly specified interfaces.

5. The proof rules will be of interest to implementors who take seriously their obligation to produce reliable programs to a known specification, to a fixed schedule, and at a fixed cost.

6. Finally, the mathematical theory gives a rigorous definition of the concept of a process, and the operators in terms of which processes are constructed. These definitions are a basis for the algebraic laws, the implementations and the proof rules.

A reader may consistently or intermittently omit or postpone any of these topics which are of lesser interest, or which present greater difficulty of understanding.

The succession of chapters in the book has also been organized to permit judicious browsing, selection, or rearrangement. The earlier sections of Chapter 1 and Chapter 2 will be a necessary introduction for all readers, but later sections may be more lightly skimmed or postponed to a second pass. Chapters 3, 4 and 5 are independent of each other, and may be started in any combination or in any order, according to the interest and inclination of the reader. So if at any stage there is any difficulty of understanding, it is advisable to continue reading at the next section or even the next chapter, since there is a reasonable expectation that the omitted material will not be immediately required again. When such a requirement arises, there will often be an explicit backward reference, which can be followed when there is sufficient motivation to do so. I hope everything in the book will in the end be found interesting and rewarding; but not everyone will wish to read and master it in the order presented.

The examples chosen to illustrate the ideas of this book will all seem very small. This is deliberate. The early examples chosen to illustrate each new idea must be so simple that the idea cannot be obscured by the complexity or unfamiliarity of the example. Some of the later examples are more subtle; the problems themselves are of the kind that could generate much confusion and complexity; and the simplicity of their solution could be due to the power of the concepts used and the elegance of the notations in which they are expressed.

Nevertheless, each reader will be familiar, perhaps painfully familiar, with problems of far greater scope, complexity and importance than the examples appropriate for an introductory text. Such problems may seem to be intractable by any mathematical theory. Please do not give way to irritation or disillusion, but rather accept the challenge of trying to apply these new methods to existing problems. Start with some grossly over-simplified version of some selected aspect of the problem, and gradually add the complexities which appear to be necessary. It is surprising how often the initial over-simplified model will convey additional insight, to assist in the solution of the problem as a whole. Perhaps the model can serve as a structure on which complex detail can later be safely superimposed. And the final surprise is that perhaps some of the additional complexity turns out to be unnecessary after all. In such cases, the effort of mastering a new method receives its most abundant reward.

Notations are a frequent complaint. A student setting out to learn the Russian language often complains at the initial hurdle of learning the unfamiliar letters of the Cyrillic alphabet, especially since many of them have strange pronunciations. If it is any consolation, this should be the least of your worries. After learning the script, you must learn the grammar and the vocabulary, and after that you must master the idiom and style, and after that you must develop fluency in the use of the language to express your own ideas. All this requires study and exercise and time, and cannot be hurried. So it is with mathematics. The symbols may initially appear to be a serious hurdle; but the real problem is to understand the meaning and properties of the symbols and how they may and may not be manipulated, and to gain fluency in using them to express new problems, solutions, and proofs. Finally, you will cultivate an appreciation of mathematical elegance and style. By that time, the symbols will be invisible; you will see straight through them to what they mean. The great advantage of mathematics is that the rules are much simpler than those of a natural language, and the vocabulary is much smaller. Consequently, when presented with something unfamiliar it is possible to work out a solution for yourself, by logical deduction and invention rather than by consulting books or experts.

That is why mathematics, like programming, can be so enjoyable. But it is not always easy. Even mathematicians find it difficult to study new branches of their subject. The theory of communicating processes is a new branch of mathematics; programmers who study it start with no disadvantage over mathematicians; but they will end with the distinct advantage of putting their knowledge to practical use.

The material of the book has been tested by presentation in informal workshops as well as on formal academic courses. It was first designed for a one-semester Master's course in software engineering, though most of it could be presented in the final or even the second year of a Bachelor's degree in computing science. The main prerequisite is some acquaintance with high-school algebra, the concepts of set theory, and the notations of the predicate calculus. These are summarised on the first page of the glossary of symbols just after this preface. The book is also a suitable basis for an intensive one-week course for experienced programmers. In such a course, the lecturer would concentrate on examples and definitions, leaving the more mathematical material for later private study. If even less time is available, a course which ends after Chapter 2 is quite worthwhile; and even in a single hour's seminar it is possible, by careful selection, to get as far as the edifying tale of the five dining philosophers.

It is great fun to present lectures and seminars on communicating sequential processes, since the examples give scope for exercise of the histrionic skills of the lecturer. Each example presents a little drama which can be acted with due emphasis on the feelings of the human participants. An audience usually finds something particularly farcical about deadlock. But they should be constantly warned about the dangers of anthropomorphism. The mathematical formulae have deliberately abstracted from the motives, preferences, and emotional responses by which the lecturer "lends an air of verisimilitude to an otherwise bald and unconvincing tale". So one must learn to concentrate attention on the cold dry text of the mathematical formulae, and cultivate an appreciation for their elegant abstraction. In particular, some of the recursively defined algorithms have something of the breathtaking beauty of a fugue composed by J. S. Bach.

SUMMARY

Chapter 1 introduces the basic concept of a process as a mathematical abstraction of the interactions between a system and its environment. It shows how the familiar technique of recursion may be used to describe processes that last a long time, or forever. The concepts are explained first by example and by pictures; a more complete explanation is given by algebraic laws, and by an implementation on a computer in a functional programming language. The second part of the chapter explains how the behaviour of a process can be recorded as a trace of the sequence of actions in which it engages. Many useful operations on traces are defined. A process can be specified in advance of implementation by describing the properties of its traces. Rules are given to help in implementation of processes which can be proved to meet their specifications.

The second chapter describes how processes can be assembled together into systems, in which the components interact with each other and with their external environment. The introduction of concurrency does not by itself introduce any element of nondeterminism. The main example of this chapter is treatment of the traditional tale of the five dining philosophers. The second part of Chapter 2 shows how processes can be conveniently adapted to new purposes by changing the names of the events in which they engage. The chapter concludes with an explanation of the mathematical theory of deterministic processes, including a simple account of the domain theory of recursion.

The third chapter gives one of the simplest known solutions to the vexed problem of nondeterminism. Nondeterminism is shown to be a valuable technique for achieving abstraction, since it arises naturally from the decision to ignore or conceal those aspects of the behaviour of a system in which we are no longer interested. It also preserves certain symmetries in the definition of the operators of the mathematical theory. Proof methods for nondeterministic processes are slightly more complicated than those for deterministic processes, since it is necessary to demonstrate that every possible nondeterministic choice will result in a behaviour which meets the given specification. Fortunately, there are techniques for avoiding nondeterminism, and these are used extensively in Chapters 4 and 5. Consequently the study or mastery of Chapter 3 can be postponed until just before Chapter 6, in which the introduction of nondeterminism can no longer be avoided.

In the later sections of Chapter 3, there is given a complete mathematical definition of the concept of a nondeterministic process. This definition will be of interest to the pure mathematician, who wishes to explore the foundations of the subject, or to verify by proof the validity of the algebraic laws and other properties of processes. Applied mathematicians (including programmers) may choose to regard the laws as self-evident or justified by their utility; and they may safely omit the more theoretical sections.

Chapter 4 at last introduces communication: it is a special case of an interaction between two processes, one of which outputs a message at the same time as the other one inputs it. Thus communication is synchronized; if buffering is required on a channel, this is achieved by interposing a buffer process between the two processes. An important objective in the design of concurrent systems is to achieve greater speed of computation in the solution of practical problems. This is illustrated by the design of some simple systolic (or iterative) array algorithms. A simple case is a pipe, defined as a sequence of processes in which each process inputs only from its predecessor and outputs only to its successor. Pipes are useful for the implementation of a single direction of a communications protocol, structured as a hierarchy of layers. Finally, the important concept of an abstract data type is modelled as a subordinate process, each instance of which communicates only with the block in which it is declared.

Chapter 5 shows how the conventional operators of sequential programming can be integrated within the framework of communicating sequential processes. It may be surprising to experienced programmers that these operators enjoy the same kind of elegant algebraic properties as the operators of familiar mathematical theories; and that sequential programs can be proved to meet their specifications in much the same way as concurrent programs. Even the externally triggered interrupt is defined and shown to be useful, and subject to elegant laws.

Chapter 6 describes how to structure and implement a system in which a limited number of physical resources such as discs and line printers can be shared among a greater number of processes, whose resource requirements vary with time. Each resource is represented as a single process. On each occasion that a resource is required by a user process, a new *virtual* resource is created. A virtual resource is a process which behaves as if it were subordinate to the user process; but it also communicates with the real resource whenever required. Such communications are interleaved with those of other concurrently active virtual processes. So the real and virtual processes play the same roles as the monitors and envelopes of PASCAL PLUS. The chapter is illustrated by the modular development of a series of complete but very simple operating systems, which are the largest examples given in this book.

Chapter 7 describes a number of alternative approaches to concurrency and communication, and explains the technical, historical, and personal motives which led to the theory expounded in the preceding chapters. Here I acknowledge my great debt to other authors, and give recommendations and an introduction to further reading in the field.

ACKNOWLEDGEMENTS

It is a great pleasure to acknowledge the profound and original work of Robin Milner, expounded in his seminal work on a *Calculus for Communicating Systems*. His original insights, his personal friendship and his professional rivalry have been a constant source of inspiration and encouragement for the work which culminated in the publication of this book.

For the last twenty years I have been considering the problems of programming for concurrent computations, and the design of a programming language to ease those problems. During that period I have profited greatly by collaboration with many scientists, including Per Brinch Hansen, Stephen Brookes, Dave Bustard, Zhou Chao Chen, Ole-Johan Dahl, Edsger W. Dijkstra, John Elder, Jeremy Jacob, Ian Hayes, Jim Kaubisch, John Kennaway, T. Y. Kong, Peter Lauer, Mike McKeag, Carroll Morgan, Ernst-Rudiger Olderog, Rudi Reinecke, Bill Roscoe, Alex Teruel, Alastair Tocher and Jim Welsh.

Finally, my special thanks go to O.-J. Dahl, E. W. Dijkstra, Leslie M. Goldschlager, Jeff Sanders and others who have carefully studied an earlier draft of this text, and who have pointed out its errors and obscurities; and in particular to the participants in the Wollongong Summer School on the Science of Computer Programming in January 1983, the attendants at my seminar in the Graduate School of the Chinese Academy of Science, April 1983, and students of the M.Sc. in Computation at Oxford University in the years 1979 to 1984.

GLOSSARY OF SYMBOLS

LOGIC

Notation	Meaning	Example
$=$	equals	$x=x$
$\neq$	is distinct from	$x\neq x+1$
$\square$	end of an example or proof	
$P\wedge Q$	P and Q (both true)	$x\leq x+1\wedge x\neq x+1$
$P\vee Q$	P or Q (one or both true)	$x\leq y\vee y\leq x$
$\neg P$	not P (P is not true)	$\neg 3>5$
$P\Rightarrow Q$	if P then Q	$x<y\Rightarrow x\leq y$
$P\equiv Q$	P if and only if Q	$x<y\equiv y>x$
$\exists x.P$	there exists an x such that P	$\exists x.x>y$
$\forall x.P$	for all x, P	$\forall x.\ x<x+1$
$\exists x{:}A.P$	there exists an x in set A such that P	
$\forall x{:}A.P$	for all x in set A, P	

SETS

Notation	Meaning	Example
$\in$	is a member of	Napoleon $\in$ mankind
$\hat{\in}$	is not a member of	Napoleon $\hat{\in}$ Russians
$\{\ \}$	the empty set (with no members)	$\neg$Napoleon$\in\{\ \}$
$\{a\}$	the singleton set of a; a is its only member	$x\in\{a\}\equiv x=a$
$\{a,b,c\}$	the set with members a,b, and c	$c\in\{a,b,c\}$
$\{x\,|\,P(x)\}$	the set of all x such that $P(x)$	$\{a\}=\{x\,|\,x=a\}$
$A\cup B$	A union B	$A\cup B=\{x\,|\,x\in A\vee x\in B\}$
$A\cap B$	A intersect B	$A\cap B=\{x\,|\,x\in A\wedge x\in B\}$
$A-B$	A minus B	$A-B=\{x\,|\,x\in A\wedge\neg x\in B\}$

18

$A \subseteq B$	A is contained in B	$A \subseteq B \equiv \forall x: A . x \in B$
$A \supseteq B$	A contains B	$A \supseteq B \equiv B \subseteq A$
$\{x: A \mid P(x)\}$	the set of x in A such that $P(x)$	
$\mathbb{N}$	the set of natural numbers	$\{0,1,2,...\}$
$\mathbb{P}A$	the power set of A	$\mathbb{P}A = \{X \mid X \subseteq A\}$
$\bigcup_{n\geq 0} A_n$	union of family of sets	$\bigcup_{n\geq 0} A_n = \{x \mid \exists n \geq 0 . x \in A_n\}$
$\bigcap_{n\geq 0} A_n$	intersection of family of sets	$\bigcap_{n\geq 0} A_n = \{x \mid \forall n \geq 0 . x \in A_n\}$

FUNCTIONS

Notation	Meaning	
$f: A \to B$	f is a function which maps each member of A to a member of B	square: $\mathbb{N} \to \mathbb{N}$
$f(x)$	that member of B to which f maps x (in A).	
injection	a function f which maps each member of A to a distinct member of B.	$x \neq y \Rightarrow f(x) \neq f(y)$
f^{-1}	inverse of an injection f.	$x = f(y) \equiv y = f^{-1}(x)$
$\{f(x) \mid P(x)\}$	the set formed by applying f to all x such that $P(x)$	$\{y \mid \exists x . y = f(x) \wedge x \in C\}$
$f(C)$	the image of C under f	square $(\{3,5\}) = \{9,15\}$
$f \circ g$	f composed with g	$f \circ g (x) = f(g(x))$
$\lambda x . f(x)$	the function which maps each value of x to $f(x)$	$(\lambda x . f(x))(3) = f(3)$

TRACES

Section	Notation	Meaning	
1.5	$\langle \rangle$	the empty trace	
1.5	$\langle a \rangle$	the trace containing only a	(singleton sequence)
1.5	$\langle a,b,c \rangle$	the trace with three symbols a then b then c	
1.6.1	$^\wedge$	(between traces) followed by	$\langle a,b,c \rangle = \langle a,b \rangle ^\wedge \langle \rangle ^\wedge \langle c \rangle$
1.6.1	s^n	s repeated n times	$\langle a,b \rangle^2 = \langle a,b,a,b \rangle$
1.6.2	$s \upharpoonright A$	s restricted to A	$\langle b,c,d,a \rangle \upharpoonright \{a,c\} = \langle c,a \rangle$
1.6.5	$s \leq t$	s is a prefix of t	$\langle a,b \rangle \leq \langle a,b,c \rangle$
4.2.2	$s \overset{n}{\leq} t$	s is like t with up to n symbols removed	$\langle a,b \rangle \overset{2}{\leq} \langle a,b,d,c \rangle$
1.6.5	s in t	s is in t	$\langle c,d \rangle$ in $\langle b,c,d,a,b \rangle$
1.6.6	$\#s$	the length of s	$\#\langle b,c,b,a \rangle = 4$

1.6.6	$s{\downarrow}b$	the count of symbol b in s	$\langle b,c,b,a\rangle{\downarrow}b=2$
1.9.6	$s{\downarrow}c$	the communications on channel c recorded in s	$\langle c.1,a.4,c.3,d.1\rangle{\downarrow}c$ $=\langle 1,3\rangle$
1.9.2	$^{\wedge}/s$	flatten s	$^{\wedge}/\langle\langle a,b\rangle,\langle\rangle, \langle c\rangle\rangle$ $=\langle a,b,c\rangle$
1.9.7	$s;t$	s successfully followed by t	$(s^{\wedge}\langle\,\checkmark\rangle);t=s^{\wedge}t$
1.6.4	A^{*}	set of sequences with elements in A	$A^{*}=\{s|s{\upharpoonright}A=s\}$
1.6.3	s_0	the head of s	$\langle a,b,c\rangle_0=a$
1.6.3	s'	the tail of s	$\langle a,b,c\rangle'=\langle b,c\rangle$
1.9.4	$s[i]$	the ith element of s	$\langle a,b,c\rangle[1]=b$
1.9.1	$f^{*}(s)$	f star of s	$\text{square}^{*}(\langle 1,5,3\rangle)$ $=\langle 1,25,9\rangle$
1.9.4	$\bar{s}$	reverse of s	$\overline{\langle a,b,c\rangle}=\langle c,b,a\rangle$

I

SPECIAL EVENTS

Section	Notation	Meaning
1.9.7	$\checkmark$	success (successful termination),
2.6.2	$l.a$	participation in event a by process named l
4.1	$c.v$	communication of value v on channel c
4.5	$l.c$	channel c of a process named l
4.5	$l.c.v$	communication of message v on channel $l.c$
5.4.1	$\frac{1}{2}$	catastrophe (lightning)
5.4.3	$\circledx$	exchange
5.4.4	$\copyright$	checkpoint for later recovery
6.2	$acquire$	acquisition of a resource
6.2	$release$	release of a resource

PROCESSES

Section	Notation	Meaning
1.1	αP	the alphabet of process P
4.1	αc	the set of messages communicable on channel c
1.1.1	$a{\rightarrow}P$	a then P
1.1.3	$(a{\rightarrow}P\,|\,b{\rightarrow}Q)$	a then P choice b then Q (provided $a{\neq}b$)
1.1.3	$(x{:}A{\rightarrow}P(x))$	(choice of) x from A then $P(x)$
1.1.2	$\mu X{:}A.F(X)$	the process X with alphabet A such that $X{=}F(X)$
1.8.3	P/s	P after (engaging in events of trace) s
2.3	$P \parallel Q$	P in parallel with Q

2.6.2	$l:P$	P with name l
2.6.4	$L:P$	P with names from set L
3.2	$P \sqcap Q$	P or Q (non-deterministic)
3.3	$P \,[]\, Q$	P choice Q
3.5	$P \backslash C$	P without C (hiding)
3.6	$P \,|||\, Q$	P interleave Q
4.4	$P \gg Q$	P chained to Q
4.5	$P // Q$	P subordinate to Q
6.4	$l :: p // Q$	remote subordination
5.1	$P;Q$	P (successfully) followed by Q
5.4	$P^\wedge Q$	P interrupted by Q
5.4.1	$P \,\overset{\iota}{\vee}\, Q$	P but on catastrophe Q
5.4.2	$\hat{P}$	restartable P
5.4.3	$P \circledx Q$	P alternating with Q
5.5	$P \triangleleft b \triangleright Q$	P if b else Q
5.1	$*P$	repeat P
5.4	$b*P$	while b repeat P
5.4	$x := e$	x becomes (value of) e
4.2	$b!e$	on (channel) b output (value of) e
4.2	$b?x$	from (channel) b input to x
6.2	$l!e?x$	call of shared subroutine named l with value parameter e and results to x
1.10.1	P **sat** S	(process) P satisfies (specification) S
1.10.1	tr	an arbitrary trace of the specified process
3.7	ref	an arbitrary refusal of the specified process
5.5.2	$x^{\cdot}$	the final value of x produced by the specified process
5.5.1	$var(P)$	set of variables assignable by P
5.5.1	$acc(P)$	set of variables accessible by P
2.8.2	$P \sqsubseteq Q$	(deterministic) Q can do at least as much as P
3.9	$P \sqsubseteq Q$	(nondeterministic) Q is as good as P or better
5.5.1	$\mathcal{D}e$	expression e is defined

ALGEBRA

Term	Meaning	
reflexive	a relation R such that	xRx
antisymmetric	a relation R such that	$xRy \wedge yRx \Rightarrow x = y$
transitive	a relation R such that	$xRy \wedge yRz \Rightarrow xRz$
partial order	a relation $\leq$ that is reflexive, antisymmetric and transitive	

bottom	a least element $\perp$ such that	$\perp \leq x$
monotonic	a function f that respects a partial order	$x \leq y \Rightarrow f(x) \leq f(y)$
strict	a function f that preserves bottom	$f(\perp) = \perp$
idempotent	a binary operator f such that	$xfx = x$
symmetric	a binary operator f such that	$xfy = yfx$
associative	a binary operator f such that	$xf(yfz) = (xfy)fz$
distributive	f distributes through g if	$xf(ygz) = (xfy)g(xfz)$ $\wedge (ygz)fx = (yfx)g(zfx)$
unit	of f is an element 1 such that	$xf1 = 1fx = x$
zero	of f is an element 0 such that	$xf0 = 0fx = 0$

GRAPHS

Term	*Meaning*
graph	a relation drawn as a picture
node	a circle in a graph representing an element in the domain or range of a relation
arc	a line or arrow in a graph connecting nodes between which the pictured relation holds
undirected graph	graph of a symmetric relation
directed graph	graph of an asymmetric relation often drawn with arrows
directed cycle	a set of nodes connected in a cycle by arrows all in the same direction
undirected cycle	a set of nodes connected in a cycle by arcs or arrows in either direction

1 PROCESSES

1.1 INTRODUCTION

Forget for a while about computers and computer programming, and think instead about objects in the world around us, which act and interact with us and with each other in accordance with some characteristic pattern of behaviour. Think of clocks and counters and telephones and board games and vending machines. To describe their patterns of behaviour, first decide what kinds of event or action will be of interest; and choose a different name for each kind. In the case of a simple vending machine, there are two kinds of event

coin   the insertion of a coin in the slot of a vending machine.
choc   the extraction of a chocolate from the dispenser of the machine.

In the case of a more complex vending machine, there may be a greater variety of events

*in*1*p*   the insertion of one penny
*in*2*p*   the insertion of a two penny coin
small   the extraction of a small biscuit or cookie
large   the extraction of a large biscuit or cookie
*out*1*p*   the extraction of one penny in change

Note that each event name denotes an event *class*; there may be many occurrences of events in a single class, separated in time. A similar distinction between a class and an occurrence should be made in the case of the letter h, of which there are many occurrences spatially separated in the text of this book.

The set of names of events which are considered relevant for a particular description of an object is called its *alphabet*. The alphabet is a permanent predefined property of an object. It is logically impossible for an object to engage in an event outside its alphabet; for example, a machine designed to sell chocolates could not suddenly deliver a toy battleship. But the converse does not hold. A machine designed to sell chocolates may actually never do so—perhaps because it has not been filled, or it is broken, or nobody wants chocolates. But once it is decided that *choc* is in the alphabet of the machine, it remains so, even if that event never actually occurs.

The choice of an alphabet usually involves a deliberate simplification, a decision to ignore many other properties and actions which are considered to be of lesser interest. For example, the colour, weight, and shape of a vending machine are not described, and certain very necessary events in its life, such as replenishing the stack of chocolates or emptying the coin box, are deliberately ignored—perhaps on the grounds that they are not (or should not be) of any concern to the customers of the machine.

The actual occurrence of each event in the life of an object should be regarded as an instantaneous or an atomic action without duration. Extended or time-consuming actions should be represented by a pair of events, the first denoting its start and the second denoting its finish. The duration of an action is represented by the interval between the occurrence of its start event and the occurrence of its finish event; during such an interval, other events may occur. Two extended actions may overlap in time if the start of each one precedes the finish of the other.

Another detail which we have deliberately chosen to ignore is the exact timing of occurrences of events. The advantage of this is that designs and reasoning about them are simplified, and furthermore can be applied to physical and computing systems of any speed and performance. In cases where timing of responses is critical, these concerns can be treated independently of the logical correctness of the design. Independence of timing has always been a necessary condition of the success of high-level programming languages.

A consequence of ignoring time is that we refuse to answer or even to ask whether one event occurs exactly simultaneously with another. When simultaneity of a pair of events is important (e.g. in synchronization) we represent it as a single-event occurrence; and when it is not, we allow two potentially simultaneous event occurrences to be recorded in either order.

In choosing an alphabet, there is no need to make a distinction between events which are initiated by the object (perhaps *choc*) and those which are initiated by some agent outside the object (for example, *coin*). The avoidance of the concept of causality leads to considerable simplification in the theory and its application.

Let us now begin to use the word *process* to stand for the behaviour pattern of an object, insofar as it can be described in terms of the limited set of events selected as its alphabet. We shall use the following conventions.

1. Words in lower-case letters denote distinct events, e.g.,
   coin, *choc*, *in2p*, *out1p*,
   and so also do the letters, a, b, c, d, e.
2. Words in upper-case letters denote specific defined processes
   e.g. *VMS* the simple vending machine
   VMC the complex vending machine
   and the letters P, Q, R (occurring in laws) stand for arbitrary processes.
3. The letters x, y, z are variables denoting events.
4. The letters A, B, C stand for sets of events.
5. The letters X, Y are variables denoting processes.
6. The alphabet of process P is denoted αP, e.g.,
   $\alpha VMS = \{coin, choc\}$
   $\alpha VMC = \{in1p, in2p, small, large, out1p\}$

The process with alphabet A which never actually engages in any of the events of A is called $STOP_A$. This describes the behaviour of a broken object: although it is equipped with the physical capabilities to engage in the events of A, it never exercises those capabilities. Objects with different alphabets are distinguished, even if they never do anything. So $STOP_{\alpha VMS}$ might have given out a chocolate, whereas $STOP_{\alpha VMC}$ could never give out a chocolate, only a biscuit. A customer for either machine knows these facts, even if he does not know that both machines are broken.

In the remainder of this introduction, we shall define some simple notations to aid in the description of objects which actually succeed in doing something.

1.1.1 Prefix

Let x be an event and let P be a process. Then

$(x \rightarrow P)$ (pronounced "x then P")

describes an object which first engages in the event x and then behaves exactly as described by P. The process $(x \rightarrow P)$ is defined to have the same alphabet as P, so this notation must not be used unless x is in that alphabet; more formally

$\alpha(x \rightarrow P) = \alpha P$ provided $x \in \alpha P$

Examples

X1   A simple vending machine which consumes one coin before breaking

$(coin \rightarrow STOP_{\alpha VMS})$ □

X2   A simple vending machine that successfully serves two customers before breaking

$(coin \rightarrow (choc \rightarrow (coin \rightarrow (choc \rightarrow STOP_{\alpha VMS}))))$

Initially, this machine will accept insertion of a coin in its slot, but will not allow a chocolate to be extracted. But after the first coin is inserted, the coin slot closes until a chocolate is extracted. This machine will not accept two coins in a row, nor will it give out two consecutive chocolates.   □

In future, we shall omit brackets in the case of linear sequences of events, like those in X2, on the convention that $\rightarrow$ is right associative.

X3   A counter starts on the bottom left square of a board, and can move only up or right to an adjacent white square

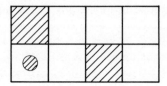

$\alpha CTR = \{up,\ right\}$
$CTR = (right \rightarrow up \rightarrow right \rightarrow right \rightarrow STOP_{\alpha CTR})$ □

Note that the operator $\rightarrow$ always takes a process on the right and a *single event* on the left. If P and Q are processes, it is syntactically incorrect to write

$P \rightarrow Q$

The correct method of describing a process which behaves first like P and then like Q is described in Chapter 4. Similarly, if x and y are events, it is syntactically incorrect to write

$x \rightarrow y$

Such a process could be correctly described

$x \rightarrow (y \rightarrow STOP)$

Thus we carefully distinguish the concept of an event from that of a process which engages in events—maybe many events or even none.

1.1.2 Recursion

The prefix notation can be used to describe the entire behaviour of a process that eventually stops. But it would be extremely tedious to write out the full behaviour of a vending machine for its maximum design life; so we need a method of describing repetitive behaviour patterns by much shorter notations. Preferably these notations should not require a prior decision on the length of the life of an object; this will permit description of objects which will continue to act and interact with their environment for as long as they are needed.

Consider the simplest possible everlasting object, a clock which never does anything but tick (the act of winding it is deliberately ignored)

$$\alpha CLOCK = \{tick\}$$

Consider next an object that behaves exactly like the clock, except that it first emits a single *tick*

$$(tick \rightarrow CLOCK)$$

The behaviour of this object is indistinguishable from that of the original clock. This reasoning leads to formulation of the equation

$$CLOCK = (tick \rightarrow CLOCK)$$

This can be regarded as an implicit definition of the behaviour of the clock, in the same way that the square root of two might be defined as the positive solution for x in the equation

$$x = x^2 + x - 2$$

The equation for the clock has some obvious consequences, which are derived by simply substituting equals for equals

$$
\begin{aligned}
CLOCK &= (tick \rightarrow CLOCK) & &\text{original equation} \\
&= (tick \rightarrow (tick \rightarrow CLOCK)) & &\text{by substitution} \\
CLOCK &= (tick \rightarrow tick \rightarrow tick \rightarrow CLOCK) & &\text{similarly}
\end{aligned}
$$

The equation can be unfolded as many times as required, and the possibility of further unfolding will still be preserved. The potentially unbounded behaviour of the *CLOCK* has been effectively defined as

$$tick \rightarrow tick \rightarrow tick \rightarrow \cdots$$

in the same way as the square root of two can be thought of as the limit of a series of decimals

1.414 ...

This method of self-referential or recursive definition of processes will work properly only if the right-hand side of the equation starts with at least one event prefixed to all recursive occurrences of the process name. For example, the recursive equation

$X = X$

does not succeed in defining anything, since everything is a solution to this equation. A process description which begins with a prefix is said to be *guarded*. If $F(X)$ is a guarded expression containing the process name X, and A is the alphabet of X, then we claim that the equation

$X = F(X)$

has an unique solution with alphabet A. It is sometimes convenient to denote this solution by the expression

$\mu X{:}A.F(X)$

Here X is a local name (bound variable), and can be changed at will, since

$\mu X{:}A.F(X) = \mu Y{:}A.F(Y)$

This equality is justified by the fact that a solution for X in the equation

$X = F(X)$

is also a solution for Y in the equation

$Y = F(Y)$

In future, we will give recursive definitions of processes either by equations, or by use of μ, whichever is more convenient. In the case of $\mu X{:}A.F(X)$, we shall often omit explicit mention of the alphabet A, where this is obvious from the content or context of the process.

Examples

X1   A perpetual clock

$CLOCK = \mu X{:}\{tick\}.\ (tick \rightarrow X)$ □

X2   At last, a simple vending machine which serves as many chocs as required

$VMS = (coin \rightarrow (choc \rightarrow VMS))$

As explained above, this equation is just an alternative for the more formal definition

$VMS = \mu X{:}\{coin,choc\}.\ (coin \rightarrow (choc \rightarrow X))$ □

X3 A machine that gives change for 5p repeatedly

$$\alpha CH5A = \{in5p, \ out2p, \ out1p\}$$
$$CH5A = (in5p \rightarrow out2p \rightarrow out1p \rightarrow out2p \rightarrow CH5A) \qquad \square$$

X4 A different change-giving machine with the same alphabet

$$CH5B = (in5p \rightarrow out1p \rightarrow out1p \rightarrow out1p \rightarrow out2p \rightarrow CH5B) \qquad \square$$

The claim that guarded equations have a solution, and that this solution is unique, may be informally justified by the method of substitution. Each time that the right-hand side of the equation is substituted for every occurrence of the process name, the expression defining the behaviour of the process gets longer, and so describes a longer initial segment of behaviour. Any finite amount of behaviour can be determined in this way. Two objects which behave the same up to every moment in time have the same behaviour, i.e., they are the same process. Those who find this reasoning incomprehensible or unconvincing should accept the claim as an axiom, whose value and relevance will gradually become more apparent. A more formal proof cannot be given without some mathematical definition of exactly what a process is. This will be done in Section 2.8.3. The account of recursion given here relies heavily on guardedness of recursive equations. A meaning for unguarded recursions will be discussed in Section 3.8.

1.1.3 Choice

By means of prefixing and recursion it is possible to describe objects with a single possible stream of behaviour. However, many objects allow their behaviour to be influenced by interaction with the environment within which they are placed. For example, a vending machine may offer a choice of slots for inserting a 2p coin or a 1p coin; and it is the customer that decides between these two events. If x and y are distinct events

$$(x \rightarrow P \,|\, y \rightarrow Q)$$

describes an object which initially engages in either of the events x or y. After the first event has occurred, the subsequent behaviour of the object is described by P if the first event was x, or by Q if the first event was y. Since x and y are different events, the choice between P and Q is determined by the first event that actually occurs. As before, we insist on constancy of alphabets, i.e.,

$$\alpha(x \rightarrow P \,|\, y \rightarrow Q) = \alpha P \qquad \text{provided } \{x,y\} \subseteq \alpha P \text{ and } \alpha P = \alpha Q$$

The bar $|$ should be pronounced "choice": "x then P choice y then Q"

Examples

X1   The possible movements of a counter on the board

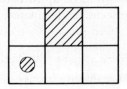

are defined by the process

$$(up \rightarrow STOP \mid right \rightarrow right \rightarrow up \rightarrow STOP)$$ □

X2   A machine which offers a choice of two combinations of change for 5p (compare 1.1.2 X3 and X4, which offer no choice)

$$CH5C = in5p \rightarrow (out1p \rightarrow out1p \rightarrow out1p \rightarrow out2p \rightarrow CH5C$$
$$\mid out2p \rightarrow out1p \rightarrow out2p \rightarrow CH5C)$$

The choice is exercised by the customer of the machine.   □

X3   A machine that serves either chocolate or toffee on each transaction

$$VMCT = \mu X.coin \rightarrow (choc \rightarrow X \mid toffee \rightarrow X)$$ □

X4   A more complicated vending machine, which offers a choice of coins and a choice of goods and change

$$VMC = (in2p \rightarrow (large \rightarrow VMC$$
$$\mid small \rightarrow out1p \rightarrow VMC)$$
$$\mid in1p \rightarrow (small \rightarrow VMC$$
$$\mid in1p \rightarrow (large \rightarrow VMC$$
$$\mid in1p \rightarrow STOP)))$$

Like many complicated machines, this has a design flaw. It is often easier to change the user manual than correct the design, so we write a notice on the machine

"WARNING: do not insert three pennies in a row."   □

X5   A machine that allows its customer to sample a chocolate, and trusts him to pay after. The normal sequence of events is also allowed

$$VMCRED = \mu X.(coin \rightarrow choc \rightarrow X$$
$$\mid choc \rightarrow coin \rightarrow X)$$ □

X6 To prevent loss, an initial payment is exacted for the privilege of using VMCRED

$$VMS2 = (coin \rightarrow VMCRED)$$

This machine will allow insertion of up to two consecutive coins before extraction of up to two consecutive chocolates; but it will never give out more chocolates than have been previously paid for. □

X7 A copying process engages in the following events

$in.0$ input of zero on its input channel
$in.1$ input of one on its input channel
$out.0$ output of zero on its output channel
$out.1$ output of one on its output channel

Its behaviour consists of a repetition of pairs of events. On each cycle, it inputs a bit and outputs the same bit

$$COPYBIT = \mu X.(in.0 \rightarrow out.0 \rightarrow X$$
$$| in.1 \rightarrow out.1 \rightarrow X)$$

Note how this process allows its environment to choose which value should be input, but no choice is offered in the case of output. That will be the main difference between input and output in our treatment of communication in Chapter 4. □

The definition of choice can readily be extended to more than two alternatives, e.g.,

$$(x \rightarrow P | y \rightarrow Q | ... | z \rightarrow R)$$

Note that the choice symbol $|$ is *not* an operator on processes; it would be syntactically incorrect to write $P | Q$, for processes P and Q. The reason for this rule is that we want to avoid the problem of giving a meaning to

$$(x \rightarrow P) | (x \rightarrow Q)$$

which appears to offer a choice of first event, but actually fails to do so. This problem is solved, at the expense of introducing nondeterminism, in Section 3.3. Meanwhile, if x,y,z are distinct events,

$$(x \rightarrow P | y \rightarrow Q | z \rightarrow R)$$

should be regarded as a single operator with three arguments P, Q, R. It cannot be regarded as equal to

$$(x \rightarrow P | (y \rightarrow Q | z \rightarrow R))$$

which is syntactically incorrect.

In general, if B is any set of events and $P(x)$ is an expression defining a process for each different x in B, then

$$(x:B \to P(x))$$

defines a process which first offers a choice of any event y in B, and then behaves like $P(y)$. It should be pronounced "x from B then P of x". In this construction, x is a local variable, so

$$(x:B \to P(x)) = (y:B \to P(y))$$

The set B defines the initial *menu* of the process, since it gives the set of actions between which a choice is to be made at the start.

Example

X8   A process which at all times can engage in any event of its alphabet A

$$\alpha RUN_A = A$$
$$RUN_A = (x:A \to RUN_A) \qquad \qquad \Box$$

In the special case that the initial menu contains only one event e,

$$(x:\{e\} \to P(x)) = (e \to P(e))$$

since e is the only possible initial event. In the even more special case that the initial menu is empty, nothing at all can happen, so

$$(x:\{\} \to P(x)) = (y:\{\} \to Q(y)) = STOP$$

The binary choice operator $|$ can also be defined using the more general notation

$$(a \to P \,|\, b \to Q) = (x:B \to R(x))$$

where $B = \{a,b\}$

and $R(x) = $ **if** $x = a$ **then** P **else** Q

Choice between three or more alternatives can be similarly expressed. Thus choice, prefixing and $STOP$ are defined as just special cases of the general choice notation. This will be a great advantage in the formulation of general laws governing processes (Section 1.3), and in their implementation (Section 1.4).

1.1.4 Mutual recursion

Recursion permits the definition of a single process as the solution of a single equation. The technique is easily generalized to the solution of sets of simultaneous equations in more than one unknown. For this to work properly, all the right-hand sides must be guarded, and each unknown process must appear exactly once on the left-hand side of one of the equations.

Example

X1 A drinks dispenser has a knob with two settings, labelled ORANGE and LEMON. The actions of setting the knob are *setorange* and *setlemon*. The actions of dispensing a drink are *orange* and *lemon*. The knob is initially in a neutral position, to which it never returns. Here are the equations defining the alphabet and behaviour of three processes

$$\alpha DD = \alpha G = \alpha W = \{setorange,\ setlemon,\ coin,\ orange,\ lemon\}$$
$$DD = (setorange \rightarrow G \,|\, setlemon \rightarrow W)$$
$$G\ \ = (coin \rightarrow orange \rightarrow G \,|\, setlemon \rightarrow W)$$
$$W\ \ = (coin \rightarrow lemon \rightarrow W \,|\, setorange \rightarrow G)$$

Informally, after the first event the drinks dispenser may be described as being in a particular one of the two states G and W. In each state it may either serve the appropriate drink or be switched to the other state. ☐

By using indexed variables, it is possible to specify infinite sets of equations.

Example

X2 An object starts on the ground, and may move *up*. At any time thereafter it may move *up* or *down*, except that when on the ground it cannot move any further down. But when it is on the ground, it may move *around*. Let n range over the natural numbers $\{0,1,2, \ldots\}$. For each n, introduce the indexed name CT_n to describe the behaviour of the object when it is n moves off the ground. Its initial behaviour is defined as

$$CT_0 = (up \rightarrow CT_1 \,|\, around \rightarrow CT_0)$$

and the remaining infinite set of equations consists of

$$CT_{n+1} = (up \rightarrow CT_{n+2} \,|\, down \rightarrow CT_n)$$

where n ranges over the natural numbers $0,1,2, \ldots$

An ordinary inductive definition is one whose validity depends on the fact that the right hand side of each equation uses only indices less than that of the left hand side. Here, CT_{n+1} is defined in terms of CT_{n+2}, and so this can be regarded only as an infinite set of mutually recursive definitions, whose validity depends on the fact that the right hand side of each equation is guarded.   □

1.2 PICTURES

It may be helpful sometimes to make a pictorial representation of a process as a tree structure, consisting of circles connected by arrows. In the traditional terminology of state machines, the circles represent states of the process, and the arrows represent transitions between the states. The single circle at the root of the tree (usually drawn at the top of the page) is the starting state; and the process moves downward along the arrows. Each arrow is labelled by the event which occurs on making that transition. The arrows leading from the same node must all have different labels.

Examples (1.1.1 X1, X2; 1.1.3 X3)

In these three examples, every branch of each tree ends in $STOP$, represented as a circle with no arrows leading out of it. To represent processes with unbounded behaviour it is necessary to introduce another convention, namely an unlabelled arrow leading from a leaf circle back to some earlier circle in the tree. The convention is that when a process reaches the node at the tail of the arrow, it immediately and imperceptibly goes back to the node to which the arrow points.

X4   **X5**

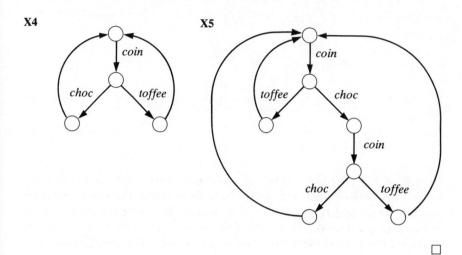

Clearly, these two different pictures illustrate exactly the same process (1.1.3 X3). It is one of the weaknesses of pictures that proofs of such an equality are difficult to conduct pictorially.

Another problem with pictures is that they cannot illustrate processes with a very large or infinite number of states, for example CT_0

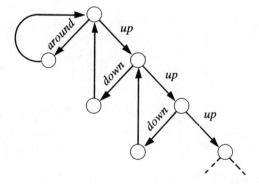

There is never room enough to draw the whole picture. A counter with only 65 536 different states would take a long time to draw.

1.3   LAWS

Even with the very restricted set of notations introduced so far, there are many different ways of describing the same behaviour. For example, it obviously should not matter in which order a choice between events is presented

$$(x{\rightarrow}P\,|\,y{\rightarrow}Q) = (y{\rightarrow}Q\,|\,x{\rightarrow}P).$$

On the other hand, a process that can do something is not the same as one that cannot do anything

$$(x{\rightarrow}P) \neq STOP$$

In order to understand a notation properly and to use it effectively, we must learn to recognize which expressions describe the same object and which do not, just as everyone who understands arithmetic knows that $(x+y)$ is the same number as $(y+x)$. Identity of processes with the same alphabet may be proved or disproved by appeal to algebraic laws very like those of arithmetic.

The first law (L1 below) deals with the choice operator (1.1.3). It states that two processes defined by choice are different if they offer different choices on the first step, or if after the same first step they behave differently. However, if the initial choices are the same, and for each initial choice the subsequent behaviours are the same, then obviously the processes are identical.

L1 $(x{:}A{\rightarrow}P(x))=(y{:}B{\rightarrow}Q(y)) \equiv (A=B \ \wedge \ \forall x{\in}A. \ P(x)=Q(x))$

Here and elsewhere, we assume without stating it that the alphabets of the processes on each side of an equation are the same.

The law L1 has a number of consequences

L1A $STOP \neq (d{\rightarrow}P)$
Proof. LHS $= (x{:}\{\}{\rightarrow}P)$ by definition (1.1.3 end)
                $\neq (x{:}\{d\}{\rightarrow}P)$ because $\{\} \neq \{d\}$
                $= $ RHS   by definition (1.1.3 end)

L1B $(c{\rightarrow}P) \neq (d{\rightarrow}Q)$ if $c \neq d$
Proof. $\{c\} \neq \{d\}$

L1C $(c{\rightarrow}P\,|\,d{\rightarrow}Q)=(d{\rightarrow}Q\,|\,c{\rightarrow}P)$
Proof. Define $R(x)=P$ if $x=c$
                  $=Q$ if $x=d$

LHS $=(x{:}\{c,d\}{\rightarrow}R(x))$	by definition
$=(x{:}\{d,c\}{\rightarrow}R(x))$	because $\{c,d\}=\{d,c\}$
$=$ RHS	by definition

L1D $(c{\rightarrow}P)=(c{\rightarrow}Q)\equiv P=Q$
Proof. $\{c\}=\{c\}$.

These laws permit proof of simple theorems.

Examples

X1 $(coin{\rightarrow}choc{\rightarrow}coin{\rightarrow}choc{\rightarrow}STOP)\neq(coin{\rightarrow}STOP)$
Proof: by L1D then L1A.   □

X2 $\mu X.(coin{\rightarrow}(choc{\rightarrow}X\,|\,toffee{\rightarrow}X))$
        $=\mu X.(coin{\rightarrow}(toffee{\rightarrow}X\,|\,choc{\rightarrow}X))$
Proof: by L1C.   □

To prove more general theorems about recursively defined processes, it is necessary to introduce a law which states that every properly guarded recursive equation has only one solution.

L2 If $F(X)$ is a guarded expression,

$$(Y=F(Y))\equiv(Y=\mu X.F(X))$$

An immediate but important corollary states that $\mu X.F(X)$ is indeed a solution of the relevant equation

L2A $\mu X.F(X)=F(\mu X.F(X))$

Example

X3 Let $VM1=(coin{\rightarrow}VM2)$
     and $VM2=(choc{\rightarrow}VM1)$

Required to prove $VM1=VMS$.

Proof. $VM1=(coin{\rightarrow}VM2)$	def. $VM1$
$=(coin{\rightarrow}(choc{\rightarrow}VM1))$	def. $VM2$

Therefore $VM1$ is a solution of the same recursive equation as VMS. Since the equation is guarded, there is only one solution. So *VM1* and *VMS* are just different names for this unique solution.

This theorem may seem so obviously true that its proof in no way adds to its credibility. The only purpose of the proof is to show by example that the laws are powerful enough to establish facts of this kind. When proving obvious facts from less obvious laws, it is important to justify every line of the proof in full, as a check that the proof is not circular.   □

The law L2 can be extended to mutual recursion. A set of mutually recursive equations can be written in the general form using subscripts

$$X_i = F(i,X) \qquad \text{for all } i \text{ in } S$$

where S is an indexing set with one member for each equation,
and X is an *array* of processes with indices ranging over the set S,
and $F(i,X)$ is a guarded expression.

Under these conditions, the law L3 states that there is only one array X whose elements satisfies all the equations

L3   Under the conditions explained above

if $(\forall i:S.(X_i = F(i,X) \wedge Y_i = F(i,Y)))$ then $X = Y$

1.4   IMPLEMENTATION OF PROCESSES

Every process P expressible in the notations introduced so far can be written in the form

$$(x:B \rightarrow F(x))$$

where F is a function from symbols to processes, and where B may be empty (in the case of *STOP*), or may contain only one member (in the case of prefix), or may contain more than one member (in the case of choice). In the case of a recursively defined process, we have insisted that the recursion should be guarded, so that it may be written

$$\mu X.(x:B \rightarrow F(x,X))$$

and this may be unfolded to the required form using L2A

$$(x:B \rightarrow F(x,\mu X.(x:B \rightarrow F(x,X))))$$

Thus every process may be regarded as a *function F* with a domain B, defining the set of events in which the process is initially prepared to engage; and for each x in B, $F(x)$ defines the future behaviour of the process if the first event was x.

This insight permits every process to be represented as a function in some suitable functional programming language such as LISP. Each event in the alphabet of a process is represented as an atom, for example *"COIN*, *"TOFFEE*. A process is a function which can be applied to such a symbol as argument. If the symbol is *not* a possible first event for the process, the function gives as its result a special symbol *"BLEEP*, which is used only for this purpose. For example, since *STOP* never engages in any event, this is the only result it can ever give, and so it is defined

$$STOP = \lambda x."BLEEP$$

But if the actual argument is a possible event for the process, the function gives back as its result another function, representing the subsequent behaviour of the process. Thus $(coin \rightarrow STOP)$ is represented as the function

$\lambda x.$ if $x = "COIN$ then $STOP$
            else $"BLEEP$

This last example takes advantage of the facility of LISP for returning a function (e.g., *STOP*) as the result of a function. LISP also allows a function to be passed as an argument to a function, a facility used in representing a general prefixing operation $(c \rightarrow P)$

$prefix(c,P) = \lambda x.$ if $x = c$ then P
                        else $"BLEEP$

A function to represent a general binary choice $(c \rightarrow P \,|\, d \rightarrow Q)$ requires four parameters

$choice2(c,P,d,Q) = \lambda x.$ if $x = c$ then P
                              else if $x = d$ then Q
                                      else $"BLEEP$

Recursively defined processes may be represented with the aid of the *LABEL* feature of LISP. For example, the simple vending machine $(\mu X.coin \rightarrow choc \rightarrow X)$ is represented as

$$LABEL\ X.prefix("COIN, prefix\ ("CHOC,X))$$

The *LABEL* may also be used to represent mutual recursion. For example *CT* (1.1.4 X2) may be regarded as a function from natural numbers to processes (which are themselves functions—but let not that be a worry). So *CT* may be defined

$CT = LABEL\ X.\lambda n.$
      if $n = 0$ then $choice2("AROUND,X(0),"UP,X(1))$
            else $choice2("UP,X(n+1),"DOWN,X(n-1))$

The process that starts on the ground is $CT(0)$.

If P is a function representing a process, and A is a list containing the symbols of its alphabet, the LISP function

$menu(A,P)$

gives a list of all those symbols of A which can occur as the first event in tħe life of P

$menu(A,P) =$ **if** $A = NIL$ **then** NIL
  else if $P(car(A)) = "BLEEP$ **then** $menu(cdr(A),P)$
    else $cons(car(A),\ menu(cdr(A),P))$

If x is in $menu(A,P)$, $P(x)$ is not $"BLEEP$, and is therefore a function defining the future behaviour of P after engaging in x. Thus if y is in $menu(A,P(x))$, then $P(x)(y)$ will give its later behaviour, after both x and y have occurred. This suggests a useful method of exploring the behaviour of a process. Write a program which first outputs the value of $menu(A,P)$ on a screen, and then inputs a symbol from the keyboard. If the symbol is not in the menu, it should be greeted with an audible bleep and then ignored. Otherwise the symbol is accepted, and the process is repeated with P replaced by the result of applying P to the accepted symbol. The process is terminated by typing an $"END$ symbol. Thus if k is the sequence of symbols input from the keyboard, the following function gives the sequence of outputs required

$interact(A,P,k) = cons(menu(A,P),$
    if $car(k) = "END$ **then** NIL
  else if $P(car(k)) = "BLEEP$ **then**
      $cons("BLEEP,\ interact(A,P,cdr(k)))$
    else $interact(A,P(car(k)),cdr(k)))$

The notations used above for defining LISP functions are very informal, and they will need to be translated to the specific conventional S-expression form of some particular implementation of LISP. For example in LISPkit, the prefix function can be defined

(prefix
  lambda
    (a p)
    (lambda (x) (if (eq x a) p (quote BLEEP))))

Fortunately, we shall use only a very small subset of pure functional LISP, so there should be little difficulty in translating and running these processes in a variety of dialects on a variety of machines.

If there are several versions of LISP available, choose one with proper static binding of variables. A LISP with lazy evaluation is also more convenient, since it permits direct encoding of recursive equations, without using LABEL, thus

$$VMS = prefix("COIN, prefix("CHOC, VMS))$$

If input and output are implemented by lazy evaluation, the *interact* function may be called with the keyboard as its third parameter; and the menu for the process *P* will appear as the first output. By selecting and inputting a symbol from the successive menus, a user can interactively explore the behaviour of the process *P*. In other versions of LISP, the *interact* function should be rewritten, using explicit input and output to achieve the same effect. When this has been done, it is possible to observe the computer executing any process that has been represented as a LISP function. In this sense, such a LISP function may be regarded as an *implementation* of the corresponding process. Furthermore, a LISP function such as *prefix* which operates on these representations may be regarded as an implementation of the corresponding operator on processes.

1.5 TRACES

A *trace* of the behaviour of a process is a finite sequence of symbols recording the events in which the process has engaged up to some moment in time. Imagine there is an observer with a notebook who watches the process and writes down the name of each event as it occurs. We can validly ignore the possibility that two events occur simultaneously; for if they did, the observer would still have to record one of them first and then the other, and the order in which he records them would not matter.

A trace will be denoted as a sequence of symbols, separated by commas and enclosed in angular brackets

$\langle x, y \rangle$ consists of two events, x followed by y.

$\langle x \rangle$ is a sequence containing only the event x.

$\langle \rangle$ is the empty sequence containing no events.

Examples

X1 A trace of the simple vending machine *VMS* (1.1.2 X2) at the moment it has completed service of its first two customers

$\langle coin, choc, coin, choc \rangle$ ☐

X2 A trace of the same machine before the second customer has extracted his *choc*

$$\langle coin, choc, coin \rangle$$

Neither the process nor its observer understands the concept of a completed transaction. The hunger of the expectant customer, and the readiness of the machine to satisfy it are not in the alphabet of these processes, and cannot be observed or recorded. □

X3 Before a process has engaged in any events, the notebook of the observer is empty. This is represented by the empty trace

$$\langle \rangle$$

Every process has this as its shortest possible trace. □

X4 The complex vending machine *VMC* (1.1.3 X4) has the following seven traces of length two or less

$$\langle \rangle$$

$$\langle in2p \rangle \qquad\qquad\qquad\qquad \langle in1p \rangle$$

$$\langle in2p, large \rangle \quad \langle in2p, small \rangle \qquad \langle in1p, in1p \rangle \quad \langle in1p, small \rangle$$

Only one of the four traces of length two can actually occur for a given machine. The choice between them will be determined by the wishes of the first customer to use the machine. □

X5 A trace of *VMC* if its first customer has ignored the warning is

$$\langle in1p, in1p, in1p \rangle$$

The trace does not actually record the breakage of the machine. Breakage is only indicated by the fact that among all the possible traces of the machine there is no trace which extends this one, i.e., there is no event x such that

$$\langle in1p, in1p, in1p, x \rangle$$

is a possible trace of *VMC*. The customer may fret and fume; the observer may watch eagerly with pencil poised; but not another single event can occur, and not another symbol will ever be written in the notebook. The ultimate disposal of customer and machine are not in our chosen alphabet. □

1.6   OPERATIONS ON TRACES

Traces play a central role in recording, describing, and understanding the behaviour of processes. In this section we explore some of the general properties of traces and of operations on them. We will use the following conventions

s, t, u	stand for traces
S, T, U	stand for sets of traces
f, g, h	stand for functions

1.6.1   Catenation

By far the most important operation on traces is catenation, which constructs a trace from a pair of operands s and t by simply putting them together in this order; the result will be denoted

$$s^\wedge t$$

For example

$$\langle coin,\ choc \rangle^\wedge \langle coin,\ toffee \rangle = \langle coin,\ choc,\ coin,\ toffee \rangle$$
$$\langle in1p \rangle^\wedge \langle in1p \rangle = \langle in1p,\ in1p \rangle$$
$$\langle in1p,\ in1p \rangle^\wedge \langle \rangle = \langle in1p,\ in1p \rangle$$

The most important properties of catenation are that it is associative, and has $\langle \rangle$ as its unit

L1 $s^\wedge \langle \rangle = \langle \rangle^\wedge s = s$

L2 $s^\wedge (t^\wedge u) = (s^\wedge t)^\wedge u$

The following laws are both obvious and useful

L3 $s^\wedge t = s^\wedge u \equiv t = u$

L4 $s^\wedge t = u^\wedge t \equiv s = u$

L5 $s^\wedge t = \langle \rangle \equiv s = \langle \rangle \wedge t = \langle \rangle$

Let f stand for a function which maps traces to traces. The function is said to be *strict* if it maps the empty trace to the empty trace

$$f(\langle \rangle) = \langle \rangle$$

It is said to be *distributive* if it distributes through catenation

$$f(s^\wedge t) = f(s)^\wedge f(t)$$

All distributive functions are strict.

If n is a natural number, we define t^n as n copies of t catenated with each other. It is readily defined by induction on n

L6 $t^0 = \langle \rangle$

L7 $t^{n+1} = t^\wedge t^n$

This definition itself gives two useful laws; here are two more which can be proved from them

L8 $t^{n+1} = t^{n\wedge} t$

L9 $(s^\wedge t)^{n+1} = s^\wedge (t^\wedge s)^{n\wedge} t$

1.6.2 Restriction

The expression $(t \upharpoonright A)$ denotes the trace t when *restricted* to symbols in the set A; it is formed from t simply by omitting all symbols outside A. For example

$$\langle around,\ up,\ down,\ around \rangle \upharpoonright \{up,\ down\} = \langle up,\ down \rangle$$

Restriction is distributive and therefore strict

L1 $\langle \rangle \upharpoonright A = \langle \rangle$

L2 $(s^\wedge t) \upharpoonright A = (s \upharpoonright A)^\wedge (t \upharpoonright A)$

Its effect on singleton sequences is obvious

L3 $\langle x \rangle \upharpoonright A = \langle x \rangle$ if $x \in A$

L4 $\langle y \rangle \upharpoonright A = \langle \rangle$ if $y \notin A$

A distributive function is uniquely defined by defining its effect on singleton sequences, since its effect on all longer sequences can be calculated by distributing the function to each individual element of the sequence and catenating the results. For example, if $y \neq x$

$$
\begin{aligned}
\langle x, y, x \rangle \upharpoonright \{x\} &= (\langle x \rangle^\wedge \langle y \rangle^\wedge \langle x \rangle) \upharpoonright \{x\} \\
&= (\langle x \rangle \upharpoonright \{x\})^\wedge (\langle y \rangle \upharpoonright \{x\})^\wedge (\langle x \rangle \upharpoonright \{x\}) && \text{by L2} \\
&= \langle x \rangle \qquad {}^\wedge \langle \rangle \qquad {}^\wedge \langle x \rangle && \text{by L3, L4} \\
&= \langle x, x \rangle
\end{aligned}
$$

The following laws show the relationship between restriction and set operations. A trace restricted to the empty set of symbols leaves nothing; and a successive restriction by two sets is the same as a single restriction by the intersection of the two sets. These laws can be proved by induction on the length of s

L5 $s \upharpoonright \{ \} = \langle \rangle$

L6 $(s \upharpoonright A) \upharpoonright B = s \upharpoonright (A \cap B)$

1.6.3 Head and tail

If s is a nonempty sequence, its first symbol is denoted s_0, and the result of removing the first symbol is s'. For example

$$\langle x, y, x\rangle_0 = x$$
$$\langle x, y, x\rangle' = \langle y, x\rangle$$

Both of these operations are undefined for the empty sequence.

L1 $(\langle x\rangle^\wedge s)_0 = x$

L2 $(\langle x\rangle^\wedge s)' = s$

L3 $s = (\langle s_0\rangle^\wedge s')$ if $s \neq \langle\rangle$

The following law gives a convenient method of proving whether two traces are equal

L4 $s=t \equiv (s=t=\langle\rangle \vee (s_0=t_0 \wedge s'=t'))$

1.6.4 Star

The set A^* is the set of all finite traces (including $\langle\rangle$) which are formed from symbols in the set A. When such traces are restricted to A, they remain unchanged. This fact permits a simple definition

$$A^* = \{s \mid s \upharpoonright A = s\}.$$

The following laws are consequences of this definition

L1 $\langle\rangle \in A^*$

L2 $\langle x\rangle \in A^* \equiv x \in A$

L3 $(s^\wedge t) \in A^* \equiv s \in A^* \wedge t \in A^*$

They are sufficiently powerful to determine whether a trace is a member of A^* or not. For example, if $x \in A$ and $y \tilde{\in} A$

$$\begin{aligned}
\langle x, y\rangle \in A^* &\equiv (\langle x\rangle^\wedge \langle y\rangle) \in A^* \\
&\equiv (\langle x\rangle \in A^*) \wedge (\langle y\rangle \in A^*) && \text{by L3} \\
&\equiv true \wedge false && \text{by L2} \\
&\equiv false
\end{aligned}$$

Another useful law could serve as a recursive definition of A^*

L4 $A^* = \{t \mid t = \langle\rangle \vee (t_0 \in A \wedge t' \in A^*)\}$

1.6.5 Ordering

If s is a copy of an initial subsequence of t, it is possible to find some extension u of s such that $s^\wedge u = t$. We therefore define an ordering relation

$$s \leq t = (\exists u . s^\wedge u = t)$$

and say that s is a *prefix* of t. For example,

$$\langle x, y \rangle \leq \langle x, y, x, w \rangle$$
$$\langle x, y \rangle \leq \langle z, y, x \rangle \equiv x = z$$

The $\leq$ relation is a partial ordering, and its least element is $\langle \rangle$, as stated in laws L1 to L4

L1 $\langle \rangle \leq s$ least element

L2 $s \leq s$ reflexive

L3 $s \leq t \wedge t \leq s \Rightarrow s = t$ antisymmetric

L4 $s \leq t \wedge t \leq u \Rightarrow s \leq u$ transitive

The following law, together with L1, gives a method for computing whether $s \leq t$ or not

L5 $(\langle x \rangle^\wedge s) \leq t \equiv t \neq \langle \rangle \wedge x = t_0 \wedge s \leq t'$

The prefixes of a given sequence are totally ordered

L6 $s \leq u \wedge t \leq u \Rightarrow s \leq t \vee t \leq s$

If s is a subsequence of t (not necessarily initial), we say s is **in** t; this may be defined

$$s \text{ in } t = (\exists u, v . \ t = u^\wedge s^\wedge v)$$

This relation is also a partial ordering, in that it satisfies laws L1 to L4 above. It also satisfies

L7 $(\langle x \rangle^\wedge s) \text{ in } t \equiv t \neq \langle \rangle \wedge ((t_0 = x \wedge s \leq t') \vee (\langle x \rangle^\wedge s) \text{ in } t')$

A function f from traces to traces is said to be *monotonic* if it respects the ordering $\leq$, i.e.,

$$f(s) \leq f(t) \qquad \text{whenever } s \leq t$$

All distributive functions are monotonic, for example

L8 $s \leq t \Rightarrow (s \upharpoonright A) \leq (t \upharpoonright A)$

A dyadic function may be monotonic in either argument, keeping the other argument constant. For example, catenation is monotonic in its second argument (but not in its first)

L9 $t \leq u \Rightarrow (s^\wedge t) \leq (s^\wedge u)$.

A function which is monotonic in all its arguments is said simply to be monotonic.

1.6.6 Length

The length of the trace t is denoted $\#t$. For example

$$\#\langle x, y, x \rangle = 3$$

The laws which define $\#$ are

L1 $\#\langle \rangle = 0$

L2 $\#\langle x \rangle = 1$

L2 $\#\langle s^\wedge t \rangle = (\#s) + (\#t)$

The number of occurrences in t of symbols from A is counted by $\#(t{\restriction}A)$.

L4 $\#(t{\restriction}(A \cup B)) = \#(t{\restriction}A) + \#(t{\restriction}B) - \#(t{\restriction}(A \cap B))$

L5 $s \leq t \Rightarrow \#s \leq \#t$

L6 $\#(t^n) = n \times (\#t)$

The number of occurrences of a symbol x in a trace s is defined

$$s{\downarrow}x = \#(s{\restriction}\{x\})$$

1.7 IMPLEMENTATION OF TRACES

In order to represent traces in a computer and to implement operations on them, we need a high-level list-processing language. Fortunately, LISP is very suitable for this purpose. Traces are represented in the obvious way by lists of atoms representing their events

$$\langle \rangle = NIL$$
$$\langle coin \rangle = cons("COIN, NIL)$$
$$\langle coin, choc \rangle = "(COIN\ CHOC)$$
which means $cons("COIN, cons("CHOC, NIL))$

Operations on traces can be readily implemented as functions on lists. For example, the head and tail of a nonempty list are given by the primitive functions *car* and *cdr*

$$t_0 = car(t)$$
$$t' = cdr(t)$$
$$\langle x \rangle^\wedge s = cons(x,s)$$

General catenation is implemented as the familiar *append* function, which is defined by recursion

$$s^\wedge t = append(s,t)$$

where $append(s,t) = $ **if** $s=NIL$ **then** t **else** $cons(car(s), append(cdr(s), t))$

The correctness of this definition follows from the laws

$$\langle \rangle^\wedge t = t$$
$$s^\wedge t = \langle s_0 \rangle^\wedge (s'^\wedge t) \qquad\qquad\qquad \text{whenever } s \neq \langle \rangle$$

The termination of the LISP append function is guaranteed by the fact that the list supplied as first argument of each recursive call is shorter than it was at the previous level of recursion. Similar arguments establish the correctness of the implementations of the other operations defined below.

To implement restriction, we represent a finite set B as a list of its members. The test $(x \in B)$ is accomplished by a call on the function

$ismember(x,B) = $ **if** $B=NIL$ **then** *false*
      else if $x=car(B)$ **then** *true*
          else $ismember(x, cdr(B))$

$(s \restriction B)$ can now be implemented by the function

$restrict(s,B) = $ **if** $s=NIL$ **then** NIL
      else if $ismember(car(s), B)$
         then $cons(car(s), restrict(cdr(s), B))$
         else $restrict(cdr(s), B)$

A test of $(s \leq t)$ is implemented as a function which delivers the answer *true* or *false*; it relies on 1.6.5 L1 and L5

$isprefix(s,t) = $ **if** $s=NIL$ **then** *true*
      else if $t=NIL$ **then** *false*
         else $car(s)=car(t) \wedge isprefix(cdr(s), cdr(t))$

1.8   TRACES OF A PROCESS

In section 1.6 a trace of a process was introduced as a sequential record of the behaviour of a process up to some moment in time. Before the process starts, it is not known which of its possible traces will actually be recorded: the choice will depend on environmental factors beyond the control of the process. However the complete set of all possible traces of a process *P can* be known in advance, and we define a function *traces(P)* to yield that set.

Examples

X1   The only trace of the behaviour of the process *STOP* is $\langle\rangle$. The notebook of the observer of this process remains forever blank

$$traces(STOP) = \{\langle\rangle\}$$ □

X2   There are only two traces of the machine that ingests a coin before breaking

$$traces(coin{\rightarrow}STOP) = \{\langle\rangle, \langle coin\rangle\}$$ □

X3   A clock that does nothing but *tick*

$$traces(\mu X.tick{\rightarrow}X) = \{\langle\rangle, \langle tick\rangle, \langle tick, tick\rangle, ...\}$$
$$= \{tick\}^*$$

As with most interesting processes, the set of traces is infinite, although of course each individual trace is finite.   □

X4   A simple vending machine

$$traces(\mu X.coin{\rightarrow}choc{\rightarrow}X) = \{s \mid \exists n.\ s \leq \langle coin, choc\rangle^n\}$$ □

1.8.1   Laws

In this section we show how to calculate the set of traces of any process defined using the notations introduced so far. As mentioned above, *STOP* has only one trace

L1 $traces(STOP) = \{t \mid t = \langle\rangle\} = \{\langle\rangle\}$

A trace of $(c{\rightarrow}P)$ may be empty, because $\langle\rangle$ is a trace of the behaviour of every process up to the moment that it engages in its very first action. Every nonempty trace begins with c, and its tail must be a possible trace of P

L2 $traces(c{\rightarrow}P) = \{t \mid t = \langle\rangle \vee (t_0 = c \wedge t' \in traces(P))\}$
$$= \{\langle\rangle\} \cup \{\langle c\rangle^{\wedge}t \mid t \in traces(P)\}$$

A trace of the behaviour of a process which offers a choice between initial events must be a trace of one of the alternatives

L3 $traces(c{\rightarrow}P \,|\, d{\rightarrow}Q) =$
$$\{t \,|\, t=\langle\rangle \vee (t_0=c \wedge t'\in traces(P)) \vee (t_0=d \wedge t'\in traces(Q))\}$$

These three laws are summarized in the single general law governing choice

L4 $traces(x{:}B{\rightarrow}P(x)) = \{t \,|\, t=\langle\rangle \vee (t_0\in B \wedge t'\in traces(P(t_0)))\}$

To discover the set of traces of a recursively defined process is a bit more difficult. A recursively defined process is the solution of an equation

$$X = F(X)$$

First, we define iteration of the function F by induction

$$F^0(X) = X$$
$$\begin{aligned}
F^{n+1}(X) &= F(F^n(X))\\
&= F^n(F(X))\\
&= \underbrace{F(...(F(F(X)))...)}_{n\ \text{times}}
\end{aligned}$$

Then, provided that F is guarded, we can define

L5 $traces(\mu X{:}A.F(X)) = \displaystyle\bigcup_{n\geq 0} traces(F^n(STOP_A))$

Examples

X1   Recall that RUN_A was defined in 1.1.3 X8 as

$$\mu X{:}A.F(X)$$

where $F(X) = (x{:}A{\rightarrow}X)$

We wish to prove that

$$traces(RUN_A) = A^*$$

Proof. $A^* = \displaystyle\bigcup_{n\geq 0} \{s \,|\, s\in A^* \wedge \#s \leq n\}$

Therefore by L5 it is sufficient to prove for all n that

$$traces(F^n(STOP_A)) = \{s \,|\, s\in A^* \wedge \#s \leq n\}$$

This is done by induction on n.

(1)   For $n=0$
$$\begin{aligned}
traces(STOP_A) &= \{\langle\rangle\}\\
&= \{s \,|\, s\in A^* \wedge \#s \leq 0\}
\end{aligned}$$

(2) $traces(F^{n+1}(STOP_A))$

$\qquad = traces(x:A \to F^n(STOP_A))$ def F, F^{n+1}

$\qquad = \{t \mid t = \langle\rangle \vee (t_0 \in A \wedge t' \in traces(F^n(STOP_A)))\}$ L4

$\qquad = \{t \mid t = \langle\rangle \vee (t_0 \in A \wedge (t' \in A^* \wedge \#t' \leq n))\}$ induction hyp.

$\qquad = \{t \mid (t = \langle\rangle \vee (t_0 \in A \wedge t' \in A^*)) \wedge \#t \leq n+1\}$ property of $\#$

$\qquad = \{t \mid t \in A^* \wedge \#t \leq n+1\}$ 1.6.4 L4 $\square$

X2   We want to prove 1.8 X4, i.e.,

$$traces(VMS) = \bigcup_{n \geq 0} \{s \mid s \leq \langle coin, choc\rangle^n\}$$

Proof.   The induction hypothesis is

$$traces(F^n(VMS)) = \{t \mid t \leq \langle coin, choc\rangle^n\}$$

where $F(X) = (coin \to choc \to X)$

(1) $traces(STOP) = \{\langle\rangle\} = \{s \mid s \leq \langle coin, choc\rangle^0\}$ 1.6.1 L6

(2) $traces(coin \to choc \to F^n(STOP))$

$\qquad = \{\langle\rangle, \langle coin\rangle\} \cup \{\langle coin, choc\rangle^\smallfrown t \mid t \in traces(F^n(STOP))\}$ L2 (twice)

$\qquad = \{\langle\rangle, \langle coin\rangle\} \cup \{\langle coin, choc\rangle^\smallfrown t \mid t \leq \langle coin, choc\rangle^n\}$ induction hyp.

$\qquad = \{s \mid s = \langle\rangle \vee s = \langle coin\rangle \vee \exists t. s = \langle coin, choc\rangle^\smallfrown t \wedge t \leq \langle coin, choc\rangle^n\}$

$\qquad = \{s \mid s \leq \langle coin, choc\rangle^{n+1}\}$

The conclusion follows by L5. $\square$

As mentioned in Section 1.5, a trace is a sequence of symbols recording the events in which a process P has engaged up to some moment in time. From this it follows that $\langle\rangle$ is a trace of every process up to the moment in which it engages in its very first event. Furthermore, if $(s^\smallfrown t)$ is a trace of a process up to some moment, then s must have been a trace of that process up to some earlier moment. Finally, every event that occurs must be in the alphabet of the process. These three facts are formalized in the laws

L6 $\langle\rangle \in traces(P)$

L7 $s^\smallfrown t \in traces(P) \Rightarrow s \in traces(P)$

L8 $traces(P) \subseteq (\alpha P)^*$

There is a close relationship between the traces of a process and the picture of its behaviour drawn as a tree. For any node on the tree, the trace of the behaviour of a process up to the time when it reaches that node is just the sequence of labels encountered on the path leading from the root of the tree to that node. For example, in the tree for VMC shown in Fig. 1.1, the trace corresponding to the path from the root to the black node is

$\qquad \langle in2p, small, out1p\rangle$

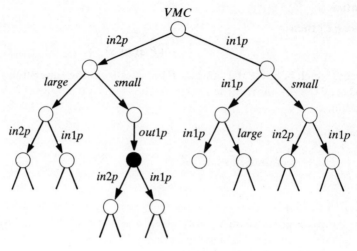

Figure 1.1

Clearly, all initial subpaths of a path in a tree are also paths in the same tree; this is stated more formally in L7 above. The empty trace defines the path from the root to itself, which justifies the law L6. The traces of a process are just the set of all paths leading from the root to some node in the tree.

Conversely, because the branches leading from each node are all labelled with different events, each trace of a process uniquely specifies a path leading from the root of the tree to a particular node. Thus any set of traces satisfying laws L6 and L7 constitutes a convenient mathematical representation for a tree with no duplicate labels on branches emerging from a single node.

1.8.2 Implementation

Suppose a process has been implemented as a LISP function P, and let s be a trace. Then it is possible to test whether s is a possible trace of P by the function

$istrace(s,P) =$ **if** $s=NIL$ **then** *true*
        else if $P(s_0)="BLEEP$ **then** *false* **else** *istrace* $(s',P(s_0))$

Since s is finite, the recursion involved here will terminate, having explored only a finite initial segment of the behaviour of the process P. It is because we avoid infinite exploration that we can safely define a process as an infinite object, i.e., a function whose result is a function whose result is a function whose result ...

1.8.3 After

If $s \in traces(P)$ then

$$P/s \qquad\qquad\qquad (P \text{ after } s)$$

is a process which behaves the same as P behaves from the time after P has engaged in all the actions recorded in the trace s. If s is not a trace of P, (P/s) is not defined.

Examples

X1 $(VMS/\langle coin \rangle) = (choc \rightarrow VMS)$ □

X2 $(VMS/\langle coin, choc \rangle) = VMS$ □

X3 $(VMC/\langle in1p \rangle^3) = STOP$ □

X4 To avoid loss arising from installation of $VMCRED$ (1.1.3 $X5$, $X6$), the owner decides to eat the first chocolate himself

$$(VMCRED/\langle choc \rangle) = VMS2 \qquad\qquad\qquad □$$

In a tree picture of P (Fig. 1.1), (P/s) denotes the whole subtree whose root lies at the end of the path labelled by the symbols of s. Thus the subtree below the black node in the Fig. 1.1 is denoted by

$$VMC/\langle in2p, small, out1p \rangle$$

The following laws describe the meaning of the operator $/$. After doing nothing, a process remains unchanged

L1 $P/\langle \rangle = P$

After engaging in $s^\smallfrown t$, the behaviour of P is the same as that of (P/s) after engaging in t

L2 $P/(s^\smallfrown t) = (P/s)/t$

After engaging in the single event c, the behaviour of a process is as defined by this initial choice

L3 $(x:B \rightarrow P(x))/\langle c \rangle = P(c)$ provided that $c \in B$

A corollary shows that $/\langle c \rangle$ is the inverse of the prefixing operator $c \rightarrow$

L3A $(c \rightarrow P)/\langle c \rangle = P$

The traces of (P/s) are defined

L4 $traces(P/s) = \{t \mid s^\smallfrown t \in traces(P)\}$ provided that $s \in traces(P)$.

In order to prove that a process P never stops it is sufficient to prove that

$$P/s \neq STOP \qquad\qquad\qquad \text{for all } s \in traces\ (P)$$

Another desirable property of a process is *cyclicity*; a process P is defined as cyclic if in all circumstances it is possible for it to return to its initial state, i.e.,

$$\forall s : traces(P). \; \exists t. \; (P/(s^\wedge t) = P)$$

STOP is trivially cyclic; but if any other process is cyclic, then it also has the desirable property of never stopping.

Examples

X1   The following processes are cyclic (1.1.3 X8, 1.1.2 X2, 1.1.3 X3, 1.1.4 X2)

$$RUN_A, \; VMS, \; (choc{\rightarrow}VMS), \; VMCT, \; CT_7 \qquad\qquad \square$$

X2   The following are not cyclic, because it is not possible to return them to their initial state (1.1.2 X2, 1.1.3 X3, 1.1.3 X2)

$$(coin{\rightarrow}VMS), \; (choc{\rightarrow}VMCT), \; (around{\rightarrow}CT_7)$$

For example, in the initial state of $(choc{\rightarrow}VMCT)$ only a chocolate is obtainable, but subsequently whenever *choc* is obtainable a choice of toffee is also possible; consequently none of these subsequent states is equal to the initial state. $\qquad \square$

Warning.   The use of / in a recursively defined process has the unfortunate consequence of invalidating its guards, thereby introducing the danger of multiple solutions to the recursion equations. For example

$$X = (a{\rightarrow}(X/\langle a \rangle))$$

is not guarded, and has as its solution *any* process of the form

$$a{\rightarrow}P$$

for any P.

Proof. $(a{\rightarrow}((a{\rightarrow}P)/\langle a \rangle)) = (a{\rightarrow}P)$ $\qquad\qquad\qquad$ by L3A.

For this reason, we will never use the / operator in recursive process definitions.

1.9   MORE OPERATIONS ON TRACES

This section describes some further operations on traces; it may be skipped at this stage, since backward references will be given in later chapters where the operations are used.

1.9.1   Change of symbol

Let f be a function mapping symbols from a set A to symbols in a set B. From f we can derive a new function f^* which maps a sequence of symbols in A^* to a sequence in B^* by applying f to each element of the sequence. For example, if *double* is a function which doubles its integer argument

$$double^*(\langle 1,5,3,1 \rangle) = \langle 2,10,6,2 \rangle$$

A starred function is obviously distributive and therefore strict

L1 $f^*(\langle \rangle) = \langle \rangle$

L2 $f^*(\langle x \rangle) = \langle f(x) \rangle$

L3 $f^*(s^\wedge t) = f^*(s)^\wedge f^*(t)$

Other laws are obvious consequences

L4 $f^*(s)_0 = \langle f(s_0) \rangle$ $\qquad\qquad$ if $s \neq \langle \rangle$

L5 $\# f^*(s) = \# s$

But here is an "obvious" law which is unfortunately not generally true

$$f^*(s \restriction A) = f^*(s) \restriction f(A)$$

where $f(A) = \{ f(x) \,|\, x \in A \}$.

The simplest counterexample is given by the function f such that

$$f(b) = f(c) = c \qquad\qquad \text{where } b \neq c$$

Therefore $f^*(\langle b \rangle \restriction \{c\}) = f^*(\langle \rangle)$ $\qquad\qquad$ since $b \neq c$
$$\begin{aligned} &= \langle \rangle && \text{L1} \\ &\neq \langle c \rangle \\ &= \langle c \rangle \restriction \{c\} \\ &= f^*(\langle c \rangle) \restriction f(\{c\}) && \text{since } f(c) = c \end{aligned}$$

However, the law is true if f is a one-one function (injection)

L6 $f^*(s \restriction A) = f^*(s) \restriction f(A)$ $\qquad\qquad$ provided that f is an injection.

1.9.2   Catenation

Let s be a sequence, each of whose elements is itself a sequence. Then $^\wedge\!/s$ is obtained by catenating all the elements together in the original order. For example

$$\begin{aligned} ^\wedge\!/\langle \langle 1,3 \rangle, \langle \rangle, \langle 7 \rangle \rangle &= \langle 1,3 \rangle^\wedge \langle \rangle^\wedge \langle 7 \rangle \\ &= \langle 1,3,7 \rangle \end{aligned}$$

This operator is distributive

L1 $^\wedge/\langle\rangle = \langle\rangle$

L2 $^\wedge/\langle s\rangle = s$

L3 $^\wedge/(s^\wedge t) = (^\wedge/s)^\wedge(^\wedge/t)$

1.9.3 Interleaving

A sequence s is an interleaving of two sequences t and u if it can be split into a series of subsequences, with alternate subsequences extracted from t and u. For example

$$s = \langle 1,6,3,1,5,4,2,7\rangle$$

is an interleaving of t and u, where

$$t = \langle 1,6,5,2,7\rangle \quad \text{and} \quad u = \langle 3,1,4\rangle$$

A recursive definition of interleaving can be given by means of the following laws

L1 $\langle\rangle\ interleaves(t,u) \equiv (t=\langle\rangle \wedge u=\langle\rangle)$

L2 $s\ interleaves(t,u) \equiv s\ interleaves\,(u,t)$

L3 $(\langle x\rangle^\wedge s)\ interleaves(t,u) \equiv (t\neq\langle\rangle \wedge t_0=x \wedge s\ interleaves(t',u))$
$$\vee\,(u\neq\langle\rangle \wedge u_0=x \wedge s\ interleaves(t,u'))$$

1.9.4 Subscription

If $0\leq i < \#s$, we use the conventional notation $s[i]$ to denote the ith element of the sequence s as described by L1

L1 $s[0]=s_0 \wedge s[i+1]=s'[i]$ $\qquad\qquad\qquad$ provided $s\neq\langle\rangle$

L2 $(f^*(s))[i] = f(s[i])$ $\qquad\qquad\qquad\qquad\qquad$ for $i<\#s$

1.9.5 Reversal

If s is a sequence, $\bar{s}$ is formed by taking its elements in reverse order. For example

$$\overline{\langle 3,5,37\rangle} = \langle 37,5,3\rangle$$

Reversal is defined fully by the following laws:

L1 $\overline{\langle\rangle} = \langle\rangle$

L2 $\overline{\langle x \rangle} = \langle x \rangle$

L3 $\overline{s \,^{\wedge} t} = \overline{t} \,^{\wedge} \overline{s}$

Reversal enjoys a number of simple algebraic properties, including

L4 $\overline{\overline{s}} = s$

Exploration of other properties is left to the reader. One of the useful facts about reversal is that $\overline{s}_0$ is the *last* element of the sequence, and in general

L5 $\overline{s}[i] = s[\#s - i - 1]$ for $i < \#s$

1.9.6   Selection

If s is a sequence of pairs, we define $s \downarrow x$ as the result of selecting from s all those pairs whose first element is x and then replacing each pair by its second element. We write a pair with a dot between its two components. Thus if

$$s = \langle a.7, \; b.9, \; a.8, \; c.0 \rangle$$

then $s \downarrow a = \langle 7, 8 \rangle$
and $s \downarrow d = \langle \rangle$

L1 $\langle \rangle \downarrow x = \langle \rangle$

L2 $(\langle y.z \rangle \,^{\wedge} t) \downarrow x = t \downarrow x$ if $y \neq x$

L3 $(\langle x.z \rangle \,^{\wedge} t) \downarrow x = \langle z \rangle \,^{\wedge} (t \downarrow x)$

If s is not a sequence of pairs, $s \downarrow a$ denotes the number of occurrences of a in s (as defined in Section 1.6.6).

1.9.7   Composition

Let $\sqrt{}$ be a symbol denoting successful termination of the process which engages in it. As a result, this symbol can appear only at the end of a trace. Let t be a trace recording a sequence of events which start when s has successfully terminated. The composition of s and t is denoted $(s;t)$. If $\sqrt{}$ does not occur in s, then t cannot start

L1 $s;t = s$ if $\neg(\langle \sqrt{} \rangle \text{ in } s)$

If $\sqrt{}$ does occur at the end of s, it is removed and t is appended to the result

L2 $(s \,^{\wedge} \langle \sqrt{} \rangle);t = s \,^{\wedge} t$ if $\neg(\langle \sqrt{} \rangle \text{ in } s)$

The symbol $\sqrt{}$ may be regarded as a sort of glue which sticks s and t together; in the absence of the glue, t cannot stick (L1). If $\sqrt{}$ occurs (incorrectly) in the middle of a trace, we stipulate for the sake of completeness that all symbols after the first occurrence are irrelevant and should be discarded

L2A $(s^\wedge \langle \sqrt{} \rangle^\wedge u);t = s^\wedge t$ if $\neg(\langle \sqrt{} \rangle$ **in** $s)$

This unfamiliar composition operator enjoys a number of familiar algebraic properties. Like catenation it is associative. Unlike catenation, it is monotonic in its first as well as its second argument. Also, it is strict in its first argument, and has $\langle \sqrt{} \rangle$ as its left unit

L3 $s;(t;u) = (s;t);u$

L4A $s \leq t \Rightarrow ((u;s) \leq (u;t))$

L4B $s \leq t \Rightarrow ((s;u) \leq (t;u))$

L5 $\langle \rangle;t = \langle \rangle$

L6 $\langle \sqrt{} \rangle;t = t$

If $\sqrt{}$ never occurs except at the end of a trace, $\langle \sqrt{} \rangle$ is a right unit as well

L7 $s;\langle \sqrt{} \rangle = s$ provided $\neg(\langle \sqrt{} \rangle$ **in** $(\mathfrak{I})')$

1.10   SPECIFICATIONS

A specification of a product is a description of the way it is intended to behave. This description is a predicate containing free variables, each of which stands for some observable aspect of the behaviour of the product. For example, the specification of an electronic amplifier, with an input range of one volt and with an approximate gain of 10, is given by the predicate

$$AMP10 = (0 \leq v \leq 1 \Rightarrow |v' - 10^*v| \leq 1)$$

In this specificiation, it is understood that v stands for the input voltage and v' stands for the output voltage. Such an understanding of the meaning of variables is essential to the use of mathematics in science and engineering.

In the case of a process, the most obviously relevant observation of its behaviour is the trace of events that occur up to a given moment in time. We will use the special variable tr to stand for an arbitrary trace of the process being specified, just as v and v' are used for arbitrary observations of voltage in the previous example.

Examples

X1 The owner of a vending machine does not wish to make a loss by installing it. He therefore specifies that the number of chocolates dispensed must never exceed the number of coins inserted

$$NOLOSS = (\#(tr\upharpoonright\{choc\}) \leq \#(tr\upharpoonright\{coin\}))$$ □

In future we will use the abbreviation (introduced in 1.6.6)

$$tr{\downarrow}c = \#(tr\upharpoonright\{c\})$$

to stand for the number of occurrences of the symbol c in tr.

X2 The customer of a vending machine wants to ensure that it will not absorb further coins until it has dispensed the chocolate already paid for

$$FAIR1 = ((tr{\downarrow}coin) \leq (tr{\downarrow}choc)+1)$$ □

X3 The manufacturer of a simple vending machine must meet the requirements both of its owner and of its customer

$$VMSPEC = NOLOSS{\wedge}FAIR1$$
$$= (0 \leq ((tr{\downarrow}coin)-(tr{\downarrow}choc)) \leq 1)$$ □

X4 The specification of a correction to the complex vending machine forbids it to accept three pennies in a row

$$VMCFIX = (\neg\langle in1p\rangle^3 \textbf{ in } tr)$$ □

X5 The specification of a mended machine

$$MENDVMC = (tr{\in}traces(VMC){\wedge}VMCFIX)$$ □

X6 The specification of $VMS2$ (1.1.3 X6)

$$0 \leq ((tr{\downarrow}coin)-(tr{\downarrow}choc)) \leq 2$$ □

1.10.1 Satisfaction

If P is a product which meets a specification S, we say that P *satisfies* S, abbreviated to

$$P \textbf{ sat } S$$

This means that every possible observation of the behaviour of P is described by S; or in other words, S is true whenever its variables take values observed from the product P, or more formally $\forall tr.tr{\in}traces(P){\Rightarrow}S$. For example, the following table gives some observations of the properties of an amplifier

	1	2	3	4	5
v	0	.5	.5	2	.1
v'	0	5	4	1	3

All observations except the last are described by $AMP10$. The second and third columns illustrate the fact that the output of the amplifier is not completely determined by its input. The fourth column shows that if the input voltage is outside its specified range, the output voltage can be anything at all, without violating the specification. (In this simple example we have ignored the possibility that excessive input may break the product.)

The following laws give the most general properties of the *satisfies* relation. The specification *true* which places no constraints whatever on observations of a product will be satisfied by all products; even a broken product satisfies such a weak and undemanding specification

L1 P **sat** *true*

If a product satisfies two different specifications, it also satisfies their conjunction

L2A   If P **sat** S
   and P **sat** T
   then P **sat** $(S \land T)$

The law L2A generalizes to infinite conjunctions, i.e., to universal quantification. Let $S(n)$ be a predicate containing the variable n

L2   If $\forall n.\ (P$ **sat** $S(n))$
   then P **sat** $(\forall n.S(n))$

provided that P does not depend on n.

If a specification S logically implies another specification T, then every observation described by S is also described by T. Consequently every product which satisfies S must also satisfy the weaker specification T

L3   If P **sat** S
   and $S \Rightarrow T$
   then P **sat** T

In the light of this law, we will sometimes lay out proofs as a chain; so if $S \Rightarrow T$, we write

   P **sat** S
      $\Rightarrow T$

as an abbreviation for the fuller proof

> P **sat** S
> $S \Rightarrow T$
> P **sat** T by L3

The laws and their explanations given above apply to all kinds of products and all kinds of specifications. In the next section we shall give the additional laws which apply to processes.

1.10.2 Proofs

In the design of a product, the designer has a responsibility to ensure that it will satisfy its specification; this responsibility may be discharged by the reasoning methods of the relevant branches of mathematics, for example, geometry or the differential and integral calculus. In this section we shall give a collection of laws which permit the use of mathematical reasoning to ensure that a process P meets its specification S.

We will sometimes write the specification as $S(tr)$, suggesting that a specification will normally contain tr as a free variable. However, the real reason for making tr explicit is to indicate how tr may be substituted by some more elaborate expression, as for example in $S(tr'')$. It is important to note that both S and $S(tr)$ can have other free variables besides tr.

Any observation of the process $STOP$ will always be an empty trace, since this process never does anything

L4A $STOP$ **sat** $(tr=\langle\rangle)$

A trace of the process $(c{\rightarrow}P)$ is initially empty. Every subsequent trace begins with c, and its tail is a trace of P. Consequently its tail must be described by any specification of P

L4B   If P **sat** $S(tr)$
     then $(c{\rightarrow}P)$ **sat** $(tr=\langle\rangle\vee(tr_0=c\wedge S(tr')))$

A corollary of this law deals with double prefixing

L4C   If P **sat** $S(tr)$
     then $(c{\rightarrow}d{\rightarrow}P)$ **sat** $(tr\leq\langle c,d\rangle\vee(tr\geq\langle c,d\rangle\wedge S(tr'')))$

Binary choice is similar to prefixing, except that the trace may begin with either of the two alternative events, and its tail must be described by the specification of the chosen alternative

L4D   If P **sat** $S(tr)$
     and Q **sat** $T(tr)$
     then $(c{\rightarrow}P\,|\,d{\rightarrow}Q)$ **sat** $(tr=\langle\rangle\vee(tr_0=c\wedge S(tr'))\vee(tr_0=d\wedge T(tr')))$

All the laws given above are special cases of the law for general choice

L4   If $\forall x \in B.\ (P(x)$ **sat** $S(tr, x))$
  then $(x:B \to P(x))$ **sat** $(tr = \langle \rangle \vee (tr_0 \in B \wedge S(tr', tr_0)))$

The law governing the after operator is surprisingly simple. If tr is a trace of (P/s), $s^\wedge tr$ is a trace of P, and therefore must be described by any specification which P satisfies

L5   If P **sat** $S(tr)$
  and $s \in traces(P)$
  then (P/s) **sat** $S(s^\wedge tr)$

Finally, we need a law to establish the correctness of a recursively defined process

L6   If $F(X)$ is guarded
  and $STOP$ **sat** S
  and $((X$ **sat** $S) \Rightarrow (F(X)$ **sat** $S))$
  then $(\mu X.F(X))$ **sat** S

The antecedents of this law ensure (by induction) that

$$F^n(STOP) \text{ sat } S \qquad\qquad \text{for all } n.$$

Since F is guarded, $F^n(STOP)$ fully describes at least the first n steps of the behaviour of $\mu X.F(X)$. So each trace of $\mu X.F(X)$ is a trace of $F^n(STOP)$ for some n. This trace must therefore satisfy the same specification as $F^n(STOP)$, which (for all n) is S. A more formal proof can be given in terms of the mathematical theory of Section 2.8.

Example

X1   We want to prove (1.1.2 X2, 1.10 X3) that

   VMS **sat** $VMSPEC$

Proof.   (1) $STOP$ **sat** $tr = \langle \rangle$ L4A

$$\Rightarrow 0 \le (tr{\downarrow}coin - tr{\downarrow}choc) \le 1$$
$$\text{since } (\langle \rangle {\downarrow} coin) = (\langle \rangle {\downarrow} choc) = 0$$

The conclusion follows by an (implicit) appeal to L3.

(2) Assume X **sat** $(0 \le ((tr{\downarrow}coin) - (tr{\downarrow}choc)) \le 1)$

Therefore $(coin \to choc \to X)$ **sat** $(tr \le \langle coin, choc \rangle$
$$\vee (tr \ge \langle coin, choc \rangle$$
$$\wedge 0 \le ((tr''{\downarrow}coin) - (tr''{\downarrow}choc)) \le 1))\qquad \text{L4C}$$

$$\Rightarrow 0 \le ((tr{\downarrow}coin) - (tr{\downarrow}choc)) \le 1$$

since $\langle\rangle{\downarrow}coin = \langle\rangle{\downarrow}choc = \langle coin\rangle{\downarrow}choc = 0$

and $\langle coin\rangle{\downarrow}coin = (\langle coin, choc\rangle{\downarrow}coin) = \langle coin, choc\rangle{\downarrow}choc = 1$

and $tr \geq \langle coin, choc\rangle \Rightarrow (tr{\downarrow}coin = tr''{\downarrow}coin + 1 \wedge tr{\downarrow}choc = tr''{\downarrow}choc + 1)$

The conclusion follows by appeal to L3 and then L6. □

The fact that a process P satisfies its specification does not necessarily mean that it is going to be satisfactory in use. For example, since

$$tr = \langle\rangle \Rightarrow 0 \leq (tr{\downarrow}coin - tr{\downarrow}choc) \leq 1$$

one can prove by L3 and L4A that

$$STOP \text{ sat } 0 \leq (tr{\downarrow}coin - tr{\downarrow}choc) \leq 1.$$

Yet $STOP$ will not serve as an adequate vending machine, either for its owner or for the customer. It certainly avoids doing anything wrong; but only by the lazy expedient of doing nothing at all. For this reason, $STOP$ satisfies every specification which is satisfiable by any process.

Fortunately, it is obvious by independent reasoning that VMS will never stop. In fact any process defined solely by prefixing, choice, and guarded recursions will never stop. The only way to write a process that can stop is to include explicitly the process $STOP$, or the process $(x:B \rightarrow P(x))$ where B is the empty set. By avoiding such elementary mistakes one can guarantee to write processes that never stop. However, after introduction of concurrency in the next chapter, such simple precautions are no longer adequate. A more general method of specifying and proving that a process will never stop is described in Section 3.7.

2 CONCURRENCY

2.1 INTRODUCTION

A process is defined by describing the whole range of its potential behaviour. Frequently, there will be a choice between several different actions, for example, the insertion of a large coin or a small one into a vending machine *VMC* (1.1.3 X4). On each such occasion, the choice of which event will actually occur can be controlled by the environment within which the process evolves. For example, it is the customer of the vending machine who may select what coin to insert. Fortunately, the environment of a process itself may be described as a process, with its behaviour defined by familiar notations. This permits investigation of the behaviour of a complete system composed from the process together with its environment, acting and interacting with each other as they evolve concurrently. The complete system should also be regarded as a process, whose range of behaviour is definable in terms of the behaviour of its component processes; and the system may in turn be placed within a yet wider environment. In fact, it is best to forget the distinction between processes, environments, and systems; they are all of them just processes whose behaviour may be prescribed, described, recorded and analysed in a simple and homogeneous fashion.

2.2 INTERACTION

When two processes are brought together to evolve concurrently, the usual intention is that they will interact with each other. These interactions may be regarded as events that require simultaneous participation of both the processes involved. For the time being, let us confine attention to such events, and ignore all others. Thus we will assume that the alphabets of the two processes are the same. Consequently, each event that actually occurs must be a possible event in the independent behaviour of each process separately. For example, a chocolate can be extracted from a vending machine only when its customer wants it and only when the vending machine is prepared to give it. If P and Q are processes with the same alphabet, we introduce the notation

$$P \| Q$$

to denote the process which behaves like the system composed of processes P and Q interacting in lock-step synchronization as described above.

Examples

X1 A greedy customer of a vending machine is perfectly happy to obtain a toffee or even a chocolate without paying. However, if thwarted in these desires, he is reluctantly prepared to pay a coin, but then he insists on taking a chocolate

$$
\begin{aligned}
GRCUST = (\,&toffee{\rightarrow}GRCUST \\
| \,&choc{\rightarrow}GRCUST \\
| \,&coin{\rightarrow}choc{\rightarrow}GRCUST\,)
\end{aligned}
$$

When this customer is brought together with the machine $VMCT$ (1.1.3 X3) his greed is frustrated, since the vending machine does not allow goods to be extracted before payment. Similarly, $VMCT$ never gives a toffee, because the customer never wants one after he has paid

$$(GRCUST \| VMCT) = \mu X.(coin{\rightarrow}choc{\rightarrow}X)$$

This example shows how a process which has been defined as a composition of two subprocesses may also be described as a simple single process, without using the concurrency operator $\|$. □

X2 A foolish customer wants a large biscuit, so he puts his coin in the vending machine VMC. He does not notice whether he has inserted a large coin or a small one; nevertheless, he is determined on a large biscuit

$$FOOLCUST = (in2p{\rightarrow}large{\rightarrow}FOOLCUST \,|\, in1p{\rightarrow}large{\rightarrow}FOOLCUST)$$

Unfortunately, the vending machine is not prepared to yield a large biscuit for only a small coin

$$(FOOLCUST \| VMC) = \mu X.(in2p{\rightarrow}large{\rightarrow}X \,|\, in1p{\rightarrow}STOP)$$

The *STOP* that supervenes after the first *in1p* is known as *deadlock*. Although each component process is prepared to engage in some further action, these actions are different; since the processes cannot agree on what the next action shall be, nothing further can happen.   □

The stories that accompany these examples show a sad betrayal of proper standards of scientific abstraction and objectivity. It is important to remember that events are intended to be neutral transitions which could be observed and recorded by some dispassionate visitor from another planet, who knows nothing of the pleasures of eating biscuits, or of the hunger suffered by the foolish customer as he vainly tries to obtain sustenance. We have deliberately chosen the alphabet of relevant events to exclude such internal emotional states; if and when desired, further events can be introduced to model internal state changes, as shown in 2.3 X1.

2.2.1   Laws

The laws governing the behaviour of $(P \| Q)$ are exceptionally simple and regular. The first law expresses the logical symmetry between a process and its environment

L1 $P \| Q = Q \| P$

The next law shows that when three processes are assembled, it does not matter in which order they are put together

L2 $P \| (Q \| R) = (P \| Q) \| R$

Thirdly, a deadlocked process infects the whole system with deadlock; but composition with $RUN_{\alpha P}$ (1.1.3 X8) makes no difference

L3A $P \| STOP_{\alpha P} = STOP_{\alpha P}$

L3B $P \| RUN_{\alpha P} = P$

The next laws show how a pair of processes either engage simultaneously in the same action, or deadlock if they disagree on what the first action should be

L4A $(c \rightarrow P) \| (c \rightarrow Q) = (c \rightarrow (P \| Q))$

L4B $(c \rightarrow P) \| (d \rightarrow Q) = STOP$ if $c \neq d$

These laws readily generalize to cases when one or both processes offer a choice of initial event; only events which they both offer will remain possible when the processes are combined

L4 $(x{:}A \rightarrow P(x)) \| (y{:}B \rightarrow Q(y)) = (z{:}(A \cap B) \rightarrow (P(z) \| Q(z)))$

It is this law which permits a system defined in terms of concurrency to be given an alternative description without concurrency.

Example

X1   Let $P = (a \rightarrow b \rightarrow P \mid b \rightarrow P)$
and $Q = (a \rightarrow (b \rightarrow Q \mid c \rightarrow Q))$

Then $(P \| Q) = a \rightarrow ((b \rightarrow P) \| (b \rightarrow Q \mid c \rightarrow Q))$ by L4A

$= a \rightarrow (b \rightarrow (P \| Q))$ by L4A

$= \mu X.(a \rightarrow b \rightarrow X)$ since the recursion is guarded. $\square$

2.2.2 Implementation

The implementation of the $\|$ combinator is clearly based on L4

$intersect(P, Q) = \lambda z.$
    if $P(z) = "BLEEP \vee Q(z) = "BLEEP$ **then** $"BLEEP$
                                    else $intersect(P(z), \ Q(z))$

2.2.3 Traces

Since each action of $(P \| Q)$ requires simultaneous participation of both P and Q, each sequence of such actions must be possible for both these operands. For the same reason, $/s$ distributes through $\|$.

L1 $traces(P \| Q) = traces(P) \cap traces(Q)$

L2 $(P \| Q)/s = (P/s) \| (Q/s)$

2.3 CONCURRENCY

The operator described in the previous section can be generalized to the case when its operands P and Q have different alphabets

$\alpha P \neq \alpha Q$

When such processes are assembled to run concurrently, events that are in both their alphabets (as explained in the previous section) require simultaneous participation of both P and Q. However, events in the alphabet of P but not in the alphabet of Q are of no concern to Q, which is physically incapable of controlling or even of noticing them. Such events may occur independently of Q whenever P engages in them. Similarly, Q may engage alone in events which are in the alphabet of Q but not of P. Thus the set of all events that are logically possible for the system is simply the union of the alphabets of the component processes

$$\alpha(P\|Q) = \alpha P \cup \alpha Q$$

This is a rare example of an operator which takes operands with different alphabets, and yields a result with yet a third alphabet. However in the case when the two operands have the same alphabet, so does the resulting combination, and $(P\|Q)$ has exactly the meaning described in the previous section.

Examples

X1 Let $\alpha NOISYVM = \{coin, choc, clink, clunk, toffee\}$

where *clink* is the sound of a coin dropping into the moneybox of a noisy vending machine

and   *clunk* is the sound made by the vending machine on completion of a transaction.

The noisy vending machine has run out of toffee

$$NOISYVM = (coin{\rightarrow}clink{\rightarrow}choc{\rightarrow}clunk{\rightarrow}NOISYVM)$$

The customer of this machine definitely prefers toffee; the *curse* is what he utters when he fails to get it; he then has to take a chocolate instead

$$\alpha CUST = \{coin, choc, curse, toffee\}$$

$$CUST = (coin{\rightarrow}(toffee{\rightarrow}CUST \mid curse{\rightarrow}choc{\rightarrow}CUST))$$

The result of the concurrent activity of these two processes is

$$(NOISYVM\|CUST) = \mu X.(coin{\rightarrow}(clink{\rightarrow}curse{\rightarrow}choc{\rightarrow}clunk{\rightarrow}X$$
$$\mid curse{\rightarrow}clink{\rightarrow}choc{\rightarrow}clunk{\rightarrow}X))$$

Note that the *clink* may occur before the *curse*, or the other way round. They may even occur simultaneously, and it will not matter in which order they are recorded. Note also that the mathematical formula in no way represents the fact that the customer prefers to get a toffee rather than utter a curse. The formula is an abstraction from reality, which ignores human emotions and concentrates on describing only the possibilities of occurrence and non-occurrence of events within the alphabet of the processes, whether these events are desired or not.   □

X2

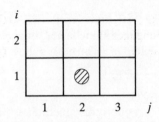

A counter starts at the middle bottom square of the board, and may move within the board either *up, down, left* or *right*.

Let $\alpha P = \{up,\ down\}$
   $P = (up \rightarrow down \rightarrow P)$
   $\alpha Q = \{left,\ right\}$
   $Q = (right \rightarrow left \rightarrow Q$
       $|\ left \rightarrow right \rightarrow Q)$

The behaviour of the counter may be defined

   $P \| Q$

In this example, the alphabets αP and αQ have *no* event in common. Consequently, the movements of the counter are an arbitrary interleaving of actions from the process P with actions from the process Q. Such interleavings are very laborious to describe without concurrency. For example, let R_{ij} stand for the behaviour of the counter (X2) when situated in row i and column j of the board, for $i \in \{1,2\}$, $j \in \{1,2,3\}$.

Then $(P \| Q) = R_{12}$, where
   $R_{21} = (down \rightarrow R_{11} | right \rightarrow R_{22})$
   $R_{11} = (up \rightarrow R_{21} | right \rightarrow R_{12})$
   $R_{22} = (down \rightarrow R_{12} | left \rightarrow R_{21} | right \rightarrow R_{23})$
   $R_{12} = (up \rightarrow R_{22} | left \rightarrow R_{11} | right \rightarrow R_{13})$
   $R_{23} = (down \rightarrow R_{13} | left \rightarrow R_{22})$
   $R_{13} = (up \rightarrow R_{23} | left \rightarrow R_{12})$ □

2.3.1 Laws

The first three laws for the extended form of concurrency are similar to those for interaction (Section 2.2.1)

L1,2 $\|$ is symmetric and associative

L3A $P \| STOP_{\alpha P} = STOP_{\alpha P}$

L3B $P \| RUN_{\alpha P} = P$

Let $a \in (\alpha P - \alpha Q)$, $b \in (\alpha Q - \alpha P)$ and $\{c, d\} \subseteq (\alpha P \cap \alpha Q)$. The following laws show the way in which P engages alone in a, Q engages alone in b, but c and d require simultaneous participation of both P and Q

L4A $(c \rightarrow P) \| (c \rightarrow Q) = c \rightarrow (P \| Q)$

L4B $(c \rightarrow P) \| (d \rightarrow Q) = STOP$ if $c \neq d$

L5A $(a \rightarrow P) \| (c \rightarrow Q) = a \rightarrow (P \| (c \rightarrow Q))$

L5B $(c \rightarrow P) \| (b \rightarrow Q) = b \rightarrow ((c \rightarrow P) \| Q)$

L6 $(a \rightarrow P) \| (b \rightarrow Q) = (a \rightarrow (P \| (b \rightarrow Q)) \,|\, b \rightarrow ((a \rightarrow P) \| Q))$

These laws can be generalized to deal with the general choice operator

L7 Let $P = (x : A \rightarrow P(x))$
and $Q = (y : B \rightarrow Q(y))$

Then $(P \| Q) = (z : C \rightarrow P' \| Q')$

where $C = (A \cap B) \cup (A - \alpha Q) \cup (B - \alpha P)$
and $P' = P(z)$ if $z \in A$
         $= P$ otherwise
and $Q' = Q(z)$ if $z \in B$
         $= Q$ otherwise.

These laws permit a process defined by concurrency to be redefined without that operator, as shown in the following example

Example

X1 Let $\alpha P = \{a, c\}$, $\alpha Q = \{b, c\}$
     Let $P = (a \rightarrow c \rightarrow P)$
     Let $Q = (c \rightarrow b \rightarrow Q)$

Therefore $P \| Q = (a \rightarrow c \rightarrow P) \| (c \rightarrow b \rightarrow Q)$ by definition
              $= a \rightarrow ((c \rightarrow P) \| (c \rightarrow b \rightarrow Q))$ by L5
              $= a \rightarrow c \rightarrow (P \| (b \rightarrow Q))$ by L4...(1)

Also $P \| (b \rightarrow Q) = (a \rightarrow (c \rightarrow P) \| (b \rightarrow Q)$
                 $| \, b \rightarrow (P \| Q))$ by L6
                $= (a \rightarrow b \rightarrow ((c \rightarrow P) \| Q)$
                 $| \, b \rightarrow (P \| Q))$ by L5
                $= (a \rightarrow b \rightarrow c \rightarrow (P \| (b \rightarrow Q))$ $\Big\{$ by L4
                 $| \, b \rightarrow a \rightarrow c \rightarrow (P \| (b \rightarrow Q)))$ and (1) above
                $= \mu X . (a \rightarrow b \rightarrow c \rightarrow X$ $\Big\{$ since this
                 $| \, b \rightarrow a \rightarrow c \rightarrow X)$ is guarded

Therefore $(P \| Q) = (a \rightarrow c \rightarrow \mu X . (a \rightarrow b \rightarrow c \rightarrow X$
                         $| \, b \rightarrow a \rightarrow c \rightarrow X))$ by (1) above $\square$

2.3.2 Implementation

The implementation of the operator $\parallel$ is derived directly from the law L7. The alphabets of the operands are represented as finite lists of symbols, A and B. Test of membership uses the function $ismember(x, A)$ defined in Section 1.7.

$(P\|Q)$ is implemented by calling a function

$\qquad concurrent(P,\ \alpha P,\ \alpha Q,\ Q)$

which is defined as follows

$\qquad concurrent(P,\ A,\ B,\ Q) = aux(P,\ Q)$

where $aux(P,\ Q) =$
$\lambda x.$ **if** $P="BLEEP$ **or** $Q="BLEEP$ **then** $"BLEEP$
else if $ismember(x,\ A) \wedge ismember(x,\ B)$ **then** $aux(P(x),\ Q(x))$
else if $ismember(x,\ A)$ **then** $aux(P(x),\ Q)$
else if $ismember(x,\ B)$ **then** $aux(P,\ Q(x))$
$\qquad\qquad\qquad$ **else** $"BLEEP$

2.3.3 Traces

Let t be a trace of $(P\|Q)$. Then every event in t which belongs to the alphabet of P has been an event in the life of P; and every event in t which does not belong to αP has occurred without the participation of P. Thus $(t\restriction\alpha P)$ is a trace of all those events in which P has participated, and is therefore a trace of P. By a similar argument $(t\restriction\alpha Q)$ is a trace of Q. Furthermore, every event in t must be in either αP or αQ. This reasoning suggests the law

L1 $traces(P\|Q) = \{t|(t\restriction\alpha P)\in traces(P)\wedge(t\restriction\alpha Q)\in traces(Q)\wedge t\in(\alpha P\cup\alpha Q)^*\}$

The next law shows how the $/s$ operator distributes through parallel composition

L2 $(P\|Q)/s = (P/(s\restriction\alpha P))\|(Q/(s\restriction\alpha Q))$

When $\alpha P = \alpha Q$, it follows that

$\qquad s\restriction\alpha P = s\restriction\alpha Q = s$

and these laws are then the same as in Section 2.2.3.

Example

X1 See 2.3 X1.

Let $t1 = \langle coin, \ clink, \ curse \rangle$
Then $t1 \upharpoonright \alpha NOISYVM = \langle coin, \ clink \rangle$ which is in $traces(NOISYVM)$
and $t1 \upharpoonright \alpha CUST = \langle coin, \ curse \rangle$ which is in $traces(CUST)$
Therefore $t1 \in traces(NOISYVM \| CUST)$

Similar reasoning shows that

$$\langle coin, \ curse, \ clink \rangle \in traces(NOISYVM \| CUST)$$

This shows that the *curse* and the *clink* may be recorded one after the other in either order. They may even occur simultaneously, but we have made the decision to provide no way of recording this. ☐

In summary, a trace of $(P \| Q)$ is a kind of interleaving of a trace of P with a trace of Q, in which events which are in the alphabet of both of them occur only once. If $\alpha P \cap \alpha Q = \{\}$ then the traces are pure interleavings (Section 1.9.3), as shown in 2.3 X2. At the other extreme, where $\alpha P = \alpha Q$, every event belongs to both of the alphabets, and the meaning of $(P \| Q)$ is exactly as defined for interaction (Section 2.2).

L3A If $\alpha P \cap \alpha Q = \{\}$
$traces(P \| Q) = \{s \mid \exists t : traces(P). \ \exists u : traces(Q). \ s \ interleaves(t, u)\}$

    L3B If $\alpha P = \alpha Q$
    $traces(P \| Q) = traces(P) \cap traces(Q)$

2.4 PICTURES

A process P with alphabet $\{a,b,c\}$ is pictured as a box labelled P, from which emerge a number of lines, each labelled with a different event from its alphabet (Fig. 2.1). Similarly, Q with alphabet $\{b,c,d\}$ may be pictured as in Fig. 2.2.

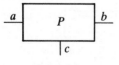

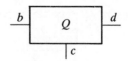

      Figure 2.1   **Figure 2.2**

When these two processes are put together to evolve concurrently, the resulting system may be pictured as a network in which similarly labelled lines are connected, but lines labelled by events in the alphabet of only one process are left free (Fig. 2.3). A third process R with $\alpha R=\{c,e\}$ may be

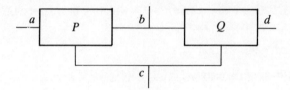

Figure 2.3

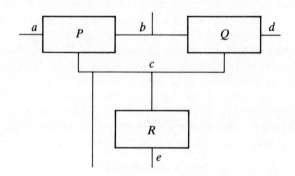

Figure 2.4

added, as shown in Fig. 2.4. This diagram shows that the event c requires participation of all three processes, b requires participation of P and Q, whereas each remaining event is the sole concern of a single process. Pictures of this kind will be known as connection diagrams.

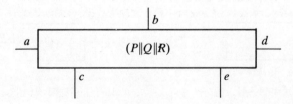

Figure 2.5

But these pictures could be quite misleading. A system constructed from three processes is still only a single process, and should therefore be pictured as a single box (Fig. 2.5). The number 60 can be constructed as the product of three other numbers ($3\times4\times5$); but after it has been so constructed it is still only a single number, and the manner of its construction is no longer relevant or even observable.

2.5   EXAMPLE: THE DINING PHILOSOPHERS

In ancient times, a wealthy philanthropist endowed a College to accommodate five eminent philosophers. Each philosopher had a room in which he could engage in his professional activity of thinking; there was also a common dining room, furnished with a circular table, surrounded by five chairs, each labelled by the name of the philosopher who was to sit in it. The names of the philosophers were $PHIL_0$, $PHIL_1$, $PHIL_2$, $PHIL_3$, $PHIL_4$, and they were disposed in this order anticlockwise round the table. To the left of each philosopher there was laid a golden fork, and in the centre stood a large bowl of spaghetti, which was constantly replenished.

A philosopher was expected to spend most of his time thinking; but when he felt hungry, he went to the dining room, sat down in his own chair, picked up his own fork on his left, and plunged it into the spaghetti. But such is the tangled nature of spaghetti that a second fork is required to carry it to the mouth. The philosopher therefore had also to pick up the fork on his right. When he was finished he would put down both his forks, get up from his chair, and continue thinking. Of course, a fork can be used by only one philosopher at a time. If the other philosopher wants it, he just has to wait until the fork is available again.

2.5.1   Alphabets

We shall now construct a mathematical model of this system. First we must select the relevant sets of events. For $PHIL_i$, the set is defined

$$\alpha PHIL_i = \{i.sits\ down, i.gets\ up,$$
$$i.picks\ up\ fork.i, i.picks\ up\ fork.(i \oplus 1),$$
$$i.puts\ down\ fork.i, i.puts\ down\ fork.(i \oplus 1)\}$$

where $\oplus$ is addition modulo 5, so $i \oplus 1$ identifies the right-hand neighbour of the ith philosopher.

Note that the alphabets of the philosophers are mutually disjoint. There is no event in which they participate jointly, so there is no way whatsoever in which they can interact or communicate with each other—a realistic reflection of the behaviour of philosophers in those days.

The other actors in our little drama are the five forks, each of which bears the same number as the philosopher who owns it. A fork is picked up and put down either by this philosopher, or by his neighbour on the other side. The alphabet of the ith fork is defined

$$\alpha FORK_i = \{i.picks\ up\ fork.i,\ (i\ominus 1).picks\ up\ fork.i,$$
$$i.puts\ down\ fork.i,\ (i\ominus 1).puts\ down\ fork.i\}$$

where $\ominus$ denotes subtraction modulo 5.

Thus each event except sitting down and getting up requires participation of exactly two adjacent actors, a philosopher and a fork, as shown in the connection diagram of Fig. 2.6.

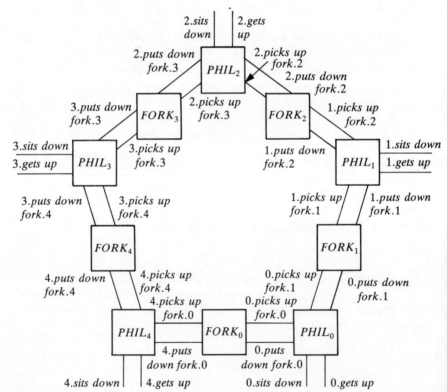

Figure 2.6

2.5.2   Behaviour

Apart from thinking and eating which we have chosen to ignore, the life of each philosopher is described as the repetition of a cycle of six events

$$PHIL_i = (i.sitsdown \rightarrow i.picks \ up \ fork.i \rightarrow i.picks \ up \ fork.(i \oplus 1) \rightarrow$$
$$i.puts \ down \ fork.i \rightarrow i.puts \ down \ fork.(i \oplus 1) \rightarrow$$
$$i.gets \ up \rightarrow PHIL_i)$$

The rôle of a fork is a simple one; it is repeatedly picked up and put down by one of its adjacent philosophers (the same one on both occasions)

$$FORK_i = (i.picks \ up \ fork.i \rightarrow i.puts \ down \ fork.i \rightarrow FORK_i$$
$$| \ (i \ominus 1).picks \ up \ fork.i \rightarrow (i \ominus 1).puts \ down \ fork.i \rightarrow FORK_i)$$

The behaviour of the whole College is the concurrent combination of the behaviour of each of these components

$$PHILOS \quad = (PHIL_0 \| PHIL_1 \| PHIL_2 \| PHIL_3 \| PHIL_4)$$
$$FORKS \quad = (FORK_0 \| FORK_1 \| FORK_2 \| FORK_3 \| FORK_4)$$
$$COLLEGE = (PHILOS \| FORKS)$$

An interesting variation of this story allows the philosophers to pick up their two forks in either order, or put them down in either order. Consider the behaviour of each philosopher's hand separately. Each hand is capable of picking up the relevant fork, but both hands are needed for sitting down and getting up

$$\alpha LEFT_i \quad = \{i.picks \ up \ fork.i, \ i.puts \ down \ fork.i,$$
$$i.sits \ down, \ i.gets \ up\}$$
$$\alpha RIGHT_i = \{i.picks \ up \ fork.(i \oplus 1), \ i.puts \ down \ fork.(i \oplus 1),$$
$$i.sits \ down, \ i.gets \ up\}$$
$$LEFT_i \quad = (i.sits \ down \rightarrow i.picks \ up \ fork.i \rightarrow$$
$$i.puts \ down \ fork.i \rightarrow i.gets \ up \rightarrow LEFT_i)$$
$$RIGHT_i = (i.sits \ down \rightarrow i.picks \ up \ fork.(i \oplus 1) \rightarrow$$
$$i.puts \ down \ fork.(i \oplus 1) \rightarrow i.gets \ up \rightarrow RIGHT_i)$$
$$PHIL_i \quad = LEFT_i \| RIGHT_i$$

Synchronization of sitting down and getting up by both $LEFT_i$ and $RIGHT_i$ ensures that no fork can be raised except when the relevant philosopher is seated. Apart from this, operations on the two forks are arbitrarily interleaved.

In yet another variation of the story, each fork may be picked up and put down many times on each occasion that the philosopher sits down. Thus the behaviour of the hands is modified to contain an iteration, for example

$LEFT_i = (i.sits\ down \rightarrow$
$\quad \mu X.(i.picks\ up\ fork.i \rightarrow i.puts\ down\ fork.i \rightarrow X$
$\quad |\ i.gets\ up \rightarrow LEFT_i))$

2.5.3 Deadlock!

When a mathematical model had been constructed, it revealed a serious danger. Suppose all the philosophers get hungry at about the same time; they all sit down; they all pick up their own forks; and they all reach out for the other fork—which isn't there. In this undignified situation, they will all inevitably starve. Although each actor is capable of further action, there is no action which any pair of them can agree to do next.

However, our story does not end so sadly. Once the danger was detected, there were suggested many ways to avert it. For example, one of the philosophers could always pick up the wrong fork first—if only they could have agreed which one it should be! The purchase of a single additional fork was ruled out for similar reasons, whereas the purchase of five more forks was much too expensive.

The solution finally adopted was the appointment of a footman, whose duty it was to assist each philosopher into and out of his chair. His alphabet was defined as

$$\bigcup_{i=0}^{4} \{i.sits\ down,\ i.gets\ up\}$$

This footman was given secret instructions never to allow more than four philosophers to be seated simultaneously. His behaviour is most simply defined by mutual recursion.

Let $U = \bigcup_{i=0}^{4} \{i.gets\ up\}, \qquad D = \bigcup_{i=0}^{4} \{i.sits\ down\}$

$FOOT_j$ defines the behaviour of the footman with j philosophers seated

$FOOT_0 = (x:D \rightarrow FOOT_1)$
$FOOT_j = (x:D \rightarrow FOOT_{j+1} |\ y:U \rightarrow FOOT_{j-1}) \qquad$ for $j \in \{1,\ 2,\ 3\}$
$FOOT_4 = (y:U \rightarrow FOOT_3)$

A college free of deadlock is defined

$NEWCOLLEGE = (COLLEGE \| FOOT_0)$

The edifying tale of the dining philosophers is due to Edsger W. Dijkstra. The footman is due to Carel S. Scholten.

2.5.4   Proof of absence of deadlock

In the original *COLLEGE* the risk of deadlock was far from obvious; the claim that *NEWCOLLEGE* is free from deadlock should therefore be proved with some care. What we must prove can be stated formally as

$$(NEWCOLLEGE/s) \neq STOP \quad \text{for all } s \in traces(NEWCOLLEGE)$$

The proof proceeds by taking an arbitrary trace s, and showing that in all cases there is at least one event by which s can be extended and still remain in *traces(NEWCOLLEGE)*. First we define the number of seated philosophers

$$seated(s) = \#(s \restriction D) - \#(s \restriction U) \qquad \text{where } U \text{ and } D \text{ are defined above}$$

Because (by 2.3.3 L1) $s \restriction (U \cup D) \in traces(FOOT_0)$, we know that

$$seated(s) \leq 4$$

If $seated(s) \leq 3$, at least one more philosopher can sit down, so that there is no deadlock. In the remaining case that $seated(s) = 4$, consider the number of philosophers who are eating (with both their forks raised). If this is nonzero, then an eating philosopher can always put down his left fork. In the remaining case that no philosopher is eating, consider the number of raised forks. If this is three or less, then one of the seated philosophers can still pick up his left fork. If there are four raised forks, then the philosopher to the left of the vacant seat already has raised his left fork and can pick up his right one. If there are five raised forks, then at least one of the four seated philosophers must be eating.

This proof involves analysis of a number of cases, described informally in terms of the behaviour of this particular example. Let us consider an alternative proof method: program a computer to explore all possible behaviours of the system to look for deadlock. In general, we could never know whether such a program had looked far enough to guarantee absence of deadlock. But in the case of a finite-state system like the *COLLEGE* it is sufficient to consider only those traces whose length does not exceed a known upper bound on the number of states. The number of states of $(P \| Q)$ does not exceed the product of the number of states of P and the number of states of Q. Since each philosopher has six states and each fork has three states, the total number of states of the *COLLEGE* does not exceed

$$6^5 \times 3^5, \text{ or approximately 1.8 million}$$

Since the alphabet of the footman is contained in that of the *COLLEGE*, the *NEWCOLLEGE* cannot have more states than the *COLLEGE*. Since in nearly every state there are two or more possible events, the number of traces that must be examined will exceed two raised to the power of 1.8 million. There is no hope that a computer will ever be able to explore all these possibilities. Proof of the absence of deadlock, even for quite simple finite processes, will remain the responsibility of the designer of concurrent systems.

2.5.5 Infinite overtaking

Apart from deadlock, there is another danger which faces a dining philosopher—that of being infinitely often overtaken by a neighbour. Suppose that a seated philosopher has an extremely greedy left neighbour, and a rather slow left arm. Before he can pick up his left fork, his left neighbour rushes in, sits down, rapidly picks up both forks, and spends a long time eating. Eventually he puts down both forks, and leaves his seat. But then the left neighbour instantly gets hungry again, rushes in, sits down, and rapidly snatches both forks, before his long-seated and long-suffering right neighbour gets round to picking up the fork they share. Since this cycle may be repeated indefinitely, a seated philosopher may never succeed in eating.

The correct solution to this problem is probably to regard it as insoluble, because if any philosopher is as greedy as described above, then somebody (either he or his neighbours) will inevitably spend a long time hungry. There is no clever way of ensuring general satisfaction, and the only effective solution is to buy more forks, and plenty of spaghetti.

However, if it is important to guarantee that a seated philosopher will eventually eat, modify the behaviour of the footman: having helped a philosopher to his seat he waits until that philosopher has picked up both forks before he allows either of his neighbours to sit down.

But there remains a more philosophical problem about infinite overtaking. Suppose the footman conceives an irrational dislike for one of the philosophers, and persistently delays the action of escorting him to his chair, even when the philosopher is ready to engage in that event. This is a possibility that cannot be described in our conceptual framework, because we cannot distinguish it from the possibility that the philosopher himself takes an indefinitely long time to get hungry. So here is a problem, like detailed timing problems, which we have deliberately decided to ignore, or rather to delegate to a different phase of design and implementation. It is an implementor's responsibility to ensure that any desirable event that becomes possible will take place within an acceptable interval. The implementor of a conventional high-level programming language has a similar obligation not to insert arbitrary delays into the execution of a program, even though the programmer has no way of enforcing or even describing this obligation.

2.6   CHANGE OF SYMBOL

The example of the previous section involved two collections of processes, philosophers and forks; within each collection the processes have very similar behaviour, except that the names of the events in which they engage are different. In this section we introduce a convenient method of defining groups of processes with similar behaviour. Let f be a one–one function (injection) which maps the alphabet of P onto a set of symbols A

$$f : \alpha P \rightarrow A$$

We define the process $f(P)$ as one which engages in the event $f(c)$ whenever P would have engaged in c. It follows that

$$\alpha f(P) = f(\alpha P)$$

$$traces(f(P)) = \{f^*(s) \,|\, s \in traces(P)\}$$

(For the definition of f^* see 1.9.1).

Examples

X1   After a few years, the price of everything goes up. To represent the effect of inflation, we define a function f by the following equations

$$\begin{array}{ll}
f(in2p) & = in10p \\
f(in1p) & = in5p \\
f(out1p) & = out5p
\end{array}
\qquad
\begin{array}{l}
f(large) = large \\
f(small) = small
\end{array}$$

The new vending machine is

$$NEWVMC = f(VMC) \qquad\qquad\qquad \square$$

X2   A counter behaves like CT_0 (1.1.4 X2), except that it moves *right* and *left* instead of *up* and *down*

$$f(up) = right, \quad f(down) = left, \quad f(around) = around,$$

$$LR_0 = f(CT_0) \qquad\qquad\qquad\qquad \square$$

The main reason for changing event names of processes in this fashion is to enable them to be composed usefully in concurrent combination.

X3   A counter moves *left, right, up* or *down* on an infinite board with boundaries at the left and at the bottom

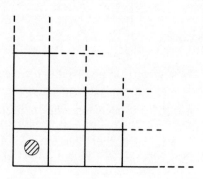

It starts at the bottom left corner. On this square alone, it can turn *around*. As in 2.3 X2, vertical and horizontal movements can be modelled as independent actions of separate processes; but *around* requires simultaneous participation of both

$$LRUD = LR_0 \| CT_0$$ □

X4   We wish to connect two instances of *COPYBIT* (1.1.3 X7) in series, so that each bit output by the first is simultaneously input by the second. First, we need to change the names of the events used for internal communication; we therefore introduce two new events *mid*.0 and *mid*.1, and define the functions f and g to change the output of one process and the input of the other

$$f(out.0) = g(in.0) = mid.0$$
$$f(out.1) = g(in.1) = mid.1$$
$$f(in.0) = in.0, \; f(in.1) = in.1$$
$$g(out.0) = out.0, \; g(out.1) = out.1$$

The answer we want is

$$CHAIN2 = f(COPYBIT) \| g(COPYBIT)$$

Note that each output of 0 or 1 by the left operand of $\|$ is (by the definition of f and g) the very same event (*mid*.0 or *mid*.1) as the input of the same 0 or 1 by the right operand. This models the synchronized communication of binary digits on a channel which connects the two operands, as shown in Fig. 2.7.

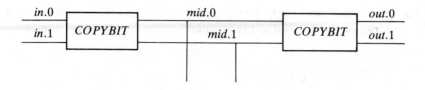

Figure 2.7

The left operand offers no choice of which value is transmitted on the connecting channel, whereas the right operand is prepared to engage in either of the events $mid.0$ or $mid.1$. It is therefore the outputting process that determines on each occasion which of these two events will occur. This method of communication between concurrent processes will be generalized in Chapter 4.

Note that the internal communications $mid.0$ and $mid.1$ are still in the alphabet of the composite process, and can be observed (or even perhaps controlled) by its environment. Sometimes one wishes to ignore or conceal such internal events; in the general case such concealment may introduce nondeterminism, so this topic is postponed to Section 3.5.   □

X5 We wish to represent the behaviour of a Boolean variable used by a computer program. The events in its alphabet are

$assign0$ assignment of value zero to the variable
$assign1$ assignment of value one to the variable
$fetch0$ access of the value of the variable at a time when it is zero
$fetch1$ access of the value of the variable at a time when it is one

The behaviour of the variable is remarkably similar to that of the drinks dispenser (1.1.4 X1), so we define

$BOOL = f(DD)$

where the definition of f is a trivial exercise. Note that this Boolean variable refuses to give its value until after a value has been first assigned. An attempt to fetch an unassigned value would result in deadlock—which is probably the kindest failure mode for incorrect programs, because the simplest postmortem will pinpoint the error.   □

The tree picture of $f(P)$ may be constructed from the tree picture of P by simply applying the function f to the labels on all the branches. Because f is a one–one function, this transformation preserves the structure of the tree and the important distinctness of labels on all branches leading from the same node. For example, a picture of $NEWVMC$ is shown in Fig. 2.8.

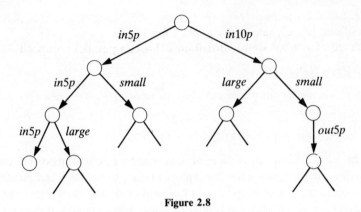

Figure 2.8

2.6.1 Laws

Change of symbol by application of a one–one function does not change the structure of the behaviour of a process. This is reflected by the fact that function application distributes through all other operators, as described in the following laws. The following auxiliary definitions are used

$f(B) = \{f(x) | x \in B\}$
f^{-1} is the inverse of f
$f \circ g$ is the composition of f and g
f^* is defined in Section 1.9.1

(the need for f^{-1} in the following laws is an important reason for insisting that f is an injection).

After change of symbol, *STOP* still performs no event from its changed alphabet

L1 $f(STOP_A) = STOP_{f(A)}$

In the case of a choice, the symbols offered for selection are changed, and the subsequent behaviour is similarly changed

L2 $f(x:B \rightarrow P(x)) = (y:f(B) \rightarrow f(P(f^{-1}(y))))$

The use of f^{-1} on the right-hand side may need explanation. Recall that P is a function delivering a process depending on selection of some x from the set B. But the variable y on the right-hand side is selected from the set $f(B)$. The corresponding event for P is $f^{-1}(y)$, which is in B (since $y \in f(B)$). The behaviour of P after this event is $P(f^{-1}(y))$, and the actions of this process must continue to be changed by application of f.

Change of symbol simply distributes through parallel composition

L3 $f(P \| Q) = f(P) \| f(Q)$

Change of symbol distributes in a slightly more complex way over recursion, changing the alphabet in the appropriate way

L4 $f(\mu X{:}A.F(X)) = (\mu Y{:}f(A).\ f(F(f^{-1}(Y))))$

Again, the use of f^{-1} on the right-hand side may be puzzling. Recall that the validity of the recursion on the left-hand side requires that F is a function which takes as argument a process with alphabet A, and delivers a process with the same alphabet. On the right-hand side, Y is a variable ranging over processes with alphabet $f(A)$, and cannot be used as an argument to F until its alphabet has been changed back to A. This is done by applying the inverse function f^{-1}. Now $F(f^{-1}(Y))$ has alphabet A, so an application of f will transform the alphabet to $f(A)$, thus ensuring validity of the recursion on the right-hand side of the law.

The composition of two changes of symbol is defined by the composition of the two symbol-changing functions

L5 $f(g(P)) = (f \circ g)\ (P)$

The traces of a process after change of symbol are obtained simply by changing the individual symbols in every trace of the original process

L6 $traces(f(P)) = \{f^*(s) | s \in traces(P)\}$

The explanation of the next and final law is similar to that of L6

L7 $f(P)/f^*(s) = f(P/s)$

2.6.2 Process labelling

Change of symbol is particularly useful in constructing groups of similar processes which operate concurrently in providing identical services to their common environment, but which do not interact with each other in any way at all. This means that they must all have different and mutually disjoint alphabets. To achieve this, each process is labelled by a different name; and each event of a labelled process is also labelled by its name. A labelled event is a pair $l.x$, where l is a label, and x is the symbol standing for the event.

A process P labelled by l is denoted by

$l{:}P$

It engages in the event $l.x$ whenever P would have engaged in x. The function required to define $l:P$ is

$$f_l(x) = l.x \qquad \text{for all } x \text{ in } \alpha P$$

and the definition of labelling is

$$l:P = f_l(P)$$

Examples

X1   A pair of vending machines standing side by side

$$(left:VMS)\,\|\,(right:VMS)$$

The alphabets of the two processes are disjoint, and every event that occurs is labelled by the name of the machine on which it occurred. If the machines were not named before being placed in parallel, every event would require participation of both of them, and the pair would be indistinguishable from a single machine; this is a consequence of the fact that

$$(VMS\|VMS) = VMS \qquad\qquad\qquad \square$$

The labelling of processes permits them to be used in the manner of variables in a high-level programming language, declared locally in the block of program which uses them.

X2   The behaviour of a Boolean variable is modelled by $BOOL$ (2.6 X5). The behaviour of a block of program is represented by a process $USER$. This process assigns and accesses the values of two Boolean variables named b and c. Thus $\alpha USER$ includes such compound events as

$b.assign0$ to assign value zero to b
$c.fetch1$ to access the current value of c when it is 1.

The $USER$ process runs in parallel with its two Boolean variables

$$b:BOOL\|c:BOOL\|USER.$$

Inside the $USER$ program, the following effects may be achieved

$b:=false;\ P$ by $(b.assign0{\rightarrow}P)$
$b:= \neg c;\ P$ by $(c.fetch0{\rightarrow}b.assign1{\rightarrow}\ P$
                        $\ |\ c.fetch1{\rightarrow}b.assign0{\rightarrow}P)$

Note how the current value of the variable is discovered by allowing the variable to make the choice between $fetch0$ and $fetch1$; and this choice affects in an appropriate way the subsequent behaviour of the $USER$. $\square$

In X2 and the following examples it would have been more convenient to define the effect of the single assignment, e.g.,

$b:=false$

rather than the pair of commands

$b:=false; P$

which explicitly mentions the rest of the program P. The means of doing this will be introduced in Chapter 5.

X3 A *USER* process needs two count variables named l and m. They are initialized to 0 and 3 respectively. The *USER* process increments each variable by $l.up$ or $m.up$, and decrements it (when positive) by $l.down$ or $m.down$. A test of zero is provided by the events $l.around$ and $m.around$. Thus the process CT (1.1.4 X2) can be used after appropriate labelling by l and by m

$$(l:CT_0\|m:CT_3\|USER)$$

Within the *USER* process the following effects (expressed in conventional notation) can be achieved

$(m:=m+1; P)$ by $(m.up{\rightarrow}P)$
if $l=0$ **then** P **else** Q by $(l.around{\rightarrow}P\mid l.down{\rightarrow}l.up{\rightarrow}Q)$

Note how the test for zero works: an attempt is made by $l.down$ to reduce the count by one, at the same time as attempting $l.around$. The count selects between these two events: if the value of the count is zero, $l.around$ is selected; and if non-zero, the other alternative. But in the latter case, the value of the count has been decremented, and it must immediately be restored to its original value by $l.up$. In the next example, restoration of the original value is more laborious.

$(m:=m+l; P)$ is implemented by ADD

where ADD is defined recursively

$$ADD = DOWN_0$$

and $DOWN_i = (l.down{\rightarrow}DOWN_{i+1}\mid l.around{\rightarrow}UP_i)$

and $UP_0 = P$

and $UP_{i+1} = l.up{\rightarrow}m.up{\rightarrow}UP_i$

The $DOWN_i$ processes discover the initial value of l by decrementing it to zero. The UP_i processes then add the discovered value to both m and to l, thereby restoring l to its initial value and adding this value to m.   □

The effect of an array variable can be achieved by a collection of concurrent processes, each labelled by its index within the array.

X4   The purpose of the process EL is to record whether the event in has occurred or not. On the first occurrence of in it responds no and on each subsequent occurrence it responds yes

$$\alpha EL = \{in,\ no,\ yes\}$$
$$EL = in \rightarrow no \rightarrow \mu X.(in \rightarrow yes \rightarrow X)$$

This process can be used in an array to mimic the behaviour of a set of small integers

$$SET3 = (0{:}EL)\|(1{:}EL)\|(2{:}EL)\|(3{:}EL)$$

The whole array can be labelled yet again before use

$$m{:}SET3\|USER$$

Each event in $\alpha(m{:}SET3)$ is a triple, e.g., $m.2.in$. Within the $USER$ process, the effect of

if $2 \in m$ **then** P **else** $(m{:}=m\cup\{2\};\ Q)$

may be achieved by

$$m.2.in \rightarrow (m.2.yes \rightarrow P \,|\, m.2.no \rightarrow Q) \qquad\qquad \square$$

2.6.3   Implementation

To implement symbol change in general, we need to know the *inverse g* of the symbol-changing function f. We also need to ensure that g will give the special answer $"BLEEP$ when applied to an argument outside the range of f. The implementation is based on 2.6.1 L4.

$$change(g,P) = \lambda x.\ \textbf{if } g(x)="BLEEP \textbf{ then } "BLEEP$$
$$\textbf{else if } P(g(x))="BLEEP \textbf{ then } "BLEEP$$
$$\textbf{else } change(g,\ P(g(x)))$$

The special case of process labelling can be implemented more simply. The compound event $l.x$ is represented as the pair of atoms $cons("l,"x)$. Now $(l{:}P)$ is implemented by

$$label(l,P) = \lambda y.\ \textbf{if } null(y) \vee atom(y) \textbf{ then } "BLEEP$$
$$\textbf{else if } car(y) \neq l \textbf{ then } "BLEEP$$
$$\textbf{else if } P(cdr(y))="BLEEP \textbf{ then } "BLEEP$$
$$\textbf{else } label(l,\ P(cdr(y)))$$

2.6.4 Multiple labelling

The definition of labelling can be extended to allow each event to take any label l from a set L. If P is a process, $(L\!:\!P)$ is defined as a process which behaves exactly like P, except that it engages in the event $l.c$ (where $l \in L$ and $c \in \alpha P$) whenever P would have done c. The choice of the label l is made independently on each occasion by the environment of $(L\!:\!P)$.

Example

X1 A lackey is a junior footman, who helps his single master to and from his seat, and stands behind his chair while he eats

$$\alpha LACKEY = \{sits\ down,\ gets\ up\}$$
$$LACKEY = (sits\ down \rightarrow gets\ up \rightarrow LACKEY)$$

To teach the lackey to share his services among five masters (but serving only one at a time), we define

$$L = \{0,1,2,3,4\}$$
$$SHARED\ LACKEY = (L\!:\!LACKEY)$$

The shared lackey could be employed to protect the dining philosophers from deadlock when the footman (2.5.3) is on holiday. Of course the philosophers may go hungrier during the holiday, since only one of them is allowed to the table at a time.   □

If L contains more than one label, the tree picture of $L\!:\!P$ is similar to that for P; but it is much more bushy in the sense that there are many more branches leading from each node. For example, the picture of the *LACKEY* is a single trunk with no branches (Fig. 2.9). However, the picture of $\{0,1\}\!:\!LACKEY$ is a complete binary tree (Fig. 2.10). The tree for the *SHARED LACKEY* is even more bushy.

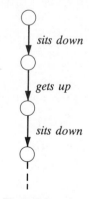

sits down

gets up

sits down

Figure 2.9

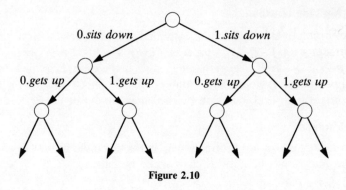

0.*sits down*   1.*sits down*

0.*gets up*   1.*gets up*   0.*gets up*   1.*gets up*

Figure 2.10

In general, multiple labelling can be used to share the services of a single process among a number of other labelled processes, provided that the set of labels is known in advance. This technique will be exploited more fully in Chapter 6.

2.7   SPECIFICATIONS

Let P and Q be processes intended to run concurrently, and suppose we have proved

P **sat** $S(tr)$

and Q **sat** $T(tr)$.

Let tr be a trace of $(P\|Q)$. It follows by 2.3.3 L1 that $(tr{\restriction}\alpha P)$ is a trace of P, and consequently it satisfies S, i.e.,

$S(tr{\restriction}\alpha P)$

Similarly, $(tr{\restriction}\alpha Q)$ is a trace of Q, so

$T(tr{\restriction}\alpha Q)$

This argument holds for every trace of $(P\|Q)$. Consequently we may deduce

$(P\|Q)$ **sat**$(S(tr{\restriction}\alpha P)\wedge T(tr{\restriction}\alpha Q))$

This informal reasoning is summarized in the law

L1   If P **sat** $S(tr)$
    and Q **sat** $T(tr)$
    then $(P\|Q)$ **sat** $(S(tr{\restriction}\alpha P)\wedge T(tr{\restriction}\alpha Q))$

Example

X1 (See 2.3.1 X1)

Let $\alpha P = \{a,c\}$, $\alpha Q = \{b,c\}$
Let $P = (a \rightarrow c \rightarrow P)$
Let $Q = (c \rightarrow b \rightarrow Q)$

We wish to prove that

$(P \| Q)$ **sat** $0 \le tr{\downarrow}a - tr{\downarrow}b \le 2$

The proof of 1.10.2 X1 can obviously be adapted to show that

P **sat** $(0 \le tr{\downarrow}a - tr{\downarrow}c \le 1)$

and Q **sat** $(0 \le tr{\downarrow}c - tr{\downarrow}b \le 1)$

By L1 it follows that

$(P \| Q)$ **sat** $(0 \le (tr{\restriction}\alpha P){\downarrow}a - (tr{\restriction}\alpha P){\downarrow}c \le 1 \wedge 0 \le (tr{\restriction}\alpha Q){\downarrow}c - (tr{\restriction}\alpha Q){\downarrow}b \le 1)$
$\Rightarrow 0 \le tr{\downarrow}a - tr{\downarrow}b \le 2$ since $(tr{\restriction}A){\downarrow}a = tr{\downarrow}a$ whenever $a \in A$. $\square$

Since the laws for **sat** allow $STOP$ to satisfy every satisfiable specification, reasoning based on these laws can never prove absence of deadlock. More powerful laws will be given in Section 3.7. Meanwhile, one way to eliminate the risk of stoppage is by careful proof, as in Section 2.5.4. Another method is to show that a process defined by the parallel combinator is equivalent to a non-stopping process defined without this combinator, as was done in 2.3.1 X1. However, such proofs involve long and tedious algebraic transformations. Wherever possible, one should appeal to some general law, such as

L2 If P and Q never stop and if $(\alpha P \cap \alpha Q)$ contains at most one event, then $(P \| Q)$ never stops.

Example

X2 The process $(P \| Q)$ defined in X1 will never stop, because

$\alpha P \cap \alpha Q = \{c\}$. $\square$

The proof rule for change of symbol is

L3 If P **sat** $S(tr)$
   then $f(P)$ **sat** $S(f^{-1^{*}}(tr))$

The use of $f^{-1^{*}}$ in the consequent of this law may need extra explanation. Let tr be a trace of $f(P)$. Then $f^{-1^{*}}(tr)$ is a trace of P. The antecedent of L3 states that every trace of P satisfies S. It follows that $f^{-1^{*}}(tr)$ satisfies S, which is exactly what is stated by the consequent of L3.

2.8 MATHEMATICAL THEORY OF DETERMINISTIC PROCESSES

In our description of processes, we have stated a large number of laws, and we have occasionally used them in proofs. The laws have been justified (if at all) by informal explanations of why we should expect and want them to be true. For a reader with the instincts of an applied mathematician or engineer, that may be enough. But the question also arises, are these laws in fact true? Are they even consistent? Should there be more of them? Or are they complete in the sense that they permit all true facts about processes to be proved from them? Could one manage with fewer and simpler laws? These are questions for which an answer must be sought in a deeper mathematical investigation.

2.8.1 The basic definitions

In constructing a mathematical model of a physical system, it is a good strategy to define the basic concepts in terms of attributes that can be directly or indirectly observed or measured. For a deterministic process P, we are familiar with two such attributes

αP the set of events in which the process is in principle capable of engaging

$traces(P)$ the set of all sequences of events in which the process can actually participate if required.

We have explained how these two sets must satisfy the three laws 1.8.1 L6, L7, L8. Consider now an arbitrary pair of sets (A,S) which satisfy these three laws. This pair uniquely identifies a process P whose traces are S constructed according to the following definitions

Let $P^0 = \{x \mid \langle x \rangle \in S\}$

and $P(x)$ be the process whose traces are $\{t \mid \langle x \rangle^\wedge t \in S\}$ for all x in P^0

Then $\alpha P = A$

and $P = (x:P^0 \rightarrow P(x))$

Furthermore, the pair (A,S) can be recovered by the equations

$A = \alpha P$
$S = traces(x:P^0 \rightarrow P(x))$

Thus there is a one–one correspondence between each process P and the pairs of sets $(\alpha P, traces(P))$. In mathematics, this is a sufficient justification for identifying the two concepts, by using one of them as the definition of the other.

D0   A deterministic process is a pair

$$(A,S)$$

where A is any set of symbols
and S is any subset of A^* which satisfies the two conditions

C0 $\langle\rangle \in S$
C1 $\forall s,t.\ s^\frown t \in S \Rightarrow s \in S.$

The simplest example of a process which meets this definition is the one that does nothing

D1 $STOP_A = (A, \{\langle\rangle\})$

At the other extreme there is the process that will do anything at any time

D2 $RUN_A = (A, A^*)$

The various operators on processes can now be formally defined by showing how the alphabet and traces of the result are derived from the alphabet and traces of the operands

D3 $(x\colon B \rightarrow (A,\ S(x))) = (A,\ \{\langle\rangle\} \cup \{\langle x \rangle^\frown s \mid x \in B \wedge s \in S(x)\})$ provided $B \subseteq A$

D4 $(A,S)/s = (A, \{t \mid (s^\frown t) \in S\})$ provided $s \in S$

D5 $\mu X\colon A.F(X) = (A, \bigcup\limits_{n \geq 0} traces(F^n(STOP_A)))$

provided F is a guarded expression

D6 $(A,S) \| (B,T) = (A \cup B,\ \{s \mid s \in (A \cup B)^* \wedge (s \restriction A) \in S \wedge (s \restriction B) \in T\})$

D7 $f(A,S) = (f(A),\ \{f^*(s) \mid s \in S\})$ provided f is one–one

Of course, it is necessary to prove that the right-hand sides of these definitions are actually processes, i.e., that they satisfy the conditions C0 and C1 of D0. Fortunately that is quite easy.

In Chapter 3, it will become apparent that D0 is not a fully adequate definition of the concept of a process, because it does not represent the possibility of nondeterminism. Consequently, a more general and more complicated definition will be required. All laws for nondeterministic processes are true for deterministic processes as well. But deterministic processes obey some additional laws, for example

$$P \| P = P$$

To avoid confusion, in this book we have avoided quoting such laws; so all quoted laws may safely be applied to nondeterministic processes as well as deterministic ones.

2.8.2 Fixed-point theory

The purpose of this section is to give an outline of a proof of the fundamental theorem of recursion, that a recursively defined process (2.8.1 D5) is indeed a solution of the corresponding recursive equation, i.e.,

$$\mu X.F(X) = F(\mu X.F(X))$$

The treatment follows the fixed-point theory of Scott.

First, we need to specify an ordering relationship $\sqsubseteq$ among processes

D1 $(A,S) \sqsubseteq (B,T) = (A = B \wedge S \subseteq T)$

Two processes are comparable in this ordering if they have the same alphabet, and one of them can do everything done by the other—and maybe more. This ordering is a partial order in the sense that

L1 $P \sqsubseteq P$

L2 $P \sqsubseteq Q \wedge Q \sqsubseteq P \Rightarrow P = Q$

L3 $P \sqsubseteq Q \wedge Q \sqsubseteq R \Rightarrow P \sqsubseteq R$

A *chain* in a partial order is an infinite sequence of elements

$$\{P_0, P_1, P_2, ...\}$$

such that

$$P_i \sqsubseteq P_{i+1} \qquad\qquad \text{for all } i$$

We define the *limit* (least upper bound) of such a chain

$$\bigsqcup_{i \geq 0} P_i = (\alpha P_0, \bigcup_{i \geq 0} traces(P_i))$$

In future, we will apply the limit operator $\bigsqcup$ only to sequences of processes that form a chain.

A partial order is said to be *complete* if it has a least element, and all chains have a least upper bound. The set of all processes with a given alphabet A form a complete partial order (c.p.o.), since it satisfies the laws

L4 $STOP_A \sqsubseteq P$ provided $\alpha P = A$

L5 $P_i \sqsubseteq \bigsqcup_{i \geq 0} P_i$

L6 $(\forall i \geq 0 . P_i \sqsubseteq Q) \Rightarrow (\bigsqcup_{i \geq 0} P_i) \sqsubseteq Q$

Furthermore the definition of μ (2.8.1 D5) can be reformulated in terms of a limit

L7 $\mu X:A.F(X) = \bigsqcup_{i \geq 0} F^i(STOP_A)$

A function F from one c.p.o. to another one (or the same one) is said to be *continuous* if it distributes over the limits of all chains, i.e.,

$$F(\bigsqcup_{i\geq0} P_i) = \bigsqcup_{i\geq0} F(P_i) \qquad \text{if } \{P_i | i\geq0\} \text{ is a chain}$$

(All continuous functions are monotonic in the sense that

$$P\sqsubseteq Q \Rightarrow F(P)\sqsubseteq F(Q) \qquad \text{for all } P \text{ and } Q,$$

so that the right-hand side of the previous equation is also the limit of an ascending chain.) A function G of several arguments is defined as continuous if it is continuous in each of its arguments separately, for example

$$G((\bigsqcup_{i\geq0} P_i),Q) = \bigsqcup_{i\geq0} G(P_i,Q) \qquad \text{for all } Q$$

and $G(Q, (\bigsqcup_{i\geq0} P_i)) = \bigsqcup_{i\geq0} G(Q,P_i) \qquad \text{for all } Q$

The composition of continuous functions is also continuous; and indeed any expression constructed by application of any number of continuous functions to any number and combination of variables is continuous in each of those variables. For example, if G, F and H are continuous

$$G(F(X), H(X,Y))$$

is continuous in X, i.e.,

$$G(F(\bigsqcup_{i\geq0} P_i), H((\bigsqcup_{i\geq0} P_i),Y)) = \bigsqcup_{i\geq0} G(F(P_i),H(P_i,Y)) \qquad \text{for all } Y$$

All the operators (except /) defined in D3 to D7 are continuous in the sense defined above

L8 $(x:B\rightarrow(\bigsqcup_{i\geq0} P_i(x))) = \bigsqcup_{i\geq0} (x:B\rightarrow P_i(x))$

L9 $\mu X{:}A.F(X,(\bigsqcup_{i\geq0} P_i)) = \bigsqcup_{i\geq0} \mu X{:}A.F(X,P_i)$ provided F is continuous

L10 $(\bigsqcup_{i\geq0} P_i)\|Q = Q\|(\bigsqcup_{i\geq0} P_i) = \bigsqcup_{i\geq0} (Q\|P_i)$

L11 $f(\bigsqcup_{i\geq0} P_i) = \bigsqcup_{i\geq0} f(P_i)$

Consequently if $F(X)$ is any expression constructed solely in terms of these operators, it will be continuous in X. Now it is possible to prove the basic fixed-point theorem

$$F(\mu X{:}A.F(X)) = F(\bigsqcup_{i\geq 0} F^i(STOP_A)) \qquad\qquad \text{def } \mu$$

$$= \bigsqcup_{i\geq 0} F(F^i(STOP_A)) \qquad\qquad \text{continuity } F$$

$$= \bigsqcup_{i\geq 1} F^i(STOP_A) \qquad\qquad \text{def } F^{i+1}$$

$$= \bigsqcup_{i\geq 0} F^i(STOP_A) \qquad\qquad STOP_A \sqsubseteq F(STOP_A)$$

$$= \mu X{:}A.F(X) \qquad\qquad \text{def } \mu$$

This proof has relied only on the fact that F is continuous. The guardedness of F is necessary only to establish uniqueness of the solution.

2.8.3 Unique solutions

In this section we treat more formally the reasoning given in Section 1.1.2 to show that an equation defining a process by guarded recursion has only one solution. In doing so, we shall make explicit more general conditions for uniqueness of such solutions. For simplicity, we deal only with single equations; the treatment easily extends to sets of simultaneous equations.

If P is a process and n is a natural number, we define $(P{\restriction}n)$ as a process which behaves like P for its first n events, and then stops; more formally

$$(A, S){\restriction}n = (A, \{s | s \in S \wedge \#s \leq n\})$$

It follows that

L1 $P{\restriction}0 = STOP$

L2 $P{\restriction}n \sqsubseteq P{\restriction}(n+1) \sqsubseteq P$

L3 $P = \bigsqcup_{n\geq 0} P{\restriction}n$

L4 $\bigsqcup_{n\geq 0} P_n = \bigsqcup_{n\geq 0} (P_n{\restriction}n)$

Let F be a monotonic function from processes to processes. F is said to be *constructive* if

$$F(X){\restriction}(n+1) = F(X{\restriction}n){\restriction}(n+1) \qquad\qquad \text{for all } X$$

This means that the behaviour of $F(X)$ on its first $n+1$ steps is determined by the behaviour of X on its first n steps only; so if $s \neq \langle\rangle$

$$s \in traces(F(X)) \equiv s \in traces(F(X{\restriction}(\#s-1)))$$

Prefixing is the primary example of a constructive function, since

$$(c{\rightarrow}P){\restriction}(n+1) = (c{\rightarrow}(P{\restriction}n)){\restriction}(n+1)$$

General choice is also constructive

$$(x:B{\to}P(x))\!\restriction\!(n+1) = (x:B{\to}(P(x)\!\restriction\!n))\!\restriction\!(n+1)$$

The identity function I is *not* constructive, since

$$I(c{\to}P)\!\restriction\!1 = c{\to}STOP$$
$$\neq STOP$$
$$= I((c{\to}P)\!\restriction\!0)$$

We can now formulate the fundamental theorem

L5   Let F be a constructive function. The equation

$$X = F(X)$$

has only one solution for X.

Proof.   Let X be an arbitrary solution.

First by induction we prove the lemma that

$$X\!\restriction\!n = F^n(STOP)\!\restriction\!n$$

Base case. $X\!\restriction\!0 = STOP = STOP\!\restriction\!0 = F^0(STOP)\!\restriction\!0.$

Induction step.

$$
\begin{aligned}
X\!\restriction\!(n+1) &= F(X)\!\restriction\!(n+1) & \text{since } X{=}F(X)\\
&= F(X\!\restriction\!n)\!\restriction\!(n+1) & F \text{ is constructive}\\
&= F(F^n(STOP)\!\restriction\!n)\!\restriction\!(n+1) & \text{hypothesis}\\
&= F(F^n(STOP))\!\restriction\!(n+1) & F \text{ is constructive}\\
&= F^{n+1}(STOP)\!\restriction\!(n+1). & \text{def } F^n
\end{aligned}
$$

Now we go back to the main theorem

$$
\begin{aligned}
X &= \bigsqcup_{n\geq0} (X\!\restriction\!n) & \text{L3}\\
&= \bigsqcup_{n\geq0} F^n(STOP)\!\restriction\!n & \text{just proved}\\
&= \bigsqcup_{n\geq0} F^n(STOP) & \text{L4}\\
&= \mu X.F(X) & 2.8.? \text{ L7}
\end{aligned}
$$

Thus all solutions of $X{=}F(X)$ are equal to $\mu X.F(X)$; or in other words, $\mu X.F(X)$ is the only solution of the equation.   □

The usefulness of this theorem is much increased if we can clearly recognize which functions are constructive and which are not. Let us define a nondestructive function G as one which satisfies

$$G(P)\!\restriction\!n = G(P\!\restriction\!n)\!\restriction\!n \qquad \text{for all } n \text{ and } P.$$

Alphabet transformation is nondestructive in this sense, since

$$f(P) \upharpoonright n = f(P \upharpoonright n) \upharpoonright n$$

So is the identity function. Any monotonic function which is constructive is also nondestructive. But the *after* operator is destructive, since

$$\begin{aligned}
((c {\rightarrow} c {\rightarrow} STOP) / \langle c \rangle) \upharpoonright 1 &= c {\rightarrow} STOP \\
&\neq STOP \\
&= (c {\rightarrow} STOP) / \langle c \rangle \\
&= (((c {\rightarrow} c {\rightarrow} STOP) \upharpoonright 1) / \langle c \rangle) \upharpoonright 1
\end{aligned}$$

Any composition of nondestructive functions (G and H) is also nondestructive, because

$$G(H(P)) \upharpoonright n = G(H(P) \upharpoonright n) \upharpoonright n = G(H(P \upharpoonright n) \upharpoonright n) \upharpoonright n = G(H(P \upharpoonright n)) \upharpoonright n$$

Even more important, any composition of a constructive function with nondestructive functions is also constructive. So if all of F, G, ..., H are nondestructive and just one of them is constructive, then

$$F(G(...(H(X))...))$$

is a constructive function of X.

The above reasoning extends readily to functions of more than one argument. For example parallel composition is nondestructive (in both its arguments) because

$$(P \| Q) \upharpoonright n = ((P \upharpoonright n) \| (Q \upharpoonright n)) \upharpoonright n$$

Let E be an expression containing the process variable X. Then E is said to be guarded in X if every occurrence of X in E has a constructive function applied to it, and no destructive function. Thus the following expression is constructive in X

$$(c {\rightarrow} X \,|\, d {\rightarrow} f(X \| P) \,|\, e {\rightarrow} (f(X) \| Q)) \;\|\; ((d {\rightarrow} X) \| R)$$

The important consequence of this is that constructiveness can be defined syntactically by the following conditions for guardedness

D0   An expression constructed solely by means of the operators concurrency, symbol change, and general choice are said to be guard-preserving.

D1   An expression which does not contain X is said to be guarded in X.

D2   A general choice

$$(x : B {\rightarrow} P(X, x))$$

is guarded in X if $P(X, x)$ is guard-preserving for all x.

D3   A symbol change $f(P(X))$ is guarded in X if $P(X)$ is guarded in X.

D4   A concurrent system $P(X)\|Q(X)$ is guarded in X if both $P(X)$ and $Q(X)$ are guarded in X.

Finally, we reach the conclusion

L6   If E is guarded in X, then the equation

$$X = E$$

has an unique solution.

3 NONDETERMINISM

3.1 INTRODUCTION

The choice operator $(x:B\rightarrow P(x))$ is used to define a process which exhibits a range of possible behaviours; and the concurrency operator $\parallel$ permits some other process to make a selection between the alternatives offered in the set B. For example, the change-giving machine $CH5C$ (1.1.3 X2) offers its customer the choice of taking his change as three small coins and one large, or two large coins and one small. Such processes are called *deterministic*, because whenever there is more than one event possible, the choice between them is determined externally by the environment of the process. It is determined either in the sense that the environment can actually make the choice, or in the weaker sense that the environment can observe which choice has been made at the very moment of that choice.

Sometimes a process has a range of possible behaviours, but the environment of the process does not have any ability to influence or even observe the selection between the alternatives. For example, a different change-giving machine may give change in either of the combinations described above; but the choice between them cannot be controlled or even predicted by its user. The choice is made, as it were internally, by the machine itself, in an arbitrary or nondeterministic fashion. The environment cannot control the choice or even observe it; it cannot even find out exactly when the choice was made, though it may later infer which choice was made from the subsequent behaviour of the process.

There is nothing mysterious about this kind of nondeterminism: it arises from a deliberate decision to ignore the factors which influence the selection. For example, the combination of change given by the machine may depend

101

on the way in which the machine has been loaded with large and small coins; but we have excluded these events from the alphabet. Thus nondeterminism is useful for maintaining a high level of abstraction in descriptions of the behaviour of physical systems and machines.

3.2 NONDETERMINISTIC OR

If P and Q are processes, then we introduce the notation

$$P \sqcap Q \qquad\qquad\qquad (P \text{ or } Q)$$

to denote a process which behaves either like P or like Q, where the selection between them is made arbitrarily, without the knowledge or control of the external environment. The alphabets of the operands are assumed to be the same

$$\alpha(P \sqcap Q) = \alpha P = \alpha Q$$

Examples

X1   A change-giving machine which always gives the right change in one of two combinations

$$CH5D = (in5p \rightarrow ((out1p \rightarrow out1p \rightarrow out1p \rightarrow out2p \rightarrow CH5D)$$
$$\sqcap (out2p \rightarrow out1p \rightarrow out2p \rightarrow CH5D)) \qquad \square$$

X2   *CH5D* may give a different combination of change on each occasion of use. Here is a machine that always gives the same combination, but we do not know initially which it will be (see 1.1.2 X3, X4)

$$CH5E = CH5A \sqcap CH5B$$

Of course, after this machine gives its first coin in change, its subsequent behaviour is entirely predictable. For this reason,

$$CH5D \neq CH5E \qquad\qquad\qquad\qquad\qquad\qquad\qquad\qquad \square$$

Nondeterminism has been introduced here in its purest and simplest form by the binary operator $\sqcap$. Of course, $\sqcap$ is not intended as a useful operator for *implementing* a process. It would be very foolish to build both P and Q, put them in a black bag, make an arbitrary choice between them, and then throw the other one away! The main advantage of nondeterminism is in *specifying* a process. A process specified as $(P \sqcap Q)$ can be implemented either by building P or by building Q. The choice can be made in advance by the implementor on grounds not relevant (and deliberately ignored) in the specification, such as low cost, fast response times, or early delivery. In fact, the $\sqcap$ operator will not often be used directly even in specifications; non-determinism arises more naturally from use of the other operators defined later in this chapter.

3.2.1 Laws

The algebraic laws governing nondeterministic choice are exceptionally simple and obvious. A choice between P and P is vacuous

L1 $\quad P \sqcap P = P$ (idempotence)

It does not matter in which order the choice is presented

L2 $\quad P \sqcap Q = Q \sqcap P$ (symmetry)

A choice between three alternatives can be split into two successive binary choices. It does not matter in which way this is done

L3 $\quad P \sqcap (Q \sqcap R) = (P \sqcap Q) \sqcap R$ (associativity)

The occasion on which a nondeterministic choice is made is not significant. A process which first does x and then makes a choice is indistinguishable from one which first makes the choice and then does x

L4 $\quad x \rightarrow (P \sqcap Q) = (x \rightarrow P) \sqcap (x \rightarrow Q)$ (distribution)

The law L4 states that the prefixing operator distributes through nondeterminism. Such operators are said to be *distributive*. A dyadic operator is said to be distributive if it distributes through $\sqcap$ in both its argument positions independently. Most of the operators defined so far for processes are distributive in this sense

L5 $\quad (x:B \rightarrow (P(x) \sqcap Q(x))) = (x:B \rightarrow P(x)) \sqcap (x:B \rightarrow Q(x))$

L6 $\quad P \| (Q \sqcap R) = (P \| Q) \sqcap (P \| R)$

L7 $\quad (P \sqcap Q) \| R = (P \| R) \sqcap (Q \| R)$

L8 $\quad f(P \sqcap Q) = f(P) \sqcap f(Q)$

However, the recursion operator is *not* distributive, except in the trivial case when the operands of $\sqcap$ are identical. This point is simply illustrated by the difference between the two processes

$$P = \mu X.((a \rightarrow X) \sqcap (b \rightarrow X))$$
$$Q = (\mu X.(a \rightarrow X)) \sqcap (\mu X.(b \rightarrow X)))$$

P can make an independent choice between a and b on each iteration, so its traces include

$$\langle a,b,b,a,b \rangle$$

Q must make a choice between always doing a and always doing b, so its traces do not include the one displayed above. However, P may choose always to do a or always to do b, so

$$traces(Q) \subseteq traces(P)$$

In some theories, nondeterminism is obliged to be *fair*, in the sense that an event that infinitely often *may* happen eventually *must* happen (though there is no limit to how long it may be delayed). In our theory, there is no such concept of fairness. Because we observe only finite traces of the behaviour of a process, if an event can be postponed indefinitely, we can never tell whether it is going to happen or not. If we want to insist that the event shall happen eventually, we must state that there is a number n such that every trace longer than n contains that event. Then the process must be designed explicitly to satisfy this constraint. For example, in the process P_0 defined below, the event a must always occur within n steps of its previous occurrence

$$P_i = (a \to P_0) \sqcap (b \to P_{i+1}) \qquad \text{for } i < n$$
$$P_n = (a \to P_0)$$

Later, we will see that both Q and P_0 are valid implementations of P.

If fairness of nondeterminism is required, this should be specified and implemented at a separate stage, for example, by ascribing nonzero probabilities to the alternatives of a nondeterministic choice. It seems highly desirable to separate complex probabilistic reasoning from concerns about the logical correctness of the behaviour of a process.

In view of laws L1 to L3 it is useful to introduce a multiple-choice operator. Let S be a finite nonempty set

$$S = \{i, j, \ldots, k\}$$

Then we define

$$\underset{x:S}{\sqcap} P(x) = P(i) \sqcap P(j) \sqcap \ldots \sqcap P(k)$$

$\underset{x:S}{\sqcap}$ is meaningless when S is either empty or infinite.

3.2.2   Implementations

As mentioned above, one of the main reasons for the introduction of nondeterminism is to abstract from details of implementation. This means that there may be many different implementations of a nondeterministic process P, each with an observably different pattern of behaviour.

The differences arise from different permitted resolutions of the non-determinism inherent in P. The choice involved may be made by the implementor before the process starts, or it may be postponed until the process is actually running.

For example, one implementation of $(P \sqcap Q)$ would be to select the first operand

$$or1(P,Q) = P$$

Another implementation is obtained by selecting the second operand, perhaps on the grounds of greater efficiency on a particular machine

$$or2(P,Q) = Q$$

Yet a third implementation postpones the decision until the process is running; it then allows the environment to make the choice, by selecting an event that is possible for one process but not the other. If the event is possible for both processes, the decision is again postponed

$$or3(P,Q) = \lambda x.\textbf{if } P(x) = "BLEEP" \textbf{ then } Q(x)$$
$$\textbf{else if } Q(x) = "BLEEP" \textbf{ then } P(x)$$
$$\textbf{else } or3(P(x), Q(x))$$

Here we have given three different possible implementations of the same operator. In fact there are many more: for example, an implementation may behave like $or3$ for the first five steps; and if all these steps are possible both for P and for Q, it then arbitrarily chooses P.

Since the designer of the process $(P \sqcap Q)$ has no control over whether P or Q will be selected, he must ensure that his system will work correctly for both choices. If there is any risk that *either P or Q* will deadlock with its environment, then $(P \sqcap Q)$ also runs that same risk. The implementation $or3$ is the one which minimizes the risk of deadlock by delaying the choice until the environment makes it, and then selecting whichever of P or Q does *not* deadlock. For this reason, the definition of $or3$ is sometimes known as *angelic nondeterminism*. But the price to be paid is high in terms of efficiency: if the choice between P and Q is not made on the first step, both P and Q have to be executed concurrently until the environment chooses an event which is possible for one but not the other. In the simple but extreme case of $or3(P,P)$, this will never happen, and the inefficiency will also be extreme.

In contrast to $or3$, the implementations $or1$ and $or2$ are asymmetric in the sense that

$$or1(P,Q) \neq or1(Q,P).$$

This seems to violate law 3.2.1 L2; but this is not so. The laws apply to processes, not to any particular implementation of them. In fact they assert the identity of the *set* of *all* implementations of their left and right hand sides. For example, since *or3* is symmetric,

$$\{or1(P,Q),\ or2(P,Q),\ or3(P,Q)\}=\{P,Q,\ or3(P,Q)\}$$
$$=\{or2(Q,P),\ or1(Q,P),\ or3(Q,P)\}$$

One of the advantages of introducing nondeterminism is to avoid the loss of symmetry that would result from selecting one of the two simple implementations, and yet to avoid the inefficiency of the symmetric implementation *or3*.

3.2.3 Traces

If s is a trace of P, then s is also a possible trace of $(P \sqcap Q)$, i.e., in the case that P is selected. Similarly if s is a trace of Q, it is also a trace of $(P \sqcap Q)$. Conversely, each trace of $(P \sqcap Q)$ must be a trace of one or both alternatives. The behaviour of $(P \sqcap Q)$ after s is defined by whichever of P or Q could engage in s; if both could, the choice remains nondeterministic.

L1 $\quad traces(P \sqcap Q) = traces(P) \cup traces(Q)$

L2 $\quad (P \sqcap Q)/s = Q/s \qquad\qquad\qquad$ if $s \in (traces(Q) - traces(P))$
$$= P/s \qquad\qquad\qquad\quad \text{if } s \in (traces(P) - traces(Q))$$
$$= (P/s) \sqcap (Q/s) \qquad\quad \text{if } s \in (traces(P) \cap traces(Q))$$

3.3 GENERAL CHOICE

The environment of $(P \sqcap Q)$ has no control or even knowledge of the choice that is made between P and Q, or even the time at which the choice is made. So $(P \sqcap Q)$ is not a helpful way of combining processes, because the environment must be prepared to deal with either P or Q; and either one of them separately would have been easier to deal with. We therefore introduce another operation $(P \;[]\; Q)$, for which the environment *can* control which of P and Q will be selected, provided that this control is exercised on the very first action. If this action is *not* a possible first action of P, then Q will be selected; but if Q cannot engage initially in the action, P will be selected. If, however, the first action is possible for both P and Q, then the choice between them is nondeterministic. (Of course, if the event is impossible for both P and Q, then it just cannot happen.) As usual

$$\alpha(P \;[]\; Q) = \alpha P = \alpha Q$$

In the case that no initial event of P is also possible for Q, the general choice operator is the same as the $|$ operator, which has been used hitherto to represent choice between different events

$$(c{\rightarrow}P \; [] \; d{\rightarrow}Q) = (c{\rightarrow}P \,|\, d{\rightarrow}Q) \qquad \text{if } c{\neq}d.$$

However if the initial events are the same, $(P \,[]\, Q)$ degenerates to nondeterministic choice

$$(c{\rightarrow}P \; [] \; c{\rightarrow}Q) = (c{\rightarrow}P) \; \sqcap \; (c{\rightarrow}Q)$$

Here we have adopted the convention that $\rightarrow$ binds more tightly than $[]$.

3.3.1 Laws

The algebraic laws for $[]$ are similar to those for $\sqcap$, and for the same reasons

L1–L3 $[]$ is idempotent, symmetric, and associative.

L4 $P \,[]\, STOP = P$

The following law formalizes the informal definition of the operation

L5 $(x{:}A{\rightarrow}P(x)) \; [] \; (y{:}B{\rightarrow}Q(y)) =$
$\qquad (z{:}(A{\cup}B){\rightarrow}(\text{if } z{\in}(A-B) \text{ then } P(z)$
$\qquad\qquad \text{else if } z{\in}(B-A) \text{ then } Q(z)$
$\qquad\qquad \text{else if } z{\in}(A{\cap}B) \text{ then } (P(z) \; \sqcap \; Q(z))))$

Like all other operators introduced so far (apart from recursion), $[]$ distributes through $\sqcap$

L6 $P \,[]\, (Q \,\sqcap\, R) = (P \,[]\, Q) \,\sqcap\, (P \,[]\, R).$

What may seem more surprising is that $\sqcap$ distributes through $[]$

L7 $P \,\sqcap\, (Q \,[]\, R) = (P \,\sqcap\, Q) \,[]\, (P \,\sqcap\, R)$

This law states that choices made nondeterministically and choices made by the environment are independent, in the sense that the selection made by one of them does not influence the choice made by the other. Let John be the agent which makes nondeterministic choices and let Mary be the environment. On the left-hand side of the law, John chooses ($\sqcap$) between P and letting Mary choose ($[]$) between Q and R. On the right-hand side, Mary chooses

either (1) to offer John the choice between P and Q
or   (2) to offer John the choice between P and R

On both sides of the equation, if John chooses P, then P will be the overall outcome. But if John does not select P, the choice between Q and R is made by Mary. Thus the results of the choice strategies described on the left- and right-hand sides of the law are always equal. Of course, the same reasoning applies to L6.

The explanation given above is rather subtle; perhaps it would be better to explain the law as the unexpected but unavoidable consequence of other more obvious definitions and laws given later in this chapter.

3.3.2 Implementation

The implementation of the choice operator follows closely the law L5. Assuming the symmetry of *or*, it is also symmetrical

$choice(P,Q) = \lambda x.$ **if** $P(x) = "BLEEP$ **then** $Q(x)$
　　　　　　　 else if $Q(x) = "BLEEP$ **then** $P(x)$
　　　　　　　　　　　　　 else $or(P(x),\ Q(x))$

3.3.3 Traces

Every trace of $(P \,[]\, Q)$ must be a trace of P or a trace of Q, and conversely

L1　$traces(P \,[]\, Q) = traces(P) \cup traces(Q)$

The next law is slightly different from the corresponding law for $\sqcap$

L2　$(P \,[]\, Q)/s = P/s$　　　　　　　　　if $s \in traces(P) - traces(Q)$
　　　　　　　　 $= Q/s$　　　　　　　　　if $s \in traces(Q) - traces(P)$
　　　　　　　　 $= (P/s) \,\sqcap\, (Q/s)$　　if $s \neq \langle\rangle$ and $s \in traces(P) \cap traces(Q)$

3.4 REFUSALS

The distinction between $(P \sqcap Q)$ and $(P \,[]\, Q)$ is quite subtle. They cannot be distinguished by their traces, because each trace of one of them is also a possible trace of the other. However it is possible to put them in an environment in which $(P \sqcap Q)$ can deadlock at its first step, but $(P \,[]\, Q)$ cannot. For example let $x \neq y$ and

$$P = (x \rightarrow P), \quad Q = (y \rightarrow Q), \quad \alpha P = \alpha Q = \{x, y\}$$

Then $(P \; [] \; Q) \| P = (x \rightarrow P)$
$$= P$$
but $(P \sqcap Q) \| P = (P \| P) \sqcap (Q \| P)$
$$= P \sqcap STOP$$

This shows that in environment P, $(P \sqcap Q)$ may reach deadlock but $(P \; [] \; Q)$ cannot. Of course, even with $(P \sqcap Q)$ we cannot be sure that deadlock will occur; and if it does not occur, we will never know that it might have. But the mere possibility of an occurrence of deadlock is enough to distinguish $(P \; [] \; Q)$ from $(P \sqcap Q)$.

In general, let X be a set of events which are offered initially by the environment of a process P, which in this context we take to have the same alphabet as P. If it is possible for P to deadlock on its first step when placed in this environment, we say that X is a *refusal* of P. The set of all such refusals of P is denoted

$$refusals(P)$$

Note that the refusals of a process constitute a family of sets of symbols. This is an unfortunate complexity, but it does seem to be unavoidable in a proper treatment of nondeterminism. Instead of refusals, it might seem more natural to use the sets of symbols which a process may be *ready* to accept; however the refusals are slightly simpler because they obey laws L9 and L10 of Section 3.4.1 (below), whereas the corresponding laws for ready sets would be more complicated.

The introduction of the concept of a refusal permits a clear formal distinction to be made between deterministic and nondeterministic processes. A process is said to be *deterministic* if it can never refuse any event in which it can engage. In other words, a set is a refusal of a deterministic process only if that set contains no event in which that process can initially engage; or more formally

$$P \text{ is deterministic} \Rightarrow (X \in refusals(P) \equiv (X \cap P^0 = \{\}))$$

where $P^0 = \{x \mid \langle x \rangle \in traces(P)\}$

This condition applies not only on the initial step of P but also after any possible sequence of actions of P. Thus we can define

$$P \text{ is deterministic} \equiv \forall s : traces(P) . (X \in refusals(P/s) \equiv (X \cap (P/s)^0 = \{\}))$$

A nondeterministic process is one that does not enjoy this property, i.e., there is at some time some event in which it can engage; but also (as a result of some internal nondeterministic choice) it may refuse to engage in that event, even though the environment is ready for it.

3.4.1   Laws

The following laws define the refusals of various simple processes. The process $STOP$ does nothing and refuses everything

L1 $refusals(STOP_A) = $ all subsets of A (including A itself)

A process $(c{\rightarrow}P)$ refuses every set that does not contain the event c

L2 $refusals(c{\rightarrow}P) = \{X \mid X \subseteq (\alpha P - \{c\})\}$

These two laws have a common generalization

L3 $refusals(x : B {\rightarrow} P(x)) = \{X \mid X \subseteq (\alpha P - B)\}$

If P can refuse X, so will $(P \sqcap Q)$ if P is selected. Similarly every refusal of Q is also a possible refusal of $(P \sqcap Q)$. These are its only refusals, so

L4 $refusals(P \sqcap Q) = refusals(P) \cup refusals(Q)$

A converse argument applies to $(P \;[]\; Q)$. If X is *not* a refusal of P, then P *cannot* refuse X, and neither can $(P \;[]\; Q)$. Similarly if X is not a refusal of Q, then it is not a refusal of $(P \;[]\; Q)$. However if *both* P and Q can refuse X, so can $(P \;[]\; Q)$

L5 $refusals(P \;[]\; Q) = refusals(P) \cap refusals(Q)$

Comparison of L5 with L4 shows the distinction between $[]$ and $\sqcap$.
   If P can refuse X and Q can refuse Y, then their combination $(P \| Q)$ can refuse all events refused by P as well as all events refused by Q, i.e., it can refuse the union of the two sets X and Y

L6 $refusals(P \| Q) = \{X \cup Y \mid X \in refusals(P) \wedge Y \in refusals(Q)\}$

For symbol change, the relevant law is clear

L7 $refusals(f(P)) = \{f(X) \mid X \in refusals(P)\}$

   There are a number of general laws about refusals. A process can refuse only events in its own alphabet. A process deadlocks when the environment offers no events; and if a process refuses a nonempty set, it can also refuse any subset of that set. Finally, any event x which cannot occur initially may be added to any set X already refused.

L8 $X \in refusals(P) \Rightarrow X \subseteq \alpha P$

L9 $\{\} \in refusals(P)$

L10 $(X \cup Y) \in refusals(P) \Rightarrow X \in refusals(P)$

L11 $X \in refusals(P) \Rightarrow (X \cup \{x\}) \in refusals(P) \vee \langle x \rangle \in traces(P)$

3.5   CONCEALMENT

In general, the alphabet of a process contains just those events which are considered to be relevant, and whose occurrence requires simultaneous participation of an environment. In describing the internal behaviour of a mechanism, we often need to consider events representing internal transitions of that mechanism. Such events may denote the interactions and communications between concurrently acting components from which the mechanism has been constructed, e.g., $CHAIN2$ (2.6 X4) and 2.6.2 X3. After construction of the mechanism, we conceal the structure of its components; and we also wish to conceal all occurrences of actions internal to the mechanism. In fact, we want these actions to occur automatically and instantaneously as soon as they can, without being observed or controlled by the environment of the process. If C is a finite set of events to be concealed in this way, then

$$P \setminus C$$

is a process which behaves like P, except that each occurrence of any event in C is concealed. Clearly it is our intention that

$$\alpha(P \setminus C) = (\alpha P) - C$$

Examples

X1   A noisy vending machine (2.3 X1) can be placed in a soundproof box

$$NOISYVM \setminus \{clink, \ clunk\}$$

Its unexercised capability of dispensing toffee can also be removed from its alphabet, without affecting its actual behaviour. The resulting process is equal to the simple vending machine

$$VMS = NOISYVM \setminus \{clink, clunk, toffee\} \qquad \qquad \square$$

When two processes have been combined to run concurrently, their mutual interactions are usually regarded as internal workings of the resulting system; they are intended to occur autonomously and as quickly as possible, without the knowledge or intervention of the system's outer environment. Thus it is the symbols in the intersection of the alphabets of the two components that need to be concealed.

X2 Let $\alpha P=\{a,c\}$, $\alpha Q=\{b,c\}$, $P=(a\rightarrow c\rightarrow P)$, $Q=(c\rightarrow b\rightarrow Q)$ (2.3.1 X1)

The action c in the alphabet of both P and Q is now regarded as an internal action, to be concealed

$$
\begin{aligned}
(P\|Q)\setminus\{c\} &= (a\rightarrow c\rightarrow\mu X.(a\rightarrow b\rightarrow c\rightarrow X \\
&\qquad\qquad | b\rightarrow a\rightarrow c\rightarrow X))\setminus\{c\} \\
&= a\rightarrow\mu X.(a\rightarrow b\rightarrow X \\
&\qquad\qquad | b\rightarrow a\rightarrow X)
\end{aligned}
$$

$\square$

3.5.1 Laws

The first laws state that concealing no symbols has no effect, and that it makes no difference in what order the symbols of a set are concealed. The remaining laws of this group show how concealment distributes through other operators.

Concealment of nothing leaves everything revealed

L1 $P\setminus\{\}=P$

To conceal one set of symbols and then some more is the same as concealing them all simultaneously

L2 $(P\setminus B)\setminus C = P\setminus(B\cup C)$

Concealment distributes in the familiar way through nondeterministic choice

L3 $(P \sqcap Q)\setminus C = (P\setminus C) \sqcap (Q\setminus C)$

Concealment does not affect the behaviour of a stopped process, only its alphabet

L4 $STOP_A\setminus C = STOP_{A-C}$

The purpose of concealment is to allow any of the concealed events to occur automatically and instantaneously, but make such occurrences totally invisible. Unconcealed events remain unchanged

L5 $(x\rightarrow P)\setminus C = x\rightarrow(P\setminus C)$ if $x\tilde{\in} C$
$\qquad\qquad = P\setminus C$ if $x\in C$

If C contains only events in which P and Q participate independently, concealment of C distributes through their concurrent composition

L6 If $\alpha P\cap\alpha Q\cap C=\{\}$
$\quad$ then $(P\|Q)\setminus C = (P\setminus C)\|(Q\setminus C)$

This is not a commonly useful law, because what we usually wish to conceal are the interactions between concurrent processes, i.e., the events of $\alpha P \cap \alpha Q$, in which they participate jointly.

Concealment distributes in the obvious way through symbol change by a one–one function

L7 $f(P \setminus C) = f(P) \setminus f(C)$

If none of the possible initial events of a choice is concealed, then the initial choice remains the same as it was before concealment

L8   If $B \cap C = \{\}$
then $(x : B \rightarrow P(x)) \setminus C = (x : B \rightarrow (P(x) \setminus C))$

Like the choice operator $[]$, the concealment of events can introduce nondeterminism. When several different concealed events can happen, it is not determined which of them will occur; but whichever does occur is concealed

L9   If $B \subseteq C$, and B is finite and not empty,
then $(x : B \rightarrow P(x)) \setminus C = \displaystyle\prod_{x : B} (P(x) \setminus C)$

In the intermediate case, when some of the initial events are concealed and some are not, the situation is rather more complicated. Consider the process

$$(c \rightarrow P \mid d \rightarrow Q) \setminus C \qquad\qquad \text{where } c \in C, \ d \hat{\in} C$$

The concealed event c may happen immediately. In this case the total behaviour will be defined by $(P \setminus C)$, and the possibility of occurrence of the event d will be withdrawn. But we cannot reliably assume that d will not happen. If the environment is ready for it, d may very well happen before the hidden event, after which the hidden event c can no longer occur. But even if d occurs, it might have been performed by $(P \setminus C)$ after the hidden occurrence of c. In this case, the total behaviour is as defined by

$$(P \setminus C) \ [] \ (d \rightarrow (Q \setminus C))$$

The choice between this and $(P \setminus C)$ is nondeterministic. This is a rather convoluted justification for the rather complex law

$$(c \rightarrow P \mid d \rightarrow Q) \setminus C = (P \setminus C) \ \sqcap \ ((P \setminus C) \ [] \ (d \rightarrow (Q \setminus C)))$$

Similar reasoning justifies the more general law

L10   If $C \cap B \neq \{\}$ and is finite
then $(x : B \rightarrow P(x)) \setminus C = Q \ \sqcap \ (Q \ [] \ (x : (B - C) \rightarrow P(x)))$

where $Q = \displaystyle\prod_{x : B \cap C} P(x) \setminus C$

A pictorial illustration of these laws is given in Section 3.5.4.

Note that $\setminus C$ does not distribute backwards through $[]$. A counterexample is

$$(c{\to}STOP\ []\ d{\to}STOP)\setminus\{c\} = STOP\ \sqcap\ (STOP\ []\ (d{\to}STOP))\qquad \text{L10}$$
$$= STOP\ \sqcap\ (d{\to}STOP)\qquad\qquad \text{3.3.1 L4}$$
$$\neq d{\to}STOP$$
$$= STOP\ []\ (d{\to}STOP)$$
$$= ((c{\to}STOP)\setminus\{c\})\ []\ ((d{\to}STOP)\setminus\{c\})$$

Concealment reduces the alphabet of a process. We can also define an operation which extends the alphabet of a process P by inclusion of symbols of a set B

$$\alpha(P_{+B}) = \alpha P \cup B$$
$$P_{+B} = (P\ \|\ STOP_B)\qquad\qquad \text{provided } B \cap \alpha P = \{\}$$

None of the new events of B will ever actually occur, so the behaviour of P_{+B} is effectively the same as that of P

L11 $traces(P_{+B}) = traces(P)$

Consequently, concealment of B reverses the extension of the alphabet by B

L12 $(P_{+B})\setminus B = P$

It is appropriate here to raise a problem that will be solved later, in Section 3.8. In simple cases, concealment distributes through recursion

$$(\mu X{:}A.(c{\to}X))\setminus\{c\} = \mu X{:}(A-\{c\}).((c{\to}X_{+\{c\}})\setminus\{c\})$$
$$= \mu X{:}(A-\{c\}).X\qquad\qquad \text{by L12, L5}$$

Thus the attempt to conceal an *infinite* sequence of consecutive events leads to the same unfortunate result as an infinite loop or unguarded recursion. The general term for this phenomenon is *divergence*.

The same problem arises even if the divergent process is infinitely often capable of some unconcealed event, for example

$$(\mu X.(c{\to}X\ []\ d{\to}P))\setminus\{c\}$$
$$= \mu X.((c{\to}X\ []\ d{\to}P)\setminus\{c\})$$
$$= \mu X.(X\setminus\{c\})\ \sqcap\ ((X\setminus\{c\})\ []\ d{\to}(P\setminus\{c\}))\qquad \text{by L10}$$

Here again, the recursion is unguarded, and leads to divergence. Even though it seems that the environment is infinitely often offered the choice of selecting d, there is no way of preventing the process from infinitely often choosing to perform the hidden event instead. This possibility seems to aid in achieving the highest efficiency of implementation. It also seems to be related to our decision not to insist on fairness of nondeterminism, as discussed in Section 3.2.1. A more rigorous discussion of divergence is given in Section 3.8.

There is a sense, an important one, in which hiding is in fact fair. Let $d \in \alpha R$, and consider the process

$$((c \rightarrow a \rightarrow P \,|\, d \rightarrow STOP) \setminus \{c\}) \parallel (a \rightarrow R)$$
$$= ((a \rightarrow P \setminus \{c\}) \sqcap (a \rightarrow P \setminus \{c\} \,[\!]\, d \rightarrow STOP)) \parallel (a \rightarrow R) \qquad \text{L10}$$
$$= (a \rightarrow P \setminus \{c\}) \parallel (a \rightarrow R) \sqcap (a \rightarrow P \setminus \{c\} \,[\!]\, d \rightarrow STOP) \parallel (a \rightarrow R)$$
$$= a \rightarrow ((P \setminus \{c\}) \parallel R)$$

This shows that a process which offers the choice between a hidden action c and a nonhidden one d cannot insist that the nonhidden action shall occur. If the environment (in this example, $a \rightarrow R$) is not prepared for d, then the hidden event must occur, so that the environment has the chance to interact with the process (e.g. $(a \rightarrow P \setminus \{c\})$) which results.

3.5.2 Implementation

For simplicity, we shall implement an operation which hides a single symbol at a time

$$hide(P,c) = P \setminus \{c\}$$

A set of two or more symbols may be hidden by hiding one after the other, since

$$P \setminus \{c1, c2, \ldots, cn\} = (\ldots((P \setminus \{c1\}) \setminus \{c2\}) \setminus \ldots) \setminus \{cn\}$$

The simplest implementation is one that always makes the hidden event occur invisibly, whenever it can and as soon as it can

$$hide(P,c) = \textbf{if } P(c) = "BLEEP \textbf{ then}$$
$$(\lambda x. \textbf{ if } P(x) = "BLEEP \textbf{ then } "BLEEP$$
$$\textbf{else } hide(P(x),c))$$
$$\textbf{else } hide(P(c),c)$$

Let us explore what happens when the hide function is applied to a process which is capable of engaging in an infinite sequence of hidden events, for example

$$hide(\mu X.(c \rightarrow X \,[\!]\, d \rightarrow P),c)$$

In this case, the test $(P(c) = "BLEEP)$ will always yield $FALSE$, so the $hide$ function will always select its **else** clause, thereby immediately calling itself recursively. There is no exit from this recursion, so no further communication with the outside world will ever occur. This is the penalty for attempting to implement a divergent process.

This implementation of concealment does not obey L2; indeed, the order in which it hides the symbols is significant, as shown by the example

$$P = (c{\rightarrow}STOP\,|\,d{\rightarrow}a{\rightarrow}STOP).$$

Then $hide(hide(P,c),d) = hide(hide(STOP,c),d)$
$$= STOP$$
and $hide(hide(P,d),c) = hide(hide((a{\rightarrow}STOP),d),c)$
$$= (a{\rightarrow}STOP)$$

But as explained in Section 3.2.2, a particular implementation of a non-deterministic operator does not have to obey the laws. It is sufficient that both the results shown above are permitted implementations of the same process

$$P\backslash\{c,d\} = (STOP \sqcap (a{\rightarrow}STOP))$$

3.5.3 Traces

If t is a trace of P, the corresponding trace of $P\backslash C$ is obtained from t simply by removing all occurrences of any of the symbols in C. Conversely each trace of $P\backslash C$ must have been obtained from some such trace of P. We therefore state

L1 $traces(P\backslash C) = \{t{\upharpoonright}(\alpha P - C)\,|\,t{:}traces(P)\}$

provided that $\forall s{:}traces(P). \ \neg diverges(P/s,C)$

The condition $diverges(P,C)$ means that P diverges immediately on concealment of C, i.e., that it can engage in an unbounded sequence of hidden events. Thus we define

$$diverges(P,C) = \forall n. \ \exists s{:}traces(P) \cap C^{*}.\#s > n$$

Corresponding to a single trace s of $P\backslash C$, there can be several traces t of the possible behaviour in which P has engaged which cannot be distinguished after the concealment, i.e., $t{\upharpoonright}(\alpha P - C) = s$. The next law states that after s it is not determined which of the possible subsequent behaviours of P will define the subsequent behaviour of $(P\backslash C)$

L2 $(P\backslash C)/s = (\displaystyle\bigcap_{t:T} P/t)\backslash C$

where $T = traces(P) \cap \{t\,|\,t{\upharpoonright}(\alpha P - C) = s\}$
provided T is finite and $s \in traces(P\backslash C)$

These laws are restricted to the case when the process does not diverge. The restrictions are not serious, because divergence is never the intended result of the attempted definition of a process. For a fuller treatment of divergence see Section 3.8.

3.5.4 Pictures

Nondeterministic choice can be represented in a picture by a node from which emerge two or more unlabelled arrows; on reaching the node, a process passes imperceptibly along one of the emergent arrows, the choice being nondeterministic.

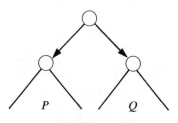

Figure 3.1

Thus $P \sqcap Q$ is pictured as in Fig. 3.1. The algebraic laws governing nondeterminism assert identities between such pictures, e.g., associativity of $\sqcap$ is illustrated in Fig. 3.2.

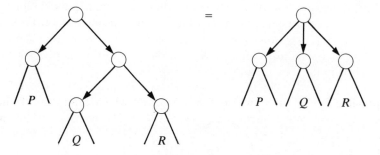

Figure 3.2

Concealment of symbols may be regarded as an operation which simply removes concealed symbols from all arrows which they label, so that these arcs turn into unlabelled arrows. The resulting nondeterminism emerges naturally, as shown in Fig. 3.3.

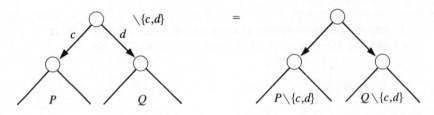

Figure 3.3

But what is the meaning of a node if some of its arcs are labelled and some are not? The answer is given by the law 3.5.1 L10. Such a node can be eliminated by redrawing·as shown in Fig. 3.4.

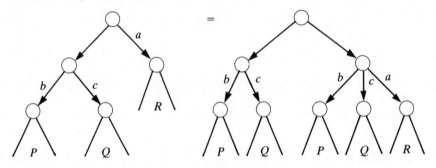

Figure 3.4

It is fairly obvious that such eliminations are always possible for finite trees. They are also possible for infinite graphs, provided that the graph contains no infinite path of consecutive unlabelled arrows, as for example in Fig. 3.5. Such a picture can arise only in the case of divergence, which we have already decided to regard as an error.

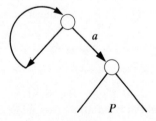

Figure 3.5

As a result of applying the transformation L10, it is possible that the node may acquire two emergent lines with the same label. Such nodes can be eliminated by the law given at the end of Section 3.3 (Fig. 3.6).

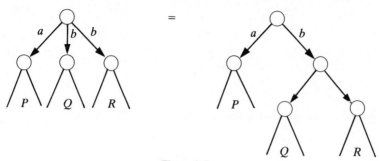

Figure 3.6

The pictorial representation of processes and the laws which govern them are included here as an aid to memory and understanding; they are not intended to be used for practical transformation or manipulation of large-scale processes.

3.6 INTERLEAVING

The $\parallel$ operator was defined in Chapter 2 in such a way that actions in the alphabet of both operands require simultaneous participation of them both, whereas the remaining actions of the system occur in an arbitrary interleaving. Using this operator, it is possible to combine interacting processes with differing alphabets into systems exhibiting concurrent activity, but without introducing nondeterminism.

However, it is sometimes useful to join processes with the same alphabet to operate concurrently without directly interacting or synchronizing with each other. In this case, each action of the system is an action of exactly one of the processes. If one of the processes cannot engage in the action, then it must have been the other one; but if both processes could have engaged in the same action, the choice between them is nondeterministic. This form of combination is denoted

$P \parallel\!\parallel\!\parallel Q$ 　　　　　　　　　　　　(P interleave Q)

and its alphabet is defined by the usual stipulation

$\alpha(P \parallel\!\parallel\!\parallel Q) = \alpha P = \alpha Q.$

Examples

X1   A vending machine that will accept up to two coins before dispensing up to two chocolates (1.1.3 X6)

$$(VMS \parallel\!\parallel\!\parallel VMS) = VMS2 \qquad\qquad\qquad \square$$

X2   A footman made from four lackeys, each serving only one philosopher at a time (see Section 2.5.3 and 2.6.4 X1)

$$L \parallel\!\parallel\!\parallel L \parallel\!\parallel\!\parallel L \parallel\!\parallel\!\parallel L$$

where $L = SHAREDLACKEY$. $\qquad\qquad\qquad\qquad\qquad\qquad \square$

3.6.1 Laws

L1–3 $\parallel\!\parallel\!\parallel$ is associative, symmetric, and distributes through $\sqcap$

L4 $P \parallel\!\parallel\!\parallel STOP = P$

L5 $P \parallel\!\parallel\!\parallel RUN = RUN$ $\qquad\qquad\qquad\qquad$ provided P does not diverge

L6 $(x \rightarrow P) \parallel\!\parallel\!\parallel (y \rightarrow Q) = (x \rightarrow (P \parallel\!\parallel\!\parallel (y \rightarrow Q)) \; \square \; y \rightarrow ((x \rightarrow P) \parallel\!\parallel\!\parallel Q))$

L7   If $P = (x{:}A \rightarrow P(x))$
and $Q = (y{:}B \rightarrow P(y))$
then $P \parallel\!\parallel\!\parallel Q = (x{:}A \rightarrow (P(x) \parallel\!\parallel\!\parallel Q) \; \square \; y{:}B \rightarrow (P \parallel\!\parallel\!\parallel Q(y)))$

Note that $\parallel\!\parallel\!\parallel$ does not distribute through $\square$. This is shown by the counterexample (where $b \neq c$)

$$
\begin{aligned}
((a \rightarrow STOP) &\parallel\!\parallel\!\parallel (b \rightarrow Q \; \square \; c \rightarrow R))/\langle a \rangle \\
&= (b \rightarrow Q \; \square \; c \rightarrow R) \\
&\neq ((b \rightarrow Q) \; \sqcap \; (c \rightarrow R)) \\
&= ((a \rightarrow STOP \; \square \; b \rightarrow Q) \parallel\!\parallel\!\parallel (a \rightarrow STOP \; \square \; c \rightarrow R))/\langle a \rangle
\end{aligned}
$$

On the left-hand end of this chain, the occurrence of a can involve progress only of the left operand of $\parallel\!\parallel\!\parallel$, so no nondeterminism is introduced. The left operand stops, and the choice between b and c is left open to the environment. On the right-hand end of the chain, the event a may be an event of either operand of $\parallel\!\parallel\!\parallel$, the choice being nondeterministic. Thus the environment can no longer choose whether the next event will be b or c.

L6 and L7 state that it is the environment which chooses between the initial events offered by the operands of $\parallel\!\parallel\!\parallel$. Nondeterminism arises only when the chosen event is possible for both operands.

Example

Let $R = (a \rightarrow b \rightarrow R)$
Then $(R \parallel\!\parallel R) = (a \rightarrow ((b \rightarrow R) \parallel\!\parallel R) \ [] \ a \rightarrow (R \parallel\!\parallel (b \rightarrow R)))$ L6
$= a \rightarrow ((b \rightarrow R) \parallel\!\parallel R) \ \sqcap \ (R \parallel\!\parallel (b \rightarrow R))$
$= a \rightarrow ((b \rightarrow R) \parallel\!\parallel R)$ L2
Also $(b \rightarrow R) \parallel\!\parallel R = (a \rightarrow ((b \rightarrow R) \parallel\!\parallel (b \rightarrow R)) \ [] \ b \rightarrow (R \parallel\!\parallel R))$ L6
$= (a \rightarrow (b \rightarrow ((b \rightarrow R) \parallel\!\parallel R))$ $\begin{cases} \text{as shown} \\ \quad \text{above} \end{cases}$
$[] \ b \rightarrow (a \rightarrow ((b \rightarrow R) \parallel\!\parallel R)))$
$= \mu X.(a \rightarrow b \rightarrow X$
$[] \ b \rightarrow a \rightarrow X)$ since the recursion is guarded.

Thus $(R \parallel\!\parallel R)$ is identical to the example 3.5 X2. A similar proof shows that $(VMS \parallel\!\parallel VMS) = VMS2$. $\square$

3.6.2   Traces and refusals

A trace of $(P \parallel\!\parallel Q)$ is an arbitrary interleaving of a trace from P with a trace from Q. For a definition of interleaving, see Section 1.9.3.

L1 $traces(P \parallel\!\parallel Q) = \{s \mid \exists t \in traces(P). \ \exists u \in traces(Q). \ s \ interleaves(t,u)\}$

$(P \parallel\!\parallel Q)$ can engage in any initial action possible for either P or Q; and it can therefore refuse only those sets which are refused by both P and Q

L2 $refusals(P \parallel\!\parallel Q) = refusals(P \ [] \ Q)$

The behaviour of $(P \parallel\!\parallel Q)$ after engaging in the events of the trace s is defined by the rather elaborate formula

L3 $(P \parallel\!\parallel Q)/s = \displaystyle\bigsqcap_{(t,u) \in T} (P/t) \parallel\!\parallel (Q/u)$

where $T = \{(t,u) \mid t \in traces(P) \wedge u \in traces(Q) \wedge s \ interleaves(t,u)\}$

This law reflects the fact that there is no way of knowing in which way a trace s of $(P \parallel\!\parallel Q)$ has been constructed as an interleaving of a trace from P and a trace from Q; thus after s, the future behaviour of $(P \parallel\!\parallel Q)$ may reflect any one of the possible interleavings. The choice between them is not known and not determined.

3.7   SPECIFICATIONS

In Section 3.4 we have seen the need to introduce refusal sets as one of the important indirectly observable aspects of the behaviour of a process. In specifying a process, we therefore need to describe the desired properties of its refusal sets as well as its traces. Let us use the variable *ref* to denote an arbitrary refusal set of a process, in the same way as we have used *tr* to denote an arbitrary trace. As a result, when *P* is a nondeterministic process the meaning of

$$P \text{ sat } S(tr, ref)$$

is revised to

$$\forall tr, ref. \ tr \in traces(P) \wedge ref \in refusals(P/tr) \Rightarrow S(tr, ref)$$

Examples

X1   When a vending machine has ingested more coins than it has dispensed chocolates, the customer specifies that it must not refuse to dispense a chocolate

$$FAIR = (tr{\downarrow}choc < tr{\downarrow}coin \Rightarrow choc \bar{\in} ref)$$

It is implicitly understood that *every* trace *tr* and *every* refusal *ref* of the specified process at all times should satisfy this specification. $\square$

X2   When a vending machine has given out as many chocolates as have been paid for, the owner specifies that it must not refuse a further coin

$$PROFIT1 = (tr{\downarrow}choc = tr{\downarrow}coin \Rightarrow coin \bar{\in} ref)$$ $\square$

X3   A simple vending machine should satisfy the combined specification

$$NEWVMSPEC = FAIR \wedge PROFIT1 \wedge (tr{\downarrow}choc \leq tr{\downarrow}coin)$$

This specification is satisfied by **VMS**. It is also satisfied by a vending machine like **VMS2** (1.1.3 X6) which will accept several coins in a row, and then give out several chocolates. $\square$

X4   If desired, one may place a limit on the balance of coins which may be accepted in a row

$$ATMOST2 = (tr{\downarrow}coin - tr{\downarrow}choc \leq 2)$$ $\square$

X5   If desired, one can insist that the machine accept at least two coins in a row whenever the customer offers them

$$ATLEAST2 = (tr{\downarrow}coin - tr{\downarrow}choc < 2 \Rightarrow coin \bar{\in} ref)$$ $\square$

X6   The process *STOP* refuses every event in its alphabet. The following predicate specifies that a process with alphabet *A* will never stop

$$NONSTOP = (ref \neq A)$$

If *P* **sat** *NONSTOP*, and if an environment allows all events in *A*, *P* must perform one of them. Since (see X3 above)

$$NEWVMSPEC \Rightarrow ref \neq \{coin, choc\}$$

it follows that any process which satisfies *NEWVMSPEC* will never stop. $\square$

These examples show how the introduction of *ref* into the specification of a process permits the expression of a number of subtle but important properties; perhaps the most important of all is the property that the process must not stop (X6). These advantages are obtained at the cost of slightly increased complexity in proof rules and in proofs.

It is also desirable to prove that a process does not diverge. Section 3.8 describes how a divergent process is one that can do anything and refuse anything. So if there is a set which *cannot* be refused, then the process is not divergent. This justifies formulation of a sufficient condition for non-divergence

$$NONDIV = (ref \neq A)$$

Fortunately

$$NONSTOP \equiv NONDIV$$

so proof of absence of divergence does not entail any more work than proof of absence of deadlock.

3.7.1 Proofs

In the following proof rules, a specification will be written in any of the forms S, $S(tr)$, $S(tr, ref)$, according to convenience. In all cases, it should be understood that the specification may contain *tr* and *ref* among its free variables.

By the definition of nondeterminism, $(P \sqcap Q)$ behaves either like P or like Q. Therefore every observation of its behaviour will be an observation possible for P or for Q or for both. This observation will therefore be described by the specification of P or by the specification of Q or by both. Consequently, the proof rule for nondeterminism has an exceptionally simple form

L1 If P **sat** S
   and Q **sat** T
   then $(P \sqcap Q)$ **sat** $(S \lor T)$

The proof rule for *STOP* states that it does nothing and refuses anything

L2A $STOP_A$ **sat** $(tr=\langle\rangle\wedge ref\subseteq A)$

Since refusals are always contained in the alphabet (3.4.1 L8) the clause $ref\subseteq A$ can be omitted. So if we omit alphabets altogether (which we shall do in future), the law L2A is identical to that for deterministic processes (1.10.2 L4A)

>   *STOP* **sat** $tr=\langle\rangle$

The previous law for prefixing (1.10.2 L4B) is also still valid, but it is not quite strong enough to prove that the process cannot stop before its initial action. The rule needs to be strengthened by mention of the fact that in the initial state, when $tr=\langle\rangle$, the initial action cannot be refused

L2B   If P **sat** $S(tr)$
   then $(c\rightarrow P)$ **sat** $((tr=\langle\rangle\wedge c\tilde{\in} ref)\vee(tr_0=c\wedge S(tr')))$

The law for general choice (1.10.2 L4) needs to be similarly strengthened

L2   If $\forall x\in B.\ P(x)$ **sat** $S(tr,x)$
   then $(x:B\rightarrow P(x))$ **sat** $((tr=\langle\rangle\wedge(B\cap ref)=\{\})\vee(tr_0\in B\wedge S(tr',tr_0)))$

The law for parallel composition given in 2.7 L1 is still valid, provided that the specifications make no mention of refusal sets. In order to deal correctly with refusals, a slightly more complicated law is required

L3   If P **sat** $S(tr,ref)$
   and Q **sat** $T(tr,ref)$
   and neither P nor Q diverges
   then $(P\|Q)$ **sat** $(\exists X,Y.ref=(X\cup Y)\wedge S(tr\upharpoonright\alpha P,X)\wedge T(tr\upharpoonright\alpha Q,Y))$

The law for change of symbol needs a similar adaptation

L4   If P **sat** $S(tr,ref)$
   then $f(P)$ **sat** $S(f^{-1*}(tr),f^{-1}(ref))$ provided f is one–one.

The law for $\square$ is surprisingly simple

L5   If P **sat** S
   and Q **sat** T
   and neither P nor Q diverges
   then $(P\ \square\ Q)$ **sat** (**if** $tr=\langle\rangle$ **then** $(S\wedge T)$ **else** $(S\vee T)$)

Initially, when $tr=\langle\rangle$, a set is refused by $(P\ \square\ Q)$ only if it is refused by both P and Q. This set must therefore be described by *both* their specifications. Subsequently, when $tr\neq\langle\rangle$, each observation of $(P\ \square\ Q)$ must be an observation either of P or of Q, and must therefore be described by one of their specifications (or both).

The law for interleaving does not need to mention refusal sets

L6 If P **sat** $S(tr)$
   and Q **sat** $T(tr)$
   and neither P nor Q diverges
   then $(P \parallel\!\!\!\mid Q)$ **sat** $(\exists s,t.(tr\ interleaves(s,t) \wedge S(s) \wedge T(t)))$

   The law for concealment is complicated by the need to guard against divergence

L7 If P **sat** $(NODIV \wedge S(tr,ref))$
   then $(P \backslash C)$ **sat** $\exists s.\ tr = s\!\upharpoonright\!(\alpha P - C) \wedge S(s,ref \cup C)$

where $NODIV$ states that the number of hidden symbols that can occur is bounded by some function of the non-hidden symbols that have occurred

$$NODIV = \#(tr\!\upharpoonright\!C) \leq f(tr\!\upharpoonright\!(\alpha P - C))$$

where f is some total function from traces to natural numbers.
   The clause $ref \cup C$ in the consequent of law L7 requires some explanation. It is due to the fact that $P \backslash C$ can refuse a set X only when P can refuse the whole set $X \cup C$, i.e., X together with *all* the hidden events. $P \backslash C$ cannot refuse to interact with its external environment until it has reached a state in which it cannot engage in any further concealed internal activities. This kind of fairness is a most important feature of any reasonable definition of concealment, as described in Section 3.5.1.
   The proof method for recursion (1.10.2 L6) also needs to be strengthened. Let $S(n)$ be a predicate containing the variable n, which ranges over the natural numbers 0,1,2, ...

L8 If $S(0)$
   and $(X$ **sat** $S(n)) \Rightarrow (F(X)$ **sat** $S(n+1))$
   then $(\mu X.F(X))$ **sat** $(\forall n.\ S(n))$

This law is valid even for an unguarded recursion, though the strongest specification which can be proved of such a process is the vacuous specification *true*.

3.8 DIVERGENCE

In previous chapters, we have observed the restriction that the equations which define a process by recursion must be *guarded* (Section 1.1.2). This restriction has ensured that the equations have only a single solution (1.3 L2). It has also released us from the obligation of giving a meaning to the infinite recursion

$$\mu X.X$$

Unfortunately, the introduction of concealment (Section 3.5) means that an apparently guarded recursion is not constructive. For example, consider the equation

$$X = c \rightarrow (X \setminus \{c\})_{+\{c\}}$$

This has as solutions both $(c \rightarrow STOP)$ and $(c \rightarrow a \rightarrow STOP)$, a fact which may be checked by substitution.

Consequently, any recursion equation which involves recursion under the hiding operator is potentially *unguarded*, and liable to have more than one solution. Which solution should be taken as the right one? We stipulate that the right solution is the least deterministic, because this allows a nondeterministic choice between all the other solutions. With this understanding, we can altogether remove the restriction that recursions must be guarded, and we can give a (possibly nondeterministic) meaning to *every* expression of the form $\mu X.F(X)$, where F is defined in terms of any of the operators introduced in this book (except /), and observing all alphabet constraints.

To explain this meaning we deal first with the simplest case, which (as so often) is also the worst case, i.e., the infinite recursion

$$\mu X.X$$

Every process is a solution of the recursive equation

$$X = X$$

Consequently $\mu X.X$ may behave like any process whatsoever. It is the most nondeterministic of all processes, the least predictable, the least controllable, and in short the worst. Let us give it an appropriate name, and define

$$CHAOS_A = \mu X{:}A.X$$

A slightly better case is the recursion given above

$$\mu X.(c \rightarrow (X \setminus \{c\})) = c \rightarrow CHAOS$$

This is a process which is different from $CHAOS$, because it can at least be relied on to engage in the initial event c before collapsing into $CHAOS$.

Apart from giving a meaning to infinite recursions, $CHAOS$ is also what results when a process can engage in an infinite sequence of consecutive hidden events. The simplest and worst case is an immediately divergent process previously quoted at the end of Section 3.5.1.

$$
\begin{aligned}
(\mu X{:}A.(c \rightarrow X)) \setminus \{c\} &= \mu X{:}(A - \{c\}).(c \rightarrow X) \setminus \{c\} \\
&= \mu X{:}A - \{c\}.(X \setminus \{c\}) && \text{by 3.5.1 L5} \\
&= \mu X{:}A - \{c\}.X \\
&= CHAOS_{A-\{c\}} && \text{def. } CHAOS
\end{aligned}
$$

3.8.1 Laws

Since $CHAOS$ is the most nondeterministic process it cannot be changed by adding yet further nondeterministic choices; it is therefore a zero of $\sqcap$

L1 $P \sqcap CHAOS = CHAOS.$

A function of processes which yields $CHAOS$ when any of its arguments is $CHAOS$ is said to be *strict*. The above law (plus symmetry) states that $\sqcap$ is strict. $CHAOS$ is such an awful process that almost any process which is defined in terms of $CHAOS$ is itself equal to $CHAOS$.

L2 The following operations are strict

$$/s, \;\|, f, \;\square, \;\backslash C, \;\interleave, \text{ and } \mu X.$$

However prefixing is not strict

L3 $CHAOS \neq (a {\rightarrow} CHAOS)$

because the right-hand side can be relied upon to do a before becoming completely unreliable.

   As mentioned before, $CHAOS$ is the most unpredictable and most uncontrollable of processes. There is nothing that it might not do; furthermore, there is nothing that it might not refuse to do!

L4 $traces(CHAOS_A) = A^*$

L5 $refusals(CHAOS_A) = $ all subsets of A.

3.8.2 Divergences

A *divergence* of a process is defined as any trace of the process after which the process behaves chaotically. The set of all divergences is defined

$$divergences(P) = \{s \,|\, s \in traces(P) \wedge (P/s) = CHAOS_{\alpha P}\}$$

It follows immediately that

L1 $divergences(P) \subseteq traces(P)$

Because $/t$ is strict,

$$CHAOS/t = CHAOS$$

and it follows that the divergences of a process are extension-closed, in the sense that

L2 $s \in divergences(P) \wedge t \in (\alpha P)^* \Rightarrow (s^\frown t) \in divergences(P)$

Since $CHAOS_A$ may refuse any subset of its alphabet A

L3 $s \in divergences(P) \wedge X \subseteq \alpha P \Rightarrow X \in refusals(P/s)$

The three laws given above state general properties of divergences of any process. The following laws show how the divergences of compound processes are determined by the divergences and traces of their components. Firstly, the process $STOP$ never diverges

L4 $divergences(STOP) = \{\}$

At the other extreme, every trace of $CHAOS$ leads to $CHAOS$

L5 $divergences(CHAOS_A) = A^*$

A process defined by choice does not diverge on its first step. Consequently, its divergences are determined by what happens after the first step

L6 $divergences(x:B \rightarrow P(x)) = \{\langle x \rangle^\wedge s \, | \, x \in B \wedge s \in divergences(P(x))\}$

Any divergence of P is also a divergence of $(P \sqcap Q)$ and of $(P \, [] \, Q)$

L7 $divergences(P \sqcap Q) = divergences(P \, [] \, Q)$
$\qquad\qquad\qquad\quad = divergences(P) \cup divergences(Q)$

Since $\|$ is strict, a divergence of $(P \| Q)$ starts with a trace of the nondivergent activity of both P and Q, which leads to divergence of either P or of Q (or of both)

L8 $divergences(P \| Q) =$
$\qquad \{s^\wedge t \, | \, t \in (\alpha P \cup \alpha Q)^* \wedge ((s \restriction \alpha P \in divergences(P) \wedge s \restriction \alpha Q \in traces(Q))$
$\qquad\qquad\qquad\quad \vee (s \restriction \alpha P \in traces(P) \wedge s \restriction \alpha Q \in divergences(Q)))\}$

A similar explanation applies to $\|\|$

L9 $divergences(P \,\|\|\, Q) =$
$\qquad \{u \, | \, \exists s, t. \; u \; interleaves(s, t) \wedge ((s \in divergences(P) \wedge t \in traces(Q))$
$\qquad\qquad\qquad\qquad\qquad \vee (s \in traces(P) \wedge t \in divergences(Q)))\}$

Divergences of a process resulting from concealment include traces derived from the original divergences, plus those resulting from the attempt to conceal an infinite sequence of symbols

L10 $divergences(P \setminus C) =$
$\qquad \{(s \restriction (\alpha P - C))^\wedge t \, | \, t \in (\alpha P - C)^*$
$\qquad\qquad\qquad \wedge (s \in divergences(P)$
$\qquad\qquad\qquad\qquad \vee (\forall n. \exists u \in C^*. \#u > n \wedge (s^\wedge u) \in traces(P)))\}$

A process defined by symbol change diverges only when its argument diverges

L11 $divergences(f(P)) = \{f^*(s) \, | \, s \in divergences(P)\}$

provided f is one–one.

It is a shame to devote so much attention to divergence, when divergence is always something we do *not* want. Unfortunately, it seems to be an inevitable consequence of any efficient or even computable method of implementation. It can arise from either concealment or unguarded recursion; and it is part of the task of a system designer to prove that for his particular design the problem will not occur. In order to prove that something can't happen, we need to use a mathematical theory in which it can!

3.9 MATHEMATICAL THEORY OF NONDETERMINISTIC PROCESSES

The laws given in this chapter are distinctly more complicated than the laws given in the two earlier chapters; and the informal justifications and examples carry correspondingly less conviction. It is therefore even more important to construct a proper mathematical definition of the concept of a nondeterministic process, and prove the correctness of the laws from the definitions of the operators.

As in Section 2.8.1, a mathematical model is based on the relevant directly or indirectly observable properties of a process. These certainly include its alphabet and its traces; but for a nondeterministic process there are also its refusals (Section 3.4) and divergences (Section 3.8). In addition to refusals at the first step of a process P, it is necessary also to take into account what P may refuse after engaging in an arbitrary trace s of its behaviour. We therefore define the *failures* of a process as a relation (set of pairs)

$$failures(P) = \{(s,X) \mid s \in traces(P) \land X \in refusals(P/s)\}$$

If (s,X) is a failure of P, this means that P can engage in the sequence of events recorded by s, and then refuse to do anything more, in spite of the fact that its environment is prepared to engage in any of the events of X. The failures of a process are more informative about the behaviour of that process than its traces or its refusals, which can both be defined in terms of failures

$$traces(P) = \{s \mid \exists X.(s,X) \in failures(P)\}$$
$$= domain(failures(P))$$
$$refusals(P) = \{X \mid (\langle\rangle,X) \in failures(P)\}$$

The various properties of traces (1.8.1 L6, L7, L8) and refusals (3.4 L8, L9, L10, L11) can be easily reformulated in terms of failures (see conditions C0, C1, C2, C3 under the definition D0 below).

We are now ready for the bold decision that a process is uniquely defined by the three sets specifying its alphabet, its failures, and its divergences; and conversely, any three sets which satisfy the relevant conditions uniquely define a process. We will first define the powerset of A as the set of all its subsets

$$\mathbb{P}A = \{X \mid X \subseteq A\}$$

D0   A process is a triple (A, F, D)

where A is any set of symbols (for simplicity finite)
    F is a relation between A^* and $\mathbb{P}A$
    D is a subset of A^*

provided that they satisfy the following conditions

C0 $(\langle\rangle, \{\}) \in F$

C1 $(s^\wedge t, X) \in F \Rightarrow (s, \{\}) \in F$

C2 $(s, Y) \in F \wedge X \subseteq Y \Rightarrow (s, X) \in F$

C3 $(s, X) \in F \wedge x \in A \Rightarrow (s, X \cup \{x\}) \in F \vee (s^\wedge \langle x \rangle, \{\}) \in F$

C4 $D \subseteq domain(F)$

C5 $s \in D \wedge t \in A^* \Rightarrow s^\wedge t \in D$

C6 $s \in D \wedge X \subseteq A \Rightarrow (s, X) \in F$

(the last three conditions reflect the laws 3.8.2 L1, L2, L3).

The simplest process which satisfies this definition is also the worst

D1 $CHAOS_A = (A, (A^* \times \mathbb{P}A), A^*)$

where $A^* \times \mathbb{P}A$ is the Cartesian product

$$\{s, X \mid s \in A^* \wedge X \in \mathbb{P}A\}$$

This is the largest process with alphabet A, since every member of A^* is both a trace and a divergence, and every subset of A is a refusal after all traces.

Another simple process is defined

D2 $STOP_A = (A, \{\langle\rangle\} \times \mathbb{P}A, \{\})$

This process never does anything, can refuse everything, and has no divergences.

An operator is defined on processes by showing how the three sets of the result can be derived from those of their operands. Of course it is necessary to show that the result of the operation satisfies the six conditions of D0; this proof is usually based on the assumption that its operands do so to start with.

The simplest operation to define is the nondeterministic or ($\sqcap$). Like many other operators, it is defined only for operands with the same alphabet

D3 $(A, F1, D1) \sqcap (A, F2, D2) = (A, F1 \cup F2, D1 \cup D2)$

The resulting process can fail or diverge in all cases that either of its two operands can do so. The laws 3.2.1 L1, L2, L3 are direct consequences of this definition.

The definitions of all the other operators can be given similarly; but it seems slightly more elegant to write separate definitions for the alphabets, failures and divergences. The definitions of the divergences have been given in Section 3.8.2, so it remains only to define the alphabets and the failures.

D4   If $\alpha P(x) = A$ for all x
  and $B \subseteq A$
  then $\alpha(x : B \rightarrow P(x)) = A$.

D5 $\alpha(P \parallel Q) = (\alpha P \cup \alpha Q)$

D6 $\alpha(f(P)) = f(\alpha P)$

D7 $\alpha(P \;[]\; Q) = \alpha(P \;|||\; Q) = \alpha P$ provided $\alpha P = \alpha Q$

D8 $\alpha(P \setminus C) = \alpha P - C$

D9 $failures(x : B \rightarrow P(x)) = \{\langle\rangle,\, X \mid X \subseteq (\alpha P - B)\}$
$\qquad\qquad\qquad\qquad \cup \{\langle x\rangle ^\frown s,\, X \mid x \in B \vee (s, X) \in failures(P(x))\}$

D10 $failures(P \parallel Q) = \{s, (X \cup Y) \mid s \in (\alpha P \cup \alpha Q)^*$
$\qquad\qquad\qquad\qquad\qquad \wedge (s \upharpoonright \alpha P, X) \in failures(P)$
$\qquad\qquad\qquad\qquad\qquad \wedge (s \upharpoonright \alpha Q, Y) \in failures(Q)\}$
$\qquad\qquad\qquad \cup \{s, X \mid s \in divergences(P \parallel Q)\}$

D11 $failures(f(P)) = \{f^*(s),\, f(X) \mid (s, X) \in failures(P)\}$

D12 $failures(P \;[]\; Q) = \{s, X \mid (s, X) \in failures(P) \cap failures(Q)$
$\qquad\qquad\qquad\qquad \vee (s \neq \langle\rangle \wedge (s, X) \in (failures(P) \cup failures(Q)))\}$
$\qquad\qquad\qquad \cup \{s, X \mid s \in divergences(P \;[]\; Q)\}$

D13 $failures(P \;|||\; Q) = \{s, X \mid \exists t, u.\ s\ interleaves(t, u)$
$\qquad\qquad\qquad\qquad\qquad \wedge (t, X) \in failures(P)$
$\qquad\qquad\qquad\qquad\qquad \wedge (u, X) \in failures(Q)\}$
$\qquad\qquad\qquad \cup \{s, X \mid s \in divergences(P \;|||\; Q)\}$

D14 $failures(P \setminus C) = \{s \upharpoonright (\alpha P - C),\, X \mid (s,\ X \cup C) \in failures(P)\}$
$\qquad\qquad\qquad \cup \{s, X \mid s \in divergences(P \setminus C)\}$

The explanation of these laws may be derived from the explanations of the corresponding traces and refusals, together with the laws for /.

It remains to give a definition for processes defined recursively by means of μ. The treatment is based on the same fixed point theory as Section 2.8.2, except that the definition of the ordering $\subseteq$ is different

D15 $(A, F1, D1) \subseteq (A, F2, D2) \equiv (F2 \subseteq F1 \wedge D2 \subseteq D1)$

$P \subseteq Q$ now means that Q is equal to P or better in the sense that it is less likely to diverge and less likely to fail. Q is more predictable and more controllable than P, because if Q can do something undesirable P can do it too; and if Q can refuse to do something desirable, P can also refuse. *CHAOS* can do anything at any time, and can refuse to do anything at any time. True to its name, it is the least predictable and controllable of all processes; or in short the worst

L1 $CHAOS \subseteq P$

This ordering is clearly a partial order. In fact it is a complete partial order, with a limit operation defined in terms of the intersections of descending chains of failures and divergences

D16 $\bigsqcup_{n \geq 0} (A, F_n, D_n) = (A, \bigcap_{n \geq 0} F_n, \bigcap_{n \geq 0} D_n)$

provided $(\forall n \geq 0.\ F_{n+1} \subseteq F_n \wedge D_{n+1} \subseteq D_n)$

The μ operation is defined in the same way as for deterministic processes (2.8.2 L7), except for the difference in the definition of the ordering, which requires that *CHAOS* be used in place of *STOP*

D17 $\mu X{:}A.F(X) = \bigsqcup_{i \geq 0} F^i(CHAOS_A)$

The proof that this is a solution (in fact the most nondeterministic solution) of the relevant equation is the same as that given in Section 2.8.2.

As before, the validity of the proof depends critically on the fact that all the operators used on the right-hand side of the recursion should be continuous in the appropriate ordering. Fortunately, all the operators defined in this book (except /) are continuous, and so is every formula constructed from them. In the case of the concealment operator, the requirement of continuity was one of the main motivations for the rather complicated treatment of divergence.

4 COMMUNICATION

4.1 INTRODUCTION

In previous chapters we have introduced and illustrated a general concept of an event as an action without duration, whose occurrence may require simultaneous participation by more than one independently described process. In this chapter we shall concentrate on a special class of event known as a *communication*. A communication is an event that is described by a pair

$$c.v$$

where c is the name of the channel on which the communication takes place and v is the value of the message which passes. Examples of this convention have already been given in *COPYBIT* (1.1.3 X7) and *CHAIN2* (2.6 X4).

The set of all messages which P can communicate on channel c is defined

$$\alpha c(P) = \{v \mid c.v \in \alpha P\}$$

We also define functions which extract channel and message components of a communication

$$channel(c.v) = c, \quad message(c.v) = v$$

All the operations introduced in this chapter can be defined in terms of the more primitive concepts introduced in earlier chapters, and most of the laws are just special cases of previously familiar laws. The reason for introducing special notations is that they are suggestive of useful applications and implementation methods; and because in some cases imposition of notational restrictions permits the use of more powerful reasoning methods.

133

4.2   INPUT AND OUTPUT

Let v be a member of $\alpha c(P)$. A process which first outputs v on the channel c and then behaves like P is defined

$$(c!v \rightarrow P) = (c.v \rightarrow P)$$

The only event in which this process is initially prepared to engage is the communication event $c.v$.

A process which is initially prepared to input any value x communicable on the channel c, and then behave like $P(x)$, is defined

$$(c?x \rightarrow P(x)) = (y:\{y \mid channel(y)=c\} \rightarrow P(message(y)))$$

Example

X0   Using the new definitions of input and output we can rewrite 1.1.3 X7

$$COPYBIT = \mu X. \ (in?x \rightarrow (out!x \rightarrow X))$$

where $\alpha in(COPYBIT) = \alpha out(COPYBIT) = \{0,1\}$ $\square$

We shall observe the convention that channels are used for communication in only one direction and between only two processes. A channel which is used only for output by a process will be called an output channel of that process; and one used only for input will be called an input channel. In both cases, we shall say loosely that the channel name is a member of the alphabet of the process.

When drawing a connection diagram (Section 2.4) of a process, the channels are drawn as arrows in the appropriate direction, and labelled with the name of the channel (Fig. 4.1).

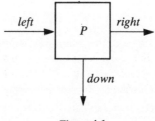

Figure 4.1

Let P and Q be processes, and let c be an output channel of P and an input channel of Q. When P and Q are composed concurrently in the system

$(P \parallel Q)$, communication will occur on channel c on each occasion that P outputs a message and Q simultaneously inputs that message. An outputting process specifies an unique value for the message, whereas the inputting process is prepared to accept any communicable value. Thus the event that will actually occur is the communication $c.v$, where v is the value specified by the outputting process. This requires the obvious constraint that the channel c must have the same alphabet at both ends, i.e.

$$\alpha c(P) = \alpha c(Q)$$

In future, we will assume satisfaction of this constraint; and where no confusion can arise we will write αc for $\alpha c(P)$. An example of the working of this model for communication has been given in $CHAIN2$ (2.6 X4); and more interesting examples will be given in Section 4.3 and subsequent sections.

In general, the value to be output by a process is specified by means of an expression containing variables to which a value has been assigned by some previous input, as illustrated in the following examples.

Examples

X1   A process which immediately copies every message it has input from the left by outputting it to the right

$$\alpha left(COPY) = \alpha right(COPY)$$
$$COPY = \mu X(left?x \rightarrow right!x \rightarrow X)$$

If $\alpha left = \{0,1\}$, $COPY$ is almost identical to $COPYBIT$ (1.1.3 X7)   □

X2   A process like $COPY$, except that every number input is doubled before it is output

$$\alpha left = \alpha right = \mathbb{N}$$
$$DOUBLE = \mu X(left?x \rightarrow right!(x+x) \rightarrow X)$$ □

X3   The value of a punched card is a sequence of eighty characters, which may be read as a single value along the left channel. A process which reads cards and outputs their characters one at a time

$$\alpha left = \{s \mid s \in \alpha right^* \wedge \#s = 80\}$$
$$UNPACK = P_{\langle \rangle}$$

where $P_{\langle \rangle} = left?s \rightarrow P_s$
and $P_{\langle x \rangle} = right!x \rightarrow P_{\langle \rangle}$
       $P_{\langle x \rangle \frown s} = right!x \rightarrow P_s$ □

X4   A process which inputs characters one at a time from the left, and assembles them into lines of 125 characters' length. Each completed line is output on the right as a single array-valued message

$$\alpha right = \{s | s \in \alpha left^* \wedge \# s = 125\}$$
$$PACK = P_{\langle \rangle}$$

where $P_s = right!s \rightarrow P_{\langle \rangle}$ if $\# s = 125$

and $P_s = left?x \rightarrow P_{s^\wedge \langle x \rangle}$ if $\# s < 125$

Here, P_s describes the behaviour of the process when it has input and packed the characters in the sequence s; they are waiting to be output when the line is long enough.   □

X5   A process which copies from left to right, except that each pair of consecutive asterisks is replaced by a single "↑"

$$\alpha left = \alpha right - \{``↑"\}$$
$$SQUASH = \mu X. \ left?x \rightarrow$$
$$\quad \text{if } x \neq ``*" \text{ then } (right!x \rightarrow X)$$
$$\quad \text{else } left?y \rightarrow (\text{if } y = ``*" \text{ then } (right!``↑" \rightarrow X)$$
$$\quad\quad\quad \text{else } (right!``*" \rightarrow right!y \rightarrow X)) \qquad □$$

A process may be prepared initially to communicate on any one of a set of channels, leaving the choice between them to the other processes with which it is connected. For this purpose we adapt the choice notation introduced in Chapter 1. If c and d are distinct channel names

$$(c?x \rightarrow P(x) \,|\, d?y \rightarrow Q(y))$$

denotes a process which initially inputs x on c and then behaves like $P(x)$, or initially inputs y on channel d and then behaves like $Q(y)$. The choice is determined by whichever of the corresponding outputs is ready first, as explained below.

Since we have decided to abstract from the timing of events and the speed of processes which engage in them, the last sentence of the previous paragraph may require explanation. Consider the case when the channels c and d are output channels of two other separate processes, which are independent in the sense that they do not directly or indirectly communicate with each other. The actions of these two processes are therefore arbitrarily interleaved. Thus if one process is making progress towards an output on c, and the other is making progress towards an output on d, it is not determined which of them reaches its output first. An implementor will be expected, but not compelled, to resolve this nondeterminism in favour of the first output to become ready. This policy also protects against the deadlock that will result if the second output is never going to occur, or if it can occur only after the first output, as in the case when both the channels c and d are connected to the same concurrent process, which outputs on one and then the other

$$(c!2 \rightarrow d!4 \rightarrow P)$$

Thus the presentation of a choice of inputs not only protects against deadlock but also achieves greater efficiency and reduces response times to proffered communications. A traveller who is waiting for a number 127 bus will in general have to wait longer than one who is prepared to travel in either a number 19 or a number 127, whichever arrives first at the bus stop. On the assumption of random arrivals, the traveller who offers a choice will wait only half as long—paradoxically, it is as though he is waiting twice as fast! To wait for the first of many possible events is the only way of achieving this: purchase of faster computers is useless.

X6 A process which accepts input on either of the two channels $left1$ or $left2$, and immediately outputs the message to the right

$$\alpha left1 = \alpha left2 = \alpha right$$
$$MERGE = (left1?x \rightarrow right!x \rightarrow MERGE$$
$$| \; left2?x \rightarrow right!x \rightarrow MERGE)$$

The output of this process is an interleaving of the messages input from $left1$ and $left2$. $\qquad\qquad\qquad\qquad\qquad\qquad\qquad\qquad\qquad\qquad\qquad$ □

X7 A process that is always prepared to input a value on the left, or to output to the right the value which it has most recently input

$$\alpha left = \alpha right$$
$$VAR = left?x \rightarrow VAR_x$$

where $VAR_x = (left?y \rightarrow VAR_y$
$\qquad\qquad\quad | \; right!x \rightarrow VAR_x)$

Here VAR_x behaves like a program variable with current value x. New values are assigned to it by communication on the left channel, and its current value is obtained by communication on the right channel. If $\alpha left = \{0,1\}$ the behaviour of VAR is almost identical to that of $BOOL$ (2.6 X5). $\qquad\qquad\qquad\qquad\qquad\qquad\qquad\qquad\qquad\qquad\qquad\qquad\qquad$ □

X8 A process which inputs from up and $left$, and outputs to $down$ a function of what it has input, before repeating

$$NODE(v) = \mu X.(up?sum \rightarrow left?prod \rightarrow$$
$$down!(sum + v*prod) \rightarrow X)$$

$\qquad\qquad\qquad\qquad\qquad\qquad\qquad\qquad\qquad\qquad\qquad\qquad\qquad\qquad\qquad\qquad\qquad$ □

X9 A process which is at all times ready to input a message on the left, and to output on its right the first message which it has input but not yet output

$$BUFFER = P_{\langle\rangle}$$

where $P_{\langle\rangle} = left?x \rightarrow P_{\langle x\rangle}$
and $P_{\langle x\rangle^\wedge s} = (left?y \rightarrow P_{\langle x\rangle^\wedge s^\wedge\langle y\rangle}$
  $\quad | right!x \rightarrow P)$

BUFFER behaves like a queue; messages join the right-hand end of the queue and leave it from the left end, in the same order as they joined, but after a possible delay, during which later messages may join the queue. $\square$

X10 A process which behaves like a stack of messages. When empty, it responds to the signal *empty*. At all times it is ready to input a new message from the left and put it on top of the stack; and whenever nonempty, it is prepared to output and remove the top element of the stack

$$STACK = P_{\langle\rangle}$$

where $P_{\langle\rangle} = (empty \rightarrow P_{\langle\rangle} | left?x \rightarrow P_{\langle x\rangle})$
and $P_{\langle x\rangle^\wedge s} = (right!x \rightarrow P_s | left?y \rightarrow P_{\langle y\rangle^\wedge\langle x\rangle^\wedge s})$

This process is very similar to the previous example, except that when empty it participates in the *empty* event, and that it puts newly arrived messages on the same end of the stored sequence as it takes them off. Thus if y is the newly input message, and x is the message currently ready for output, the *STACK* stores $\langle y\rangle^\wedge\langle x\rangle^\wedge s$ but the *BUFFER* stores $\langle x\rangle^\wedge s^\wedge\langle y\rangle$. $\square$

4.2.1 Implementation

In a LISP implementation of communicating processes, the event $c.v$ is naturally represented by the dotted pair $(c.v)$, which is constructed by

$$cons("c,v).$$

Input and output commands are conveniently implemented as functions which first take a channel name as argument. If the process is not prepared to communicate on the channel, it delivers the answer *"BLEEP*. The actual value communicated is treated separately in the next stage, as described below.

If Q is the input command

$$(c?x \rightarrow Q(x))$$

then $Q("c) \neq "BLEEP$; instead, its result is a function which expects the input value x as its argument, and delivers as its result the process $Q(x)$. Thus Q is implemented by calling the LISP function

$input("c, \lambda x.Q(x))$

which is defined

$input(c, F) = \lambda y.$ **if** $y \neq c$ **then** $"BLEEP$ **else** F.

It follows that $Q/\langle c.v\rangle$ is represented in LISP by $Q("c)(v)$, provided $\langle c.v\rangle$ is a trace of Q.

If P is the output command

$(c!v \rightarrow P')$

then $P("c) \neq "BLEEP$; instead, its result is the pair $cons(v,P')$. Thus P is implemented by calling the LISP function

$output("c, v, P')$

which is defined

$output(c, v, P) = \lambda y.$ **if** $y \neq c$ **then** $"BLEEP$ **else** $cons\ (v, P)$

It follows that $v = car(P("c))$ and $P/\langle c.v\rangle$ is represented in LISP by $cdr(P("c))$, provided $\langle c.v\rangle$ is a trace of P.

In theory, if αc is finite, it would be possible to treat $c.v$ as a single event, passed as a parameter to the input and output commands. But this would be grotesquely inefficient, since the only way of finding what value is output would be to test whether $P(c.v) \neq "BLEEP$ for all values v in αc, until the right one is found. One of the justifications for introducing specialized notation for input and output is to encourage and permit methods of implementation which are significantly more efficient. The disadvantage is that the implementation of nearly all the other operators needs to be recoded in the light of this optimisation.

Examples

X1 $COPY = LABEL\ X.\ input("left, \lambda x.output("right,x,X))$ □

X2 $PACK = P(NIL)$

where $P = LABEL\ X.$
$\quad\quad\quad \lambda s.$ **if** $length(s) = 125$ **then** $output("right,s,X(NIL))$
$\quad\quad\quad\quad$ **else** $input\ ("left, \lambda x.X(append(s,cons(x,NIL))))$ □

4.2.2 Specifications

In specifying the behaviour of a communicating process, it is convenient to describe separately the sequences of messages that pass along each of the channels. If c is a channel name, we define (see Section 1.9.6)

$$tr{\downarrow}c = message^*(tr{\upharpoonright}\alpha c)$$

It is convenient just to omit the $tr{\downarrow}$, and write $right \leq left$ instead of $tr{\downarrow}right \leq tr{\downarrow}left$.

Another useful definition places a lower bound on the length of a prefix

$$s \overset{n}{\leq} t = (s \leq t \wedge \#t \leq \#s + n)$$

This means that s is a prefix of t, with not more than n items removed. The following laws are obvious and useful

$$s \overset{0}{\leq} t \equiv (s = t)$$

$$s \overset{n}{\leq} t \wedge t \overset{m}{\leq} u \Rightarrow s \overset{n+m}{\leq} u$$

$$s \leq t \equiv \exists n. \; s \overset{n}{\leq} t$$

Examples

X1 $COPY$ **sat** $right \overset{1}{\leq} left$ □

X2 $DOUBLE$ **sat** $right \overset{1}{\leq} double^*(left)$ □

X3 $UNPACK$ **sat** $right \leq {}^\wedge\!/left$

where ${}^\wedge\!/\langle s_0, s_1, ..., s_{n-1}\rangle = s_0 {}^\wedge s_1 {}^\wedge ... {}^\wedge s_{n-1}$ (see 1.9.2)

The specification here states that the output on the right is obtained by flattening the sequence of sequences input on the left.   □

X4 $PACK$ **sat** $(({}^\wedge\!/right \overset{125}{\leq} left) \wedge (\#^*right) \in \{125\}^*)$

This specification states that each element output on the right is itself a sequence of length 125, and the catenation of all these sequences is an initial subsequence of what has been input on the left.   □

If $\oplus$ is a binary operator, it is convenient to apply it distributively to the corresponding elements of two sequences. The length of the resulting sequence is equal to that of the shorter operand

$$s \oplus t = \langle \rangle$$

$$= \langle s_0 \oplus t_0 \rangle {}^\wedge (s' \oplus t')$$

if $s = \langle \rangle$ or $t = \langle \rangle$
otherwise

Clearly $(s \oplus t)[i] = s[i] \oplus t[i]$ for $i < min(\#s, \#t)$.

and $s \overset{n}{\leq} t \Rightarrow (s \oplus u \overset{n}{\leq} t \oplus u) \wedge (u \oplus s \overset{n}{\leq} u \oplus t)$

X5 The Fibonacci sequence

$$\langle 1,1,2,3,5,8, \ldots \rangle$$

is defined by the recurrence relation

$$fib[0] = fib[1] = 1$$
$$fib[i+2] = fib[i+1] + fib[i]$$

The second line can be rewritten using the   operator to left-shift the sequence by one place

$$fib'' = fib' + fib$$

The original definition of the Fibonacci sequence may be recovered from this more cryptic form by subscripting both sides of the equation

$$fib''[i] = (fib' + fib)[i]$$

therefore $fib'[i+1] = fib'[i] + fib[i]$ (1.9.4 L1)

therefore $fib[i+2] = fib[i+1] + fib[i]$

Another explanation of the meaning of the equation is as a description of the infinite sum, where the left shift is clearly displayed

$$
\begin{array}{ll}
1 , 1 , 2 , 3 , 5 \ldots & \text{fib} \\
\quad \text{//} \ \text{//} \ \text{//} \ \text{//} & \\
1 , 2 , 3 , 5, \ldots & +\text{fib}' \\
\quad \text{//} \ \text{//} \ \text{//} & \\
2 , 3 , 5 , \ldots & =\text{fib}''
\end{array}
$$

In the above discussion, fib is regarded as an infinite sequence. If s is a finite initial subsequence of fib (with $\#s \geq 2$) then instead of the equation we get the inequality

$$s'' \leq s' + s$$

This formulation can be used to specify a process FIB which outputs the Fibonacci sequence to the right.

    FIB **sat** $(right \leq \langle 1,1 \rangle \vee (\langle 1,1 \rangle \leq right \wedge right'' \leq right' + right))$ □

X6 A variable with value x outputs on the right the value most recently input on the left, or x, if there is no such input. More formally, if the most recent action was an output, then the value which was output is equal to the last item in the sequence $\langle x \rangle^\wedge left$

    VAR_x **sat** $(channel(\overline{tr}_0) = right \Rightarrow \overline{right_0} = \overline{(\langle x \rangle^\wedge left)_0})$

where $\bar{s}_0$ is the last element of s (Section 1.9.5).

This is an example of a process that cannot be adequately specified solely in terms of the sequence of messages on its separate channels. It is also necessary to know the order in which the communications on separate channels are interleaved, for example that the latest communication is on the right. In general, this extra complexity will be necessary for processes which use the choice operator. $\Box$

X7   The *MERGE* process produces an interleaving (Section 1.9.3) of the two sequences input on *left*1 and *left*2, buffering up to one message

> $MERGE$ sat $\exists r.\ right \overset{1}{\leq} r \wedge r\ interleaves(left1,\ left2)$ $\Box$

X8   *BUFFER* sat *right≤left* $\Box$

A process which satisfies the specification (*right≤left*) describes the behaviour of a transparent communications protocol, which is guaranteed to deliver on the right only those messages which have been submitted on the left, and in the same order. A protocol achieves this in spite of the fact that the place where the messages are submitted is widely separated from the place where they are received, and the fact that the communications medium which connects the two places is somewhat unreliable. Examples will be given in Section 4.4.5.

4.3   COMMUNICATIONS

Let *P* and *Q* be processes, and let *c* be a channel used for output by *P* and for input by *Q*. Thus the set containing all communication events of the form *c.v* is within the intersection of the alphabet of *P* with the alphabet of *Q*. When these processes are composed concurrently in the system ($P \parallel Q$), a communication *c.v* can occur only when both processes engage simultaneously in that event, i.e., whenever *P* outputs a value *v* on the channel *c*, and *Q* simultaneously inputs the same value. An inputting process is prepared to accept *any* communicable value, so it is the outputting process that determines which actual message value is transmitted on each occasion, as in 2.6 X4.

Thus output may be regarded as a specialized case of the prefix operator, and input a special case of choice; and this leads to the law

L1 $(c!v{\rightarrow}P) \parallel (c?x{\rightarrow}Q(x)) = c!v{\rightarrow}(P \parallel Q(v))$

Note that *c!v* remains on the right-hand side of this equation as an observable action in the behaviour of the system. This represents the physical possibility of tapping the wires connecting the components of a system, and of thereby keeping a log of their internal communications. It is also a help in reasoning about the system. If desired, such internal operations can be concealed by applying the concealment operator described in Section 3.5 outside the parallel composition of the two processes which communicate on the same channel, as shown by the law

L2 $((c!v \rightarrow P) \parallel (c?x \rightarrow Q(x))) \setminus C = (P \parallel Q(v)) \setminus C$

where $C = \{c.v | v \in \alpha c\}$

Examples will be given in Sections 4.4 and 4.5.

The specification of the parallel composition of communicating processes takes a particularly simple form when channel names are used to denote the sequences of messages passing on them. Let c be the name of a channel along which P and Q communicate. In the specification of P, c stands for the sequence of messages communicated by P on c. Similarly, in the specification of Q, c stands for the sequence of messages communicated by Q. Fortunately, by the very nature of communication, when P and Q communicate on c, the sequences of messages sent and received must at all times be identical. Consequently this sequence must satisfy both the specification of P and the specification of Q. The same is true for all channels in the intersection of their alphabets.

Consider now a channel d in the alphabet of P but *not* of Q. This channel cannot be mentioned in the specification of Q, so the values communicated on it are constrained only by the specification of P. Similarly, it is Q that determines the properties of the communications on its own channels. Consequently a specification of the behaviour of $(P \parallel Q)$ can be simply formed as the logical conjunction of the specification of P with the specification of Q. However, this simplification is valid only when the specifications of P and Q are expressed wholly in terms of the channel names, which is not always possible, as shown by 4.2.2 X6.

Examples

X1   Let $P = (left?x \rightarrow mid!(x \times x) \rightarrow P)$
$\phantom{\textbf{X1}\quad Let\ } Q = (mid?y \rightarrow right!(173 \times y) \rightarrow Q)$

Clearly P **sat**$(mid \overset{1}{\leq} square^*(left))$

and Q **sat**$(right \overset{1}{\leq} 173 \times mid)$

where $(173 \times mid)$ multiplies each message of mid by 173.

It follows that

$(P \parallel Q)$ **sat** $(right \overset{1}{\leq} 173 \times mid) \wedge (mid \overset{1}{\leq} square^*(left))$

The specification here implies

$$right \leq 173 \times square^*(left)$$

which was presumably the original intention.   □

When communicating processes are connected by the concurrency operator ∥, the resulting formulae are highly suggestive of a physical implementation method in which electronic components are connected by wires along which they communicate. The purpose of such an implementation is to increase the speed with which useful results can be produced. The technique is particularly effective when the same calculation must be performed on each member of a stream of input data, and the results must be output at the same rate as the input, but possibly after an initial delay. Such systems are called data flow networks.

A picture of a system of communicating processes closely represents their physical realization. An output channel of one process is connected to a like-named input channel of the other process, but channels in the alphabet of only one process are left free. Thus the example X1 can be drawn, as shown in Fig. 4.2.

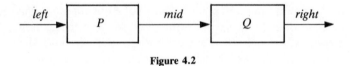

Figure 4.2

X2   Two streams of numbers are to be input from *left*1 and *left*2. For each x read from *left*1 and each y from *left*2, the number $(a \times x + b \times y)$ is to be output on the right. The speed requirement dictates that the multiplications must proceed concurrently. We therefore define two processes, and compose them

$$X21 = (left1?x \rightarrow mid!(a \times x) \rightarrow X21)$$
$$X22 = (left2?y \rightarrow mid?z \rightarrow right!(z + b \times y) \rightarrow X22)$$
$$X2 = (X21 \parallel X22)$$

Clearly, $X2$ **sat** $(mid \overset{1}{\leq} a \times left1 \wedge right \overset{1}{\leq} mid + b \times left2)$
$$\Rightarrow (right \leq a \times left1 + b \times left2)$$ □

X3   A stream of numbers is to be input on the left, and on the right is output a weighted sum of consecutive pairs of input numbers, with weights a and b. More precisely, we require that

$$right \leq a \times left + b \times left'$$

The solution can be constructed by adding a new process $X23$ to the solution of $X2$

$X3 = (X2 \parallel X23)$

where $X23$ **sat** $(left1 \overset{1}{\leq} left \wedge left2 \overset{1}{\leq} left')$.

$X23$ can be defined

$X23 = (left?x \rightarrow left1!x \rightarrow (\mu X.\ left?x \rightarrow left2!x \rightarrow left1!x \rightarrow X))$

It copies from $left$ to both $left1$ and $left2$, but omits the first element in the case of $left2$.

A picture of the network of $X3$ is shown in Fig. 4.3.   □

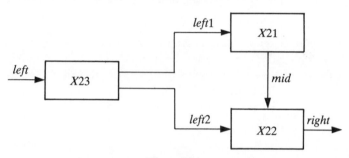

Figure 4.3

When two concurrent processes communicate with each other by output and input only on a single channel, they cannot deadlock (compare 2.7 L2). As a result, any network of nonstopping processes which is free of cycles cannot deadlock, since an acyclic graph can be decomposed into subgraphs connected by only a single arrow. However the network of X3 contains an undirected cycle, and cyclic networks cannot be decomposed into subnetworks except with connections on two or more channels; so in this case absence of deadlock cannot so easily be assured. For example, if the two outputs $left2!x \rightarrow left1!x \rightarrow$ in the loop of $X23$ were reversed, deadlock would occur rapidly. In proving absence of deadlock it is often possible to ignore the content of the messages, and regard each communication on channel c as a single event named c. Communications on unconnected channels can be ignored. Thus $X3$ can be written in terms of these events

$$(\mu X.left1 \rightarrow mid \rightarrow X)$$
$$\parallel (\mu Y.left2 \rightarrow mid \rightarrow Y)$$
$$\parallel (left1 \rightarrow (\mu Z.left2 \rightarrow left1 \rightarrow Z))$$
$$= \mu X3.(left1 \rightarrow left2 \rightarrow mid \rightarrow X3)$$

This proves that $X3$ cannot deadlock, using algebraic methods as in 2.3 X1.

These examples show how data flow networks can be set up to compute one or more streams of results from one or more streams of input data. The shape of the network corresponds closely to the structure of operands and operators appearing in the expressions to be computed. When these patterns are large but regular, it is convenient to use subscripted names for channels, and to introduce an iterated notation for concurrent combination

$$\mathop{\|}_{i<n} P(i) = (P(0) \parallel P(1) \parallel \dots \parallel P(n-1))$$

A regular network of this kind is known as an *iterative array*. If the connection diagram has no directed cycles, the term *systolic array* is often used, since data passes through the system much like blood through the chambers of the heart.

X4   The channels $\{left_j | j<n\}$ are used to input the coordinates of successive points in n-dimensional space. Each coordinate set is to be multiplied by a fixed vector V of length n, and the resulting scalar product is to be output to the right; or more formally

$$right \le \sum_{j=0}^{n-1} V_j \times left_j$$

It is specified that in each microsecond the n coordinates of one point are to be input and one scalar product is to be output. The speed of each individual processor is such that it takes nearly one microsecond to do an input, a multiplication, an addition and an output. It is therefore clear that at least n processors will be required to operate concurrently. The solution to the problem should therefore be designed as an iterative array with at least n elements.

Let us replace the Σ in the specification by its usual inductive definition

$$mid_0 = 0^*$$
$$mid_{j+1} = V_j \times left_j + mid_j \qquad\qquad \text{for } j<n$$
$$right = mid_n$$

Thus we have split the specification into a conjunction of $n+1$ component equations, each containing at most one multiplication. All that is required is to write a process for each equation

$$MULT_0 = (\mu X.\ mid_0!0 \rightarrow X)$$
$$MULT_{j+1} = (\mu X.\ left_j?x \rightarrow mid_j?y \rightarrow mid_{j+1}!(V_j \times x + y) \rightarrow X) \qquad \text{for } j<n$$
$$MULT_{n+1} = (\mu X.\ mid_n?x \rightarrow right!x \rightarrow X)$$

$$NETWORK = \mathop{\|}_{j<n+2} MULT_j$$

The connection diagram is shown in Fig. 4.4. □

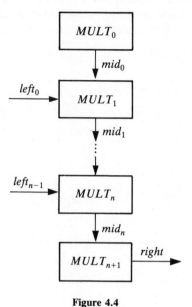

Figure 4.4

X5 This is similar to X4, except that m different scalar products of the same coordinate sets are required almost simultaneously. Effectively, the channel $left_j$ (for $j<n$) is to be used to input the jth column of an infinite array; this is to be multiplied by the $(n \times m)$ matrix M, and the ith column of the result is to be output on $right_i$ for $i<m$. In formulae

$$right_i = \sum_{j<n} M_{ij} \times left_j$$

The coordinates of the result are required as rapidly as before, so at least $m \times n$ processes are required.

The solution might find practical application in a graphics display device which automatically transforms or even rotates a two-dimensional representation of a three-dimensional object. The shape is defined by a series of points in absolute space; the iterative array applies linear transformations to compute the deflection on the x and y plates of the cathode ray tube; a third output coordinate could perhaps control the intensity of the beam.

The solution is based on Fig. 4.5. Each column of this array (except the last) is modelled on the solution to X4; but it copies each value input on its horizontal input channel to its neighbour on its horizontal output channel.

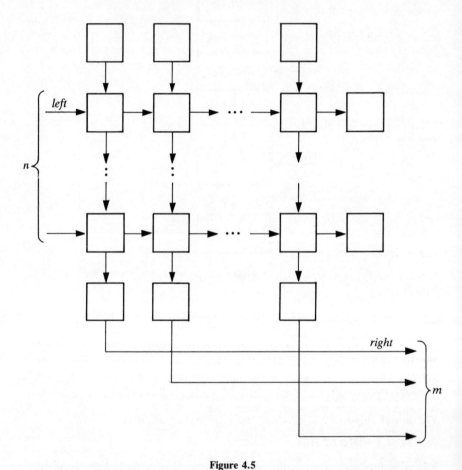

Figure 4.5

The processes on the right margin merely discard the values they input. It would be possible to economize by absorbing the functions of these marginal processors into their neighbours.

The details of the solution are left as an exercise.   □

X6 The input on channel c is to be interpreted as the successive digits of a natural number C, starting from the least significant digit, and expressed with number base b. We define the value of the input number as

$$C = \sum_{i \geq 0} c[i] \times b^i$$

where $c[i] < b$ for all i.

Given a fixed multiplier M, the output on channel d is to be the successive digits of the product $M \times C$. The digits are to be output after minimal delay.

Let us specify the problem more precisely. The desired output d is

$$d = \sum_{i \geq 0} M \times c[i] \times b^i$$

The jth element of d must be the jth digit, which can be computed by the formula

$$d[j] = ((\sum_{i \geq 0} M \times c[i] \times b^i) \div b^j) \bmod b$$

$$= (M \times c[j] + z_j) \bmod b$$

where $z_j = (\sum_{i < j} M \times c[i] \times b^i) \div b^j$

and $\div$ denotes integer division.

z_j is the carry term, and can readily be proved to satisfy the inductive definition

$$z_0 = 0$$

$$z_{j+1} = ((M \times c[j] + z_j) \div b)$$

We therefore define a process $MULT1(z)$, which keeps the carry z as a parameter

$$MULT1(z) = c?x \rightarrow d!(M \times x + z) \bmod b \rightarrow MULT1((M \times x + z) \div b)$$

The initial value of z is zero, so the required solution is

$$MULT = MULT1(0) \qquad\qquad \square$$

X7 The problem is the same as X6, except M is a multi-digit number

$$M = \sum_{i < n} M_i \times b^i$$

A single processor can multiply only single-digit numbers. However, output is to be produced at a rate which allows only one multiplication per digit. Consequently, at least n processors are required. We will get each $NODE_i$ to look after one digit M_i of the multiplier.

The basis of a solution is the traditional manual algorithm for multi-digit multiplication, except that the partial sums are added immediately to the next row of the table

..... 153091	C	the incoming number
253	M	the multiplier
.... 306182	$M_2 \times C$	computed by $NODE_2$
....765455	$M_1 \times C$	computed by $NODE_1$
.....827275	$25 \times C$	
....459273	$M_0 \times C$	computed by $NODE_0$
....732023	$M \times C$	

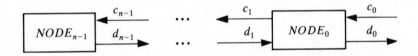

Figure 4.6

The nodes are connected as shown in Fig. 4.6. The original input comes in on c_0 and is propagated leftward on the c channels. The partial answers are propagated rightward on the d channels, and the desired answer is output on d_0. Fortunately each node can give one digit of its result before communicating with its left neighbour. Furthermore, the leftmost node can be defined to behave like the answer to X6

$$NODE_{n-1}(z) = c_{n-1}\,?\,x \to d_{n-1}\,!\,(M_{n-1} \times x + z)\ \mathbf{mod}\ b$$
$$\to NODE_{n-1}((M_{n-1} \times x + z) \div b)$$

The remaining nodes are similar, except that each of them passes the input digit to its left neighbour, and adds the result from its left neighbour to its own carry. For $k < n-1$

$$NODE_k\,(z) = c_k?x \to d_k!(M_k \times x + z)\ \mathbf{mod}\ b \to c_{k+1}!x \to d_{k+1}?y$$
$$\to NODE_k\,(y + (M_k \times x + z) \div b)$$

The whole network is defined

$$\|_{i<n} NODE_i\,(0) \qquad\qquad \Box$$

X7 is a simple example from a class of ingenious network algorithms, in which there is an essential cycle in the directed graph of communication channels. But the statement of the problem has been much simplified by the assumption that the multiplier is known in advance and fixed for all time. In a practical application, it is much more likely that such parameters would have to be input along the same channel as the subsequent data, and would have to be reinput whenever it is required to change them. The implementation of this requires great care, but little ingenuity.

A simple implementation method is to introduce a special symbol, say *reload*, to indicate that the next number or numbers are to be treated as a change of parameter; and if the number of parameters is variable, an *endreload* symbol may also be introduced.

X8 Same as X4, except that the parameters V_j are to be reloaded by the number immediately following a *reload* symbol. The definition of $MULT_{j+1}$ needs to be changed to include the multiplier as parameter

$$MULT_{j+1}(v) = left_j?x\rightarrow$$
$$\textbf{if } x=reload \textbf{ then } (left_j?y\rightarrow MULT_{j+1}(y))$$
$$\textbf{else } (mid_j?y\rightarrow mid_{j+1}!(v\times x+y)\rightarrow MULT_{j+1}(v)) \qquad \square$$

4.4   PIPES

In this section we shall confine attention to processes with only two channels in their alphabet, namely an input channel *left* and an output channel *right*. Such processes are called *pipes*, and they may be pictured as in Fig. 4.7.

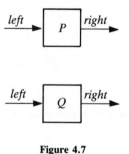

Figure 4.7

The processes *P* and *Q* may be joined together so that the right channel of *P* is connected to the left channel of *Q*, and the sequence of messages output by *P* and input by *Q* on this internal channel is concealed from their common environment. The result of the connection is denoted

$P \gg Q$

and may be pictured as the series shown in Fig. 4.8.

Figure 4.8

This connection diagram represents the concealment of the connecting channel by not giving it a name. It also shows that all messages input on the left channel of $(P \gg Q)$ are input by P, and all messages output on the right channel of $(P \gg Q)$ are output by Q. Finally $(P \gg Q)$ is itself a pipe, and may again be placed in series with other pipes

$(P \gg Q) \gg R$, $(P \gg Q) \gg (R \gg S)$, etc.

By 4.4.1 L1 $\gg$ is associative, so in future we shall omit brackets in such a series.

The validity of chaining processes by $\gg$ depends on the obvious alphabet constraints

$\alpha(P \gg Q) = \alpha left(P) \cup \alpha right(Q)$

and a further constraint states that the connected channels are capable of transmitting the same kind of message

$\alpha right(P) = \alpha left(Q)$

Examples

X1   A pipe which outputs each input value multiplied by four (4.2 X2)

$QUADRUPLE = DOUBLE \gg DOUBLE$ □

X2   A process which inputs cards of eighty characters and outputs their text, tightly packed into lines of 125 characters each (4.2 X3, X4)

$UNPACK \gg PACK$

This process is quite difficult to write using conventional structured programming techniques, because it is not clear whether the major loop should iterate once per input card, or once per output line. The problem is known by

Michael Jackson as *structure clash*. The solution given above contains a separate loop in each of the two processes, which nicely matches the structure of the original problem. □

X3 Same as X2, except that each pair of consecutive asterisks is replaced by "↑" (4.2 X5)

$$UNPACK \gg SQUASH \gg PACK$$

In a conventional sequential program, this minor change in specification could cause severe problems. It is nice to avoid such problems by the simple expedient of inserting an additional process. This kind of modularity has been introduced and exploited by the designers of operating systems. □

X4 Same as X2, except that the reading of cards may continue when the printer is held up, and later the printing can continue when the card reader is held up (4.2 X9)

$$UNPACK \gg BUFFER \gg PACK$$

The buffer holds characters which have been produced by the *UNPACK* process, but not yet consumed by the *PACK* process. They will be available for input by the *PACK* process during times when the *UNPACK* process is temporarily delayed. The buffer thus smooths out temporary variations in the rate of production and consumption. However it can never solve the problem of long-term mismatch between the rates of production and consumption. If the card reader is on average slower than the printer, the buffer will be nearly always empty, and no smoothing effect will be achieved. If the reader is faster, the buffer will expand indefinitely, until it consumes all available storage space. □

X5 In order to avoid undesirable expansion of buffers, it is usual to limit the number of messages buffered. Even the single buffer provided by the *COPY* process (4.2 X1) may be adequate. Here is a version of X4 which reads one card ahead on input and buffers one line on output

$$COPY \gg UNPACK \gg PACK \gg COPY$$

Note the alphabets of the two instances of *COPY* are different, a fact which should be understood from the context in which they are placed. □

X6 A double buffer, which accepts up to two messages before requiring output of the first

$$COPY \gg COPY$$ □

Its behaviour is rather similar to that of *CHAIN2* (2.6 X4) and even *VMS2* (1.1.3 X6).

4.4.1 Laws

The most useful algebraic property of chaining is associativity

L1 $P \gg (Q \gg R) = (P \gg Q) \gg R$

The remaining laws show how input and output can be implemented in a pipe; they enable process descriptions to be simplified by a form of symbolic execution. For example, if the process on the left of $\gg$ starts with output of a message v to the right, and the process on the right of $\gg$ starts with input from the left, the message v is transmitted from the former process to the latter; however the actual communication is concealed, as shown in the following law

L2 $(right!v \rightarrow P) \gg (left?y \rightarrow Q(y)) = P \gg Q(v)$

If one of the processes is determined to communicate with the other, but the other is prepared to communicate externally, it is the external communication that takes place first, and the internal communication is saved up for a subsequent occasion

L3 $(right!v \rightarrow P) \gg (right!w \rightarrow Q) = right!w \rightarrow ((right!v \rightarrow P) \gg Q)$

L4 $(left?x \rightarrow P(x)) \gg (left?y \rightarrow Q(y)) = left?x \rightarrow (P(x) \gg (left?y \rightarrow Q(y)))$

If both processes are prepared for external communication, then either may happen first

L5 $(left?x \rightarrow P(x)) \gg (right!w \rightarrow Q) = (left?x \rightarrow (P(x) \gg (right!w \rightarrow Q))$
$ | \ right!w \rightarrow ((left?x \rightarrow P(x)) \gg Q))$

The law L5 is equally valid when the operator $\gg$ is replaced by $\gg R \gg$, since pipes in the middle of a chain cannot communicate directly with the environment

L6 $(left?x \rightarrow P(x)) \gg R \gg (right!w \rightarrow Q) = (left?x \rightarrow (P(x) \gg R \gg (right!w \rightarrow Q))$
$ | \ right!w \rightarrow ((left?x \rightarrow P(x)) \gg R \gg Q))$

Similar generalizations may be made to the other laws

L7   If R is a chain of processes all starting with output to the right,

$R \gg (right!w \rightarrow Q) = right!w \rightarrow (R \gg Q)$

L8   If R is a chain of processes all starting with input from the left,

$(left?x \rightarrow P(x)) \gg R = left?x \rightarrow (P(x) \gg R)$

Examples

X1 Let us define

$R(y) = (right!y \rightarrow COPY) \gg COPY$

So $R(y) = (right!y \rightarrow COPY) \gg (left?x \rightarrow right!x \rightarrow COPY)$ def $COPY$
$ = COPY \gg (right!y \rightarrow COPY)$ L2 $\square$

X2 $COPY \gg COPY$

$\qquad = (left?x \rightarrow right!x \rightarrow COPY) \gg COPY$ def $COPY$

$\qquad = left?x \rightarrow ((right!x \rightarrow COPY) \gg COPY)$ L4

$\qquad = left?x \rightarrow R(x)$ def $R(x)$ ☐

X3 From the last line of X1 we deduce

$R(y) = (left?x \rightarrow right!x \rightarrow COPY) \gg (right!y \rightarrow COPY)$

$\qquad = (left?x \rightarrow ((right!x \rightarrow COPY) \gg (right!y \rightarrow COPY))$

$\qquad\quad | \; right!y \rightarrow (COPY \gg COPY))$ L5

$\qquad = (left?x \rightarrow right!y \rightarrow R(x)$ L3

$\qquad\quad | \; right!y \rightarrow left?x \rightarrow R(x))$ X2

This shows that a double buffer, after input of its first message, is prepared either to output that message or to input a second message before doing so. The reasoning of the above proofs is very similar to that of 2.3.1 X1 ☐

4.4.2 Implementation

In the implementation of $(P \gg Q)$ three cases are distinguished

(1) If communication can take place on the internal connecting channel, it does so immediately, without consideration of the external environment. If an infinite sequence of such communications is possible, the process diverges (Section 3.5.2).

(2) Otherwise, if the environment is interested in communication on the left channel, this is dealt with by P.

(3) Or if the environment is interested in the right channel, this is dealt with by Q.

For an explanation of the input and output operations, see Section 4.2.1.

$chain(P,Q) =$

    if $P("right) \neq "BLEEP \wedge Q("left) \neq "BLEEP$

        then $chain(cdr(P("right)), \; Q("left) \, (car(P("right))))$ case (1)

    else $\lambda x.$ **if** $x = "right$

           then if $Q("right) = "BLEEP$ **then** $"BLEEP$

                else $cons(car(Q("right)),$

                              $chain(P, \; cdr(Q("right)))))$ case (2)

           else if $x = "left$

                then if $P(x) = "BLEEP$ **then** $"BLEEP$

                    else $\lambda y. \; chain(P("left)(y), \; Q)$ case (3)

           else $"BLEEP$

4.4.3   Livelock

The chaining operator connects two processes by just one channel; and so it introduces no risk of deadlock. If both P and Q are nonstopping, then $(P \gg Q)$ will not stop either. Unfortunately there is a new danger that the processes P and Q will spend the whole time communicating with each other, so that $(P \gg Q)$ never again communicates with the external world. This case of divergence (Sections 3.5.1, 3.8) is illustrated by the trivial example

$$P = (right!1 \rightarrow P)$$
$$Q = (left?x \rightarrow Q).$$

$(P \gg Q)$ is obviously a useless process; it is even worse than $STOP$, in that like an endless loop it may consume unbounded computing resources without achieving anything. A less trivial example is $(P \gg Q)$, where

$$P = (right!1 \rightarrow P \,|\, left?x \rightarrow P1(x))$$
$$Q = (left?x \rightarrow Q \,|\, right!1 \rightarrow Q1)$$

In this example, divergence derives from the mere possibiity of infinite internal communication; it exists even though the choice of external communication on the left and on the right is offered on every possible occasion, and even though after such an external communication the subsequent behaviour of $(P \gg Q)$ would not diverge.

A simple method to prove $(P \gg Q)$ is free of livelock is to show that P is *left-guarded* in the sense that it can never output an infinite series of messages to the right without interspersing inputs from the left. To ensure this, we must prove that the length of the sequence output to the right is at all times bounded above by some well-defined function f of the sequence of values input from the left; or more formally, we define

$$P \text{ is left-guarded} \equiv \exists f. \ P \text{ sat } (\#right \leq f(left))$$

Left-guardedness is often obvious from the text of P.

L1   If every recursion used in the definition of P is guarded by an input from the left, then P is left-guarded.

L2   If P is left-guarded then $(P \gg Q)$ is free of livelock.

Exactly the same reasoning applies to right-guardedness of the second operand of $\gg$

L3   If Q is right-guarded then $(P \gg Q)$ is free of livelock.

Examples

X1 The following are left-guarded by L1 (4.1 X1, X2, X5, X9)

COPY, DOUBLE, SQUASH, BUFFER □

X2 The following are left-guarded in accordance with the original definition, because

$UNPACK$ **sat** $\#right \leq \#(^{\wedge}/left)$
$PACK$ **sat** $\#right \leq \#left$ □

X3 *BUFFER* is *not* right-guarded, since it can input arbitrarily many messages from the left without ever outputting to the right. □

4.4.4 Specifications

A specification of a pipe can often be expressed as a relation $S(left,right)$ between the sequence of messages input on the left channel and the sequence of messages output on the right. When two pipes are connected in series, the sequence *right* produced by the left operand is equated with the sequence *left* consumed by the right operand; and this common sequence is then concealed. All that is known of the concealed sequence is that it exists. But we also need to avert the risk of livelock. Thus we explain the rule

L1 If P **sat** $S(left,right)$
  and Q **sat** $T(left,right)$
  and if P is left-guarded or Q is right-guarded
  then $(P \gg Q)$ **sat** $\exists s.\ S(left,s) \wedge T(s,right)$.

This states that the relation between *left* and *right* which is maintained by $(P \gg Q)$ is the normal relational composition of the relation for P with the relation for Q. Since the $\gg$ operator cannot introduce deadlock in pipes, we can afford to omit reasoning about refusals.

Examples

X1 $DOUBLE$ **sat** $right \overset{1}{\leq} double^*(left)$
  $DOUBLE$ is left-guarded and right-guarded.
So $(DOUBLE \gg DOUBLE)$ **sat** $\exists s.\ (s \overset{1}{\leq} double^*(left) \wedge right \overset{1}{\leq} double^*(s))$
  $\equiv right \overset{2}{\leq} double^*(double^*(left))$
  $\equiv right \overset{2}{\leq} quadruple^*(left)$ □

X2   Let us use recursion together with $\gg$ to give an alternative definition of a buffer

$$BUFF = \mu X.(left?x \rightarrow (X \gg (right!x \rightarrow COPY)))$$

We wish to prove that

$$BUFF \text{ sat } (right \leq left)$$

Assume that

$$X \text{ sat } \#left \geq n \lor right \leq left$$

We know that

$$COPY \text{ sat } right \leq left$$

Therefore $(right!x \rightarrow COPY)$ sat $((right = left = \langle\rangle \lor (right \geq \langle x \rangle \land right' \leq left))$

$$\Rightarrow right \leq \langle x \rangle \char`\^ left$$

Since the right operand is right-guarded, by L1 and the assumption

$$(X \gg (right!x \rightarrow COPY)) \text{ sat } (\exists s.(\#left \geq n \lor s \leq left) \land right \leq \langle x \rangle \char`\^ s)$$

$$\Rightarrow (\#left \geq n \lor right \leq \langle x \rangle \char`\^ left)$$

Therefore $left?x \rightarrow (...)$ sat $right = left = \langle\rangle$
$$\lor (left > \langle\rangle \land (\#left' \geq n \lor right \leq \langle left_0 \rangle \char`\^ left'))$$

$$\Rightarrow \#left \geq n + 1 \lor right \leq left$$

The desired conclusion follows by the proof rule for recursive processes (3.7.1 L8). The simpler law (1.10.2 L6) cannot be used, because the recursion is not obviously guarded. $\square$

4.4.5   Buffers and protocols

A buffer is a process which outputs on the right exactly the same sequence of messages as it has input from the left, though possibly after some delay; furthermore, when non-empty, it is always ready to output on the right. More formally, we define a buffer to be a process P which never stops, which is free of livelock, and which meets the specification

$$P \text{ sat } (right \leq left) \land (\text{if } right = left \text{ then } left\hat{\in}ref \text{ else } right\hat{\in}ref)$$

Here $c\hat{\in}ref$ means that the process cannot refuse to communicate on channel c (Section 3.7, 3.4). It follows that all buffers are left-guarded.

Example

X1 The following processes are buffers

$COPY, (COPY \gg COPY), BUFF, BUFFER.$ □

Buffers are clearly useful for storing information which is waiting to be processed. But they are even more useful as specifications of the desired behaviour of a communications protocol, which is intended to deliver messages in the same order in which they have been submitted. Such a protocol consists of two processes, a transmitter T and a receiver R, which are connected in series $(T \gg R)$. If the protocol is correct, clearly $(T \gg R)$ must be a buffer.

In practice, the wire that connects the transmitter to the receiver is quite long, and the messages which are sent along it are subject to corruption or loss. Thus the behaviour of the wire itself can be modelled by a process $WIRE$, which may behave not quite like a buffer. It is the task of the protocol designer to ensure that in spite of the bad behaviour of the wire, the system as a whole acts as a buffer; i.e.,

$(T \gg WIRE \gg R)$ is a buffer.

A protocol is usually built in a number of layers $(T_1, R_1), (T_2, R_2), ...,$ (T_n, R_n), each one using the previous layer as its communication medium

$$T_n \gg ... \gg (T_2 \gg (T_1 \gg WIRE \gg R_1) \gg R_2) \gg ... \gg R_n$$

Of course, when the protocol is implemented in practice, all the transmitters are collected into a single transmitter at one end and all the receivers at the other, in accordance with the changed bracketing

$$(T_n \gg ... \gg T_2 \gg T_1) \gg WIRE \gg (R_1 \gg R_2 \gg ... \gg R_n)$$

The law of associativity of $\gg$ guarantees that this regrouping does not change the behaviour of the system.

In practice, protocols must be more complicated than this, since single-directional flow of messages is not adequate to achieve reliable communication on an unreliable wire: it is necessary to add channels in the reverse direction, to enable the receiver to send back acknowledgement signals for successfully received messages, so that unacknowledged messages can be retransmitted.

The following laws are useful in proving the correctness of protocols. They are due to A. W. Roscoe.

L1 If P and Q are buffers, so are $(P \gg Q)$ and $(left?x \rightarrow (P \gg (right!x \rightarrow Q)))$

L2 If $T \gg R = (left?x \rightarrow (T \gg (right!x \rightarrow R)))$ then $(T \gg R)$ is a buffer.

The following is a generalization of L2

L3   If for some function f and for all z

$$(T(z) \gg R(z)) = (left?x \rightarrow (T(f(x,z)) \gg (right!x \rightarrow R(f(x,z)))))$$

then $T(z) \gg R(z)$ is a buffer for all z.

Examples

X1   The following are buffers by L1

$COPY \gg COPY$, $BUFFER \gg COPY$, $COPY \gg BUFFER$,

$BUFFER \gg BUFFER$ $\square$

X2   It has been shown in 4.4.1 X1 and X2 that

$$(COPY \gg COPY) = (left?x \rightarrow (COPY \gg (right!y \rightarrow COPY)))$$

By L2 it is therefore a buffer. $\square$

X3   Phase encoding

A phase encoder is a process T which inputs a stream of bits, and outputs $\langle 0,1 \rangle$ for each 0 input and $\langle 1,0 \rangle$ for each 1 input. A decoder R reverses this translation

$$T = left?x \rightarrow right!x \rightarrow right!(1-x) \rightarrow T$$
$$R = left?x \rightarrow left?y \rightarrow \textbf{if } y = x \textbf{ then } FAIL \textbf{ else } (right!x \rightarrow R)$$

where the process $FAIL$ is left undefined.

We wish to prove by L2 that $(T \gg R)$ is a buffer

$$\begin{aligned}
(T \gg R) &= left?x \rightarrow ((right!x \rightarrow right!(1-x) \rightarrow T) \\
&\qquad\qquad \gg (left?x \rightarrow left?y \rightarrow \textbf{if } y = x \textbf{ then } FAIL \textbf{ else } (right!x \rightarrow R))) \\
&= left?x \rightarrow (T \gg \textbf{if}(1-x) = x \textbf{ then } FAIL \textbf{ else } (right!x \rightarrow R)) \\
&= left?x \rightarrow (T \gg (right!x \rightarrow R))
\end{aligned}$$

Therefore $(T \gg R)$ is a buffer, by L2. $\square$

X4   Bit stuffing

The transmitter T faithfully reproduces the input bits from left to right, except that after three consecutive 1-bits which have been output, it inserts a single extra 0. Thus the input 01011110 is output as 010111010. The receiver R removes these extra zeroes. Thus $(T \gg R)$ must be proved to be a buffer. The construction of T and R, and the proof of their correctness, are left as an exercise. $\square$

X5   Line sharing

It is desired to copy data from a channel *left*1 to *right*1 and from *left*2 to *right*2. This can most easily be achieved by two disjoint protocols, each using a different wire. Unfortunately, only a single wire *mid* is available, and this must be used for both streams of data, as shown by Fig. 4.9.

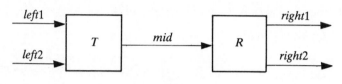

Figure 4.9

Messages input by T must be tagged before transmission along *mid*, and R must untag them and output them on the corresponding right channel

$$T = (left1?x \rightarrow mid!tag1(x) \rightarrow T$$
$$| \; left2?y \rightarrow mid!tag2(y) \rightarrow T)$$
$$R = mid?z \rightarrow \textbf{if} \, tag(z) = 1 \, \textbf{then} \, (right1!untag(z) \rightarrow R) \; \textbf{else} \, (right2!untag(z) \rightarrow R)$$

This solution is quite unsatisfactory. If two messages are input on *left*1, but the recipient is not yet ready for them, the whole system will have to wait, and transmission between *left*2 and *right*2 may be seriously delayed. To insert buffers on the channels will only postpone the problem for a short while. The correct solution is to introduce another channel in the reverse direction, and for R to send signals back to T to stop sending messages on the stream for which there seems to be little demand. This is known as flow control.   □

4.5   SUBORDINATION

Let P and Q be processes with

$$\alpha P \subseteq \alpha Q$$

In the combination $(P \| Q)$, each action of P can occur only when Q permits it to occur; whereas Q can engage independently in the actions of $(\alpha Q - \alpha P)$, without the permission and without the knowledge of its partner P. Thus P serves Q as a slave or subordinate process, while Q acts as a master or main process. When communications between a subordinate process and a main process are to be concealed from their common environment, we use the asymmetric notation

$$P//Q$$

Using the concealment operator, this can be defined

$$P//Q = (P\|Q)\setminus\alpha P$$

This notation is used only when $\alpha P \subseteq \alpha Q$; and then

$$\alpha(P//Q) = (\alpha Q - \alpha P)$$

It is usually convenient to give the subordinate process a name, say m, which is used in the main process for all interactions with its subordinate. The process naming technique described in Section 2.6.2 can be readily extended to communicating processes, by introducing compound channel names. These take the form $m.c$, where m is a process name and c is the name of one of its channels. Each communication on this channel is a triple

$$m.c.v$$

where $\alpha m.c(m\!:\!P) = \alpha c(P)$

and $v \in \alpha c(P)$.

In the construction $(m\!:\!P//Q)$, Q communicates with P along channels with compound names of the form $m.c$ and $m.d$; whereas P uses the corresponding simple channels c and d for the same communications. Thus for example

$$(m\!:\!(c!v{\rightarrow}P)//(m.c?x{\rightarrow}Q(x))) = (m\!:\!P//Q(v))$$

Since all these communications are concealed from the environment, the name m can never be detected from the outside; it therefore serves as a *local* name for the subordinate process.

Subordination can be nested, for example

$$(n\!:\!(m\!:\!P//Q)//R)$$

In this case, all occurrences of events involving the name m are concealed before the name n is attached to the remaining events, all of which are in the alphabet of Q, and not of P. There is no way that R can communicate directly with P, or even know of the existence of P or its name m.

Examples

X1   *doub*:*DOUBLE*//*Q*   (for *DOUBLE* see 4.2 X2)

The subordinate process acts as a simple subroutine called from within the main process Q. Inside Q, the value of $2 \times e$ may be obtained by a successive output of the argument e or the left channel of *doub*, and input of the result on the right channel

$$doub.left!e \rightarrow (doub.right?x \rightarrow \ldots)$$ □

X2 One subroutine may use another as a subordinate, and do so several times

$$QUADRUPLE =$$
$$(doub:DOUBLE//(\mu X.left?x \rightarrow doub.left!x \rightarrow$$
$$doub.right?y \rightarrow doub.left!y \rightarrow$$
$$doub.right?z \rightarrow right!z \rightarrow X)$$

This is designed itself to be used as a subroutine

$$quad:QUADRUPLE//Q$$

This version of $QUADRUPLE$ is similar to that of 4.4 X1, but does not have the same double-buffering effect. □

X3 A conventional program variable named m may be modelled as a subordinate process

$$m:VAR//Q$$

Inside the main process Q, the value of m can be assigned, read, and updated by input and output, as described in 2.6.2 X2

$m:=3;\ P$	is implemented by	$(m.left!3 \rightarrow P)$
$x:=m;\ P$	is implemented by	$(m.right?x \rightarrow P)$
$m:=m+3;\ P$	is implemented by	$(m.right?y \rightarrow m.left!(y+3) \rightarrow P)$ □

A subordinate process may be used to implement a data structure with a more elaborate behaviour than just a simple variable.

X4 $(q:BUFFER//Q)$ (see 4.2 X9)

The subordinate process serves as an unbounded queue named q. Within Q, the output $q.left!v$ adds v to one end of the queue, and $q.right?y$ removes an element from the other end, and gives its value to y. If the queue is empty, the queue will not respond, and the system may deadlock. □

X5 A stack with name st is declared (see 4.2 X10)

$$st:STACK//Q$$

Inside the main process Q, $st.left!v$ can be used to push the value v onto the stack, and $st.right?x$ will pop the top value. To deal with the possibility that the stack is empty, a choice construction can be used

$$(st.right?x{\rightarrow}Q1(x)\,|\,st.empty{\rightarrow}Q2)$$

If the stack is non-empty, the first alternative is selected; if empty, deadlock is avoided and the second alternative is selected.　　　　　□

A subordinate process with several channels may be used by several concurrent processes, provided that they do not use the same channel.

X6　A process Q is intended to communicate a stream of values to R; these values are to be buffered by a subordinate buffer process named b, so that output from Q will not be delayed when R is not ready for input. Q uses channel $b.left$ for its output and R uses $b.right$ for its input

$$(b{:}BUFFER//(Q\|R))$$

Note that if R attempts to input from an empty buffer, the system will not necessarily deadlock; R will simply be delayed until Q next outputs a value to the buffer. (If Q and R communicate with the buffer on the *same* channel, then that channel must be in the alphabet of both of them; and the definition of $\|$ would require them always to communicate simultaneously the same value—which would be quite wrong.)　　　　　□

The subordination operator may be used to define subroutines by recursion. Each level of recursion (except the last) declares a *new* local subroutine to deal with the recursive call(s).

X7　Factorial
$$FAC = \mu X.\ left?n{\rightarrow}(\textbf{if } n{=}0 \textbf{ then } (right!1{\rightarrow}X)$$
$$\textbf{else } (f{:}\ X//(f.left!(n{-}1){\rightarrow}f.right?y{\rightarrow}right!(n{\times}y){\rightarrow}X)))\qquad □$$

The subroutine FAC uses channels *left* and *right* to communicate parameters and results to its calling process; and it uses channels $f.left$ and $f.right$ to communicate with its subordinate process named f. In these respects it is similar to the $QUADRUPLE$ subroutine (X2). The only difference is that the subordinate process is isomorphic to FAC itself.　　　　　□

This is a boringly familiar example of recursion, expressed in an unfamiliar but rather cumbersome notational framework. A less familiar idea is that of using recursion together with subordination to implement an unbounded data structure. Each level of the recursion stores a single component of the structure, and declares a *new* local subordinate data structure to deal with the rest.

X8   Unbounded finite set

A process which implements a set inputs its members on its left channel. After each input, it outputs a *YES* if it has already input the same value, and *NO* otherwise. It is very similar to the set of 2.6.2 X4, except that it will store messages of any kind

$$SET = left?x \rightarrow right!NO \rightarrow (rest:SET // LOOP(x))$$

where $LOOP(x) =$

$$\mu X.left?y \rightarrow (\textbf{if } y=x \textbf{ then } right!YES \rightarrow X$$
$$\textbf{else } (rest.left!y \rightarrow rest.right?z \rightarrow right!z \rightarrow X))$$

The set starts empty; therefore on input of its first member x it immediately outputs *NO*. It then declares a subordinate process called *rest*, which is going to store all members of the set except x. The *LOOP* is designed to input subsequent members of the set. If the newly input member is equal to x, the answer *YES* is sent back immediately on the right channel. Otherwise, the new member is passed on for storage by *rest*. Whatever answer (*YES* or *NO*) is sent back by *rest* is passed on again, and the *LOOP* repeats.   □

X9   Binary tree

A more efficient representation of a set is as a binary tree, which relies on some given total ordering $\leq$ over its elements. Each node stores its earliest inserted element, and declares *two* subordinate trees, one to store elements smaller than the earliest, and one to store the bigger elements. The external specification of the tree is the same as X8

$$TREE = left?x \rightarrow right!NO \rightarrow$$
$$(smaller:TREE // (bigger:TREE // LOOP))$$

The design of the *LOOP* is left as an exercise.   □

4.5.1   Laws

The following obvious laws govern communications between a process and its subordinates. The first law describes concealed communication in each direction between the main and subordinate processes

L1A $(m:(c?x \rightarrow P(x)))//(m.c!v \rightarrow Q) = (m:P(v))//Q$

L1B $(m:(d!v \rightarrow P))//(m.d?x \rightarrow Q(x)) = (m:P)//Q(v)$

If b is a channel not named by m, the main process can communicate on b without affecting the subordinate

L2 $(m:P//(b!e \rightarrow Q)) = (b!e \rightarrow (m:P//Q))$

The only process capable of making a choice for a subordinate process is its main process

L3 $(m:(c?x{\to}P1(x) \mid d?y{\to}P2(y)))//(m.c!v{\to}Q) = (m:P1(v)//Q)$

If two subordinate processes have the same name, one of them is inaccessible

L4 $m:P//(m:Q//R) = (m:Q//R)$

Usually, the order in which subordinate processes are written does not matter

L5 If m and n are distinct names

$m:P//(n:Q//R) = n:Q//(m:P//R)$

The use of recursion in defining subordinate processes is sufficiently surprising to raise doubts whether it actually works. These doubts may be slightly alleviated by showing how the combination evolves. The example below uses a particular trace of behaviour of the process, and shows how that trace is produced. More important, it shows how other slightly differing traces cannot be produced.

Example

X1 A typical trace of *SET* is

$s = \langle left.1, right.NO, left.2, right.NO \rangle$

The value of *SET*/s can be calculated in a series of steps, using L1 and L2

$SET/\langle left.1 \rangle = right!NO{\to}(rest:SET//LOOP(1))$

so $SET/\langle left.1, right.NO \rangle = (rest:SET//LOOP(1))$

and $SET/\langle left.1, right.NO, left.2 \rangle$

$= (rest:SET//(rest.left!2{\to}rest.right?z{\to}right!z{\to}LOOP(1))$

$= (rest:(right!NO{\to}(rest:SET//LOOP(2)))$

$//(rest.right?z{\to}right!z{\to}LOOP(1)))$

$= rest:(rest:SET//LOOP(2))//(right!NO{\to}LOOP(1))$

Therefore $SET/s = rest:(rest:SET//LOOP(2))//LOOP(1)$

It is obvious from this that

$\langle left.1, right.NO, left.2, right.YES \rangle$

is *not* a trace of *SET*.

The reader may check that

$SET/s^\wedge \langle left.2, right.YES \rangle = SET/s$

and $SET/s^\wedge \langle left.5, right.NO \rangle = rest:(rest:(rest:SET//LOOP(5))$

$//LOOP(2))//LOOP(1)$ □

4.5.2 Connection diagrams

A subordinate process may be drawn inside the box representing the process that uses it, as shown for 4.5 X1 in Fig. 4.10.

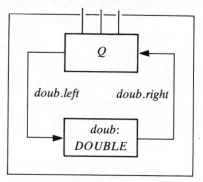

Figure 4.10

For nested subordinate processes, the boxes nest more deeply, as shown for 4.5 X2 in Fig. 4.11.

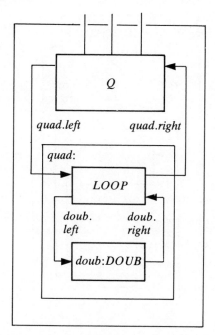

Figure 4.11

$SET/\langle left.1, right.\ NO\rangle =$

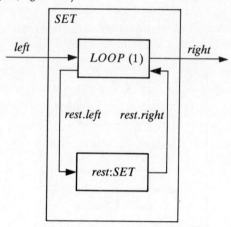

$SET/s=$

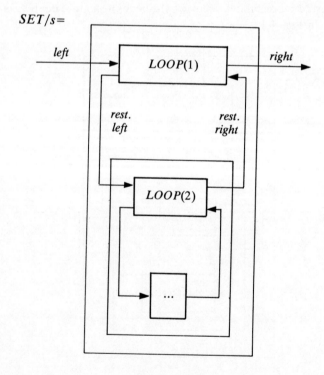

Figure 4.12

A recursive process is one that is nested inside itself, like the picture of the artist's studio, in which there stands on an easel the completed painting itself, which shows on the easel a completed painting ... Such a picture in practice can never be completed. Fortunately, for a process it is not necessary to complete the picture—it evolves automatically as needed during its activity. Thus (see 4.5.1 X1) we may picture successive stages in the early history of a set as shown in Fig. 4.12.

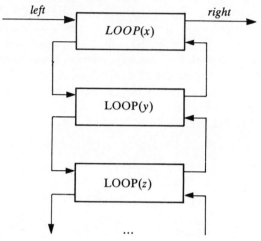

Figure 4.13

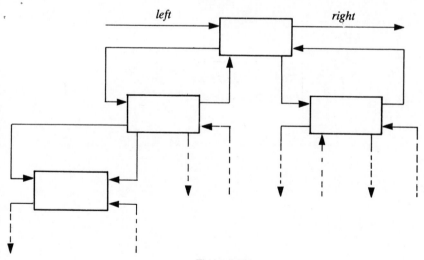

Figure 4.14

If we ignore the nesting of the boxes, this can be drawn as a linear structure as in Fig. 4.13. Similarly, the example TREE (4.5 X9) could be drawn as in Fig. 4.14.

The connection diagrams suggest how a corresponding network might be constructed from hardware components, with boxes representing integrated circuits and arrows representing wires between them. Of course in any practical realization, the recursion must be unfolded to some finite limit before the network can start its normal operation; and if this limit is exceeded during operation, the network cannot successfully continue. Dynamic reallocation and reconfiguration of hardware networks is a lot more difficult than the stack-based storage allocation which makes recursion in conventional sequential programs so efficient. Nevertheless, recursion is surely justified by the aid it gives in the invention and design of algorithms; and if not by that, then at least by the intellectual joy which it gives to those who understand it and use it.

5 SEQUENTIAL PROCESSES

5.1 INTRODUCTION

The process $STOP$ is defined as one that never engages in any action. It is not a useful process, and probably results from a deadlock or other design error, rather than a deliberate choice of the designer. However, there is one good reason why a process should do nothing more, namely that it has already accomplished everything that it was designed to do. Such a process is said to terminate successfully. In order to distinguish between this and $STOP$, it is convenient to regard successful termination as a special event, denoted by the symbol $\checkmark$ (pronounced "success"). A sequential process is defined as one which has $\checkmark$ in its alphabet; and naturally this can only be the last event in which it engages. For this reason we stipulate that $\checkmark$ cannot be an alternative in the choice construct

$$(x{:}B{\rightarrow}P(x)) \text{ is invalid if } \checkmark \in B$$

$SKIP_A$ is defined as a process which does nothing but terminate successfully

$$\alpha SKIP_A = A \cup \{\checkmark\}$$

As usual, we shall frequently omit the subscript alphabet.

Examples

X1 A vending machine that is intended to serve only one customer with chocolate or toffee and then terminate successfully

$$VMONE = (coin \rightarrow (choc \rightarrow SKIP \mid toffee \rightarrow SKIP)) \qquad \square$$

171

In designing a process to solve a complex task, it is frequently useful to split the task into two subtasks, one of which must be completed successfully before the other begins. If P and Q are sequential processes with the same alphabet, their sequential composition

$P;Q$

is a process which first behaves like P; but when P terminates successfully, $(P;Q)$ continues by behaving like Q. If P never terminates successfully, neither does $(P;Q)$.

X2 A vending machine designed to serve exactly two customers, one after the other

$VMTWO = VMONE;VMONE$ □

A process which repeats similar actions as often as required is known as a loop; it can be defined as a special case of recursion

$*P = \mu X.(P;X)$
$\quad = P;P;P;....$
$\alpha(*P) = \alpha P - \{\sqrt{}\}$

Clearly such a loop will never terminate successfully; that is why it is convenient to remove $\sqrt{}$ from its alphabet.

X3 A vending machine designed to serve any number of customers

$VMCT = *VMONE$

This is identical to $VMCT$ (1.1.3 X3).   □

A sequence of symbols is said to be a *sentence* of a process P if P terminates successfully after engaging in the corresponding sequence of actions. The set of all such sentences is called the *language* accepted by P. Thus the notations introduced for describing sequential processes may also be used to define the grammar of a simple language, such as might be used for communication between a human being and a computer.

X4 A sentence of Pidgingol consists of a noun clause followed by a predicate. A predicate is a verb followed by a noun clause. A verb is either *bites* or *scratches*. The definition of a noun clause is given more formally below

$\alpha PIDGINGOL \quad = \{a,the,cat,dog,bites,scratches\}$
$PIDGINGOL \quad = NOUNCLAUSE;PREDICATE$
$PREDICATE \quad = VERB;NOUNCLAUSE$
$VERB \quad\quad\quad = (bites{\to}SKIP\,|\,scratches{\to}SKIP)$
$NOUNCLAUSE = ARTICLE;NOUN$
$ARTICLE \quad\quad = (a{\to}SKIP\,|\,the{\to}SKIP)$
$NOUN \quad\quad\quad = (cat{\to}SKIP\,|\,dog{\to}SKIP)$

Example sentences of Pidgingol are

the cat scratches a dog
a dog bites the cat ☐

To describe languages with an unbounded number of sentences, it is necessary to use some kind of iteration or recursion.

X5 A noun clause which may contain any number of adjectives *furry* or *prize*

$$NOUNCLAUSE = ARTICLE; \mu X.(furry \rightarrow X \,|\, prize \rightarrow X$$
$$|\, cat \rightarrow SKIP \,|\, dog \rightarrow SKIP)$$

Examples of a noun clause are

the furry furry prize dog
a dog ☐

X6 A process which accepts any number of as followed by a b and then the same number of cs, after which it terminates successfully

$$A^n BC^n = \mu X.(b \rightarrow SKIP$$
$$|\, a \rightarrow (X;(c \rightarrow SKIP)))$$

If a b is accepted first, the process terminates; no as and no cs are accepted, so their numbers are the same. If the second branch is taken, the accepted sentence starts with a and ends with c, and between these is the sentence accepted by the recursive call on the process X. If we assume that the recursive call accepts an equal number of as and cs, then so will the non-recursive call on $A^n BC^n$, since it accepts just one more a at the beginning and one more c at the end.

This example shows how sequential composition, used in conjunction with recursion, can define a machine with an infinite number of states. ☐

X7 A process which first behaves like $A^n BC^n$, but then accepts a d followed by the same number of es

$$A^n BC^n DE^n = ((A^n BC^n); d \rightarrow SKIP) \| C^n DE^n$$

where $C^n DE^n = f(A^n BC^n)$ for f which maps a to c, b to d, and c to e.

In this example, the process on the left of the $\|$ is responsible for ensuring an equal number of as and cs (separated by a b). It will not allow a d until the proper number of cs have arrived; but the es (which are not in its alphabet) are ignored. The process on the right of $\|$ is responsible for ensuring an equal number of es as cs. It ignores the as and the b, which are not in its alphabet. The pair of processes terminate together when they have both completed their allotted tasks.   □

The notations for defining a language by means of an accepting process are as powerful as those of regular expressions. The use of recursion introduces some of the power of context-free grammars, but not all. A process can only define those languages that can be parsed from left to right without backtracking or look-ahead. This is because the use of the choice operator requires that the first event of each alternative is different from all its other first events. Consequently, it is not possible to use the construction of X5 to define a noun clause in which the word *prize* can be either a noun or an adjective or both, e.g. *the prize dog*, *the furry prize*. The use of [] (Section 3.3) would not help, because it introduces nondeterminism, and allows an arbitrary choice of the clause which will analyse the rest of the input. If the choice is wrong, the process will deadlock before reaching the end of the input text. What is required to solve this problem is a new kind of choice operator which provides angelic nondeterminism like *or*3 (Section 3.2.2). This new operator requires that the two alternatives run concurrently until the environment makes the choice; its definition is left as an exercise.

Without angelic nondeterminism the language-defining method described above is not so powerful as context-free grammars, because it requires left-to-right parsability without back-tracking. However, the introduction of ‖ permits definition of languages which are not context-free, for example X7.

X8   A process which accepts any interleaving of *down*s and *up*s, except that it terminates successfully on the first occasion that the number of *down*s exceeds the number of *up*s

$$POS = (down \rightarrow SKIP \mid up \rightarrow (POS; POS))$$

If the first symbol is *down*, the task of *POS* is immediately accomplished. But if the first symbol is *up*, it is then necessary to accept *two* more *down*s than *up*s. The only way of achieving this is first to accept one more *down* than *up*; and then again to accept one more *down* than *up*. Thus two successive recursive calls on *POS* are needed, one after the other.   □

X9   The process C_0 behaves like CT_0 (1.1.4 X2)

$$C_0 = (around \rightarrow C_0 \mid up \rightarrow C_1)$$
$$C_{n+1} = POS; C_n \qquad \text{for all } n \geq 0.$$
$$= \underbrace{POS; ...; POS; POS; C_0}_{n \text{ times}}$$

□

We can now solve the problem mentioned in 2.6.2 X3, and encountered again in 4.5 X3, that each operation on a subordinate process explicitly mentions the rest of the user process which follows it. The required effect can now be more conveniently achieved by means of *SKIP* and sequential composition.

X10 A *USER* process manipulates two count variables named l and m (see 2.6.2 X3)

$$l:CT_0\|m:CT_3\|USER$$

The following subprocess (inside the *USER*) adds the current value of l to m

$$ADD = (l.around \rightarrow SKIP$$
$$|\ l.down \rightarrow (ADD;(m.up \rightarrow l.up \rightarrow SKIP)))$$

If the value of l is initially zero, nothing needs to be done. Otherwise, l is decremented, and its reduced value is added to m (by the recursive call to *ADD*). Then m is incremented once more, and l is also incremented, to compensate for the initial decrementation and bring it back to its initial value. □

5.2 LAWS

The laws for sequential composition are similar to those for catenation (Section 1.6.1), with *SKIP* playing the role of the unit

L1 $SKIP;P = P;SKIP = P$

L2 $(P;Q);R = P;(Q;R)$

L3 $(x:B \rightarrow P(x));Q = (x:B \rightarrow (P(x);Q))$

The law for the choice operator has corollaries

L4 $(a \rightarrow P);Q = a \rightarrow (P;Q)$

L5 $STOP;Q = STOP$

When sequential processes are composed in parallel, the combination terminates successfully just when *both* components do so

L6 $SKIP_A \| SKIP_B = SKIP_{A \cup B}$

A successfully terminating process participates in no further event offered by a concurrent partner

L7 $((x:B \rightarrow P(x)) \| SKIP_A) = (x:(B-A) \rightarrow (P(x) \| SKIP_A))$

In a concurrent combination of a sequential with a nonsequential process, when does the combination terminate successfully? If the alphabet of the sequential process wholly contains that of its partner, termination of the partnership is determined by that of the sequential process, since the other process can do nothing when its partner has finished

L8 $STOP_A \| SKIP_B = SKIP_B$ if $\sqrt{} \hat{\in} A \wedge A \subseteq B$.

The condition for the validity of this law is a very reasonable one, which should always be observed when $\sqrt{}$ is in the alphabet of only one of a pair of processes running concurrently. In this way, we avoid the problem of a process which continues after engaging in $\sqrt{}$.

The laws L1 to L3 may be used to prove the claim made in 5.1 X9 that C_0 behaves like CT_0 (1.1.4 X2). This is done by showing that C satisfies the set of guarded recursive equations used to define CT. The equation for CT_0 is the same as that for C_0

$$C_0 = (around \rightarrow C_0 | up \rightarrow C_1) \qquad\qquad\qquad \text{def } C_0$$

For $n > 0$, we need to prove

$$C_n = (up \rightarrow C_{n+1} | down \rightarrow C_{n-1})$$

Proof $LHS = POS; C_{n-1}$ def C_n
$\qquad = (down \rightarrow SKIP | up \rightarrow POS; POS); C_{n-1}$ def POS
$\qquad = (down \rightarrow (SKIP; C_{n-1}) | up \rightarrow (POS; POS); C_{n-1})$ L3
$\qquad = (down \rightarrow C_{n-1} | up \rightarrow POS; (POS; C_{n-1}))$ L1,L2
$\qquad = (down \rightarrow C_{n-1} | up \rightarrow POS; C_n)$ def C_n
$\qquad = RHS$ def C_n

Since C_n obeys the same set of guarded recursion equations as CT_n, they are the same.

This proof has been written out in full, in order to illustrate the use of the laws, and also in order to allay suspicion of circularity. What seems most suspicious is that the proof does not use induction on n. In fact, any attempt to use induction on n will fail, because the very definition of CT_n contains the process CT_{n+1}. Fortunately, an appeal to the law of unique solutions is both simple and successful.

5.3   MATHEMATICAL TREATMENT

The mathematical definition of sequential composition must be formulated in such a way as to ensure the truth of the laws quoted in the previous section. Special care needs to be exercised on

$$P; SKIP = P$$

As usual, the treatment of deterministic processes is much simpler, and will be completed first.

5.3.1 Deterministic processes

Operations on deterministic processes are defined in terms of the traces of their results. The first and only action of the process *SKIP* is successful termination, so it has only two traces

L0 $traces(SKIP) = \{\langle\rangle, \langle\sqrt{}\rangle\}$

To define sequential composition of processes, it is convenient first to define sequential composition of their individual traces. If s and t are traces and s does not contain $\sqrt{}$

$$(s;t) = s$$
$$(s^\wedge\langle\sqrt{}\rangle);t = s^\wedge t$$

(see Section 1.9.7 for a fuller treatment). A trace of $(P;Q)$ consists of a trace of P; and if this trace ends in $\sqrt{}$, the $\sqrt{}$ is replaced by a trace of Q

L1 $traces(P;Q) = \{s;t | s \in traces(P) \wedge t \in traces(Q)\}$

An equivalent definition is

L1A $traces(P;Q) = \{s | s \in traces(P) \wedge \neg\langle\sqrt{}\rangle \text{ in } s\}$
$$\cup \{s^\wedge t | s^\wedge\langle\sqrt{}\rangle \in traces(P) \wedge t \in traces(Q)\}$$

This definition may be simpler to understand but it is more complicated to use.

The whole intention of the $\sqrt{}$ symbol is that it should terminate the process which engages in it. We therefore need the law

L2 $P/s = SKIP$ if $s^\wedge\langle\sqrt{}\rangle \in traces(P)$

This law is essential in the proof of

$$P;SKIP = P$$

Unfortunately, it is not in general true. For example, if

$$P = (SKIP_{\{\}} \| c \rightarrow STOP_{\{c\}})$$

then $traces(P) = \{\langle\rangle, \langle\sqrt{}\rangle, \langle c\rangle, \langle c,\sqrt{}\rangle, \langle\sqrt{},c\rangle\}$ and $P/\langle\rangle \neq SKIP$, even though $\langle\sqrt{}\rangle \in traces(P)$. We therefore need to impose alphabet constraints on parallel composition. $(P\|Q)$ must be regarded as invalid unless

$$\alpha P \subseteq \alpha Q \vee \alpha Q \subseteq \alpha P \vee \sqrt{} \in (\alpha P \cap \alpha Q \cup \overline{\alpha P} \cap \overline{\alpha Q})$$

For similar reasons, alphabet change must be guaranteed to leave $\sqrt{}$ unchanged, so $f(P)$ is invalid unless

$$f(\sqrt{}) = \sqrt{}$$

Furthermore, if m is a process name, we must adopt the convention that

$$m.\sqrt{} = \sqrt{}$$

Finally, we must never use $\sqrt{}$ in the choice construct

$$(\sqrt{} \rightarrow P \mid c \rightarrow Q)$$

This restriction also rules out RUN_A when $\sqrt{} \in A$.

5.3.2 Non-deterministic processes

Sequential composition of nondeterministic processes presents a number of problems. The first of them is that a nondeterministic process like $SKIP \sqcap (c \rightarrow SKIP)$ does not satisfy the law L2 of the previous section. A solution to this is to weaken 5.3.1 L2 to

L2A $s^\frown \langle \sqrt{} \rangle \in traces(P) \Rightarrow (P/s) \sqsubseteq SKIP$

This means that whenever P can terminate, it can do so without offering any alternative event to its environment. To maintain the truth of L2A, all restrictions of the previous sections must be observed, and also

$SKIP$ must never appear unguarded in an operand of $[]$
$\sqrt{}$ must not appear in the alphabet of either operand of $\|$

(It is possible that a slight change to the definitions of $[]$ and $\|$ might permit relaxation of these restrictions.)

    In addition to the laws given earlier in this chapter, sequential composition of nondeterministic processes satisfies the following laws. Firstly, a divergent process remains divergent, no matter what is specified to happen after its successful termination

L1 $CHAOS; P = CHAOS$

Sequential composition distributes through nondeterministic choice

L2A $(P \sqcap Q); R = (P;R) \sqcap (Q;R)$
L2B $R;(P \sqcap Q) = (R;P) \sqcap (R;Q)$

    To define $(P;Q)$ in the mathematical model of nondeterministic processes (Section 3.9) requires treatment of its failures and divergences. But first we describe its refusals (Section 3.4). If P can refuse X, and cannot terminate successfully, it follows that $X \cup \{\surd\}$ is also a refusal of P (3.4.1 L11). In this case X is a refusal of $(P;Q)$. But if P offers the option of successful termination, then in $(P;Q)$ this transition may occur autonomously; its occurrence is concealed, and any refusal of Q is also a refusal of $(P;Q)$. The case where successful termination of P is nondeterministic is also treated in the definition

D1 $refusals(P;Q) = \{X | (X \cup \{\surd\}) \in refusals(P)\}$
$\qquad \cup \{X | \langle \surd \rangle \in traces(P) \wedge X \in refusals(Q)\}$

The traces of $(P;Q)$ are defined in the same way as for deterministic processes. The divergences of $(P;Q)$ are defined by the remark that it diverges whenever P diverges; or when P has terminated successfully and then Q diverges

D2 $divergences(P;Q) = \{s | s \in divergences(P) \wedge \neg \langle \surd \rangle \text{ in } s\}$
$\qquad \cup \{s^\wedge t | s^\wedge \langle \surd \rangle \in traces(P) \wedge \neg \langle \surd \rangle \text{ in } s$
$\qquad \wedge t \in divergences(Q)\}$

Any failure of $(P;Q)$ is either a failure of P before P can terminate, or it is a failure of Q after P has terminated successfully

D3 $failures(P;Q) = \{(s,X) | (s, X \cup \{\surd\}) \in failures(P)\}$
$\qquad \cup \{(s^\wedge t, X) | s^\wedge \langle \surd \rangle \in traces(P) \wedge (t,X) \in failures(Q)\}$
$\qquad \cup \{(s,X) | s \in divergences(P;Q)\}$

5.3.3 Implementation

SKIP is implemented as the process which accepts only the symbol *"SUCCESS*. It does not matter what it does afterwards

$\quad SKIP = \lambda x. \text{ if } x = "SUCCESS \text{ then } STOP \text{ else } "BLEEP$

A sequential composition behaves like the second operand if the first operand terminates; otherwise, the first operand participates in the first event, and the rest of it is composed with the second operand

$\quad sequence(P,Q) = \text{if } P("SUCCESS) \neq "BLEEP \text{ then } Q$
$\qquad \text{else } \lambda x. \text{ if } P(x) = "BLEEP \text{ then } "BLEEP$
$\qquad\qquad\qquad\qquad\quad \text{else } sequence(P(x),Q)$

5.4 INTERRUPTS

In this section we define a kind of sequential composition $(P^\wedge Q)$ which does not depend on successful termination of P. Instead, the progress of P is just interrupted on occurrence of the first event of Q; and P is never resumed. It follows that a trace of $(P^\wedge Q)$ is just a trace of P up to an arbitrary point when the interrupt occurs, followed by any trace of Q

$$\alpha(P^\wedge Q) = \alpha P \cup \alpha Q$$
$$traces(P^\wedge Q) = \{s^\wedge t \mid s \in traces(P) \wedge t \in traces(Q)\}$$

To avoid problems, we specify that $\sqrt{}$ must not be in αP.

The next law states that it is the environment which determines when Q shall start, by selecting an event which is initially offered by Q but not by P

L1 $(x{:}B{\to}P(x))^\wedge Q = Q \; [] \; (x{:}B{\to}(P(x)^\wedge Q))$

If $(P^\wedge Q)$ can be interrupted by R, this is the same as P interruptible by $(Q^\wedge R)$

L2 $(P^\wedge Q)^\wedge R = P^\wedge(Q^\wedge R)$

Since *STOP* offers no first event, it can never be triggered by the environment. Similarly, if *STOP* is interruptible, only the interrupt can actually occur. Thus *STOP* is a unit of $^\wedge$

L3 $P^\wedge STOP = P = STOP^\wedge P$

The interrupt operator executes both of its operands at most once, so it distributes through nondeterministic choice

L4A $P^\wedge(Q \sqcap R) = (P^\wedge Q) \sqcap (P^\wedge R)$

L4B $(Q \sqcap R)^\wedge P = (Q^\wedge P) \sqcap (R^\wedge P)$

Finally, one cannot cure a divergent process by interrupting it; nor is it safe to specify a divergent process after the interrupt

L5 $CHAOS^\wedge P = CHAOS = P^\wedge CHAOS$

In the remainder of this section, we shall insist that the possible initial events of the interrupting process are outside the alphabet of the interrupted process. Since the occurrence of interrupt is visible and controllable by the environment, this restriction preserves determinism, and reasoning about the operators is simplified. To emphasize the preservation of determinism, we extend the definition of the choice operator. Provided that $c \hat{\in} B$

$$(x{:}B{\to}P(x) \mid c{\to}Q) \text{ is short for } (x{:}(B\cup\{c\}){\to}(\textbf{if } x{=}c \textbf{ then } Q \textbf{ else } P(x)))$$

and similarly for more operands.

5.4.1 Catastrophe

Let $\hat{\gamma}$ be a symbol standing for a catastrophic interrupt event, which it is reasonable to suppose would not be caused by P; more formally

$$\gamma \hat{\in} \alpha P$$

Then a process which behaves like P up to catastrophe and thereafter like Q is defined

$$P \overset{\wedge}{\gamma} Q = P^\wedge (\gamma \rightarrow Q)$$

Here Q is perhaps a process which is intended to effect a recovery after catastrophe. Note that the infix operator $\overset{\wedge}{\gamma}$ is distinguished from the event γ by the circumflex.

The first law is just an obvious formalization of the informal description of the operator

L1 $\quad (P \overset{\wedge}{\gamma} Q)/(s^\wedge \langle \gamma \rangle) = Q \qquad$ for $s \in traces(P)$

In the deterministic model, this single law uniquely defines the meaning of the operator. In a nondeterministic universe, uniqueness would require additional laws stating strictness and distributivity in both arguments.

The second law gives a more explicit description of the first and subsequent steps of the process. It shows how $\overset{\wedge}{\gamma}$ distributes back through $\rightarrow$

L2 $\quad (x{:}B \rightarrow P(x)) \overset{\wedge}{\gamma} Q = (x{:}B \rightarrow (P(x) \overset{\wedge}{\gamma} Q) \mid \gamma \rightarrow Q)$

This law too uniquely defines the operator on deterministic processes.

5.4.2 Restart

One possible response to catastrophe is to restart the original process again. Let P be a process such that $\gamma \hat{\in} \alpha P$. We specify $\hat{P}$ as a process which behaves like P until γ occurs, and after each γ behaves like P from the start again. Such a process is called *restartable* and is defined by the simple recursion

$$\alpha \hat{P} = \alpha P \cup \{\gamma\}$$
$$\hat{P} = \mu X.(P \overset{\wedge}{\gamma} X)$$
$$\quad = P \overset{\wedge}{\gamma}(P \overset{\wedge}{\gamma}(P \overset{\wedge}{\gamma} ...))$$

This is a guarded recursion, since the occurrence of X is guarded by γ. $\hat{P}$ is certainly a cyclic process (Section 1.8.3), even if P is not.

Catastrophe is not the only reason for a restart. Consider a process designed to play a game, interacting with its human opponent by means of a selection of keys on a keyboard (see the description of the *interact* function of Section 1.4). Humans sometimes get dissatisfied with the progress of a game, and wish to start a new game again. For this purpose, a new and special key ($\varnothing$) is provided on the keyboard; depression of this key at any point in the progress of a game will restart the game. It is convenient to define a game P independently of the restart facility and then transform it into a restartable game $\hat{P}$ by using the operator defined above. This idea is due to Alex Teruel.

The informal definition of $\hat{P}$ is expressed by the law

L1 $\hat{P}/s^\wedge\langle \varnothing \rangle = \hat{P}$ for $s \in traces(P)$

But this law does not uniquely define $\hat{P}$, since it is equally well satisfied by RUN. However, $\hat{P}$ is the smallest deterministic process that satisfies L1.

5.4.3   Alternation

Suppose P and Q are processes which play games in the manner described in Section 5.4.2; and a human player wishes to play both games simultaneously, alternating between them in the same way as a chess master plays a simultaneous match by cycling round several weaker opponents. We therefore provide a new key $\circledx$, which causes alternation between the two games P and Q. This is rather like an interrupt, in that the current game is interrupted at an arbitrary point; but it differs from the interrupt in that the current state of the current game is preserved, so that it can be resumed when the other game is later interrupted. The process which plays the games P and Q simultaneously in this way is denoted $(P\circledx Q)$, and it is most clearly specified by the laws

L1 $\circledx \in (\alpha(P\circledx Q) - \alpha P - \alpha Q)$

L2 $(P\circledx Q)/s = (P/s)\circledx Q$ if $s \in traces(P)$

L3 $(P\circledx Q)/\langle \circledx \rangle = (Q\circledx P)$

We want the smallest process that satisfies L2 and L3. A more constructive description of the operator can be derived from these laws; it shows how $\circledx$ distributes backward through $\rightarrow$

L4 $(x:B\rightarrow P(x))\circledx Q = (x:B\rightarrow(P(x)\circledx Q) \mid \circledx \rightarrow (Q\circledx P))$

The alternation operator is useful not only for playing games. A similar facility should be provided in a "friendly" operating system for alternating between system utilities. For example, you do not wish to lose your place in the editor on switching to a "help" program, nor *vice versa*.

5.4.4 Checkpoints

Let P be a process which describes the behaviour of a long-lasting data base system. When lightning ($\nrightarrow$) strikes, one of the worst responses would be to restart P in its initial state, losing all the laboriously accumulated data of the system. It would be much better to return to some recent state of the system which is known to be satisfactory. Such a state is known as a checkpoint. We therefore provide a new key Ⓒ, which should be pressed only when the current state of the system is known to be satisfactory. When $\nrightarrow$ occurs, the most recent checkpoint is restored; or if there is no checkpoint the initial state is restored. We suppose Ⓒ and $\nrightarrow$ are not in the alphabet of P, and define $Ch(P)$ as the process that behaves like P, but responds in the appropriate fashion to these two events.

The informal definition of $Ch(P)$ is most succinctly formalized in the laws

L1 $Ch(P)/(s^\wedge\langle\,\nrightarrow\rangle) = Ch(P)$ for $s\in traces(P)$

L2 $Ch(P)/s^\wedge\langle$Ⓒ$\rangle = Ch(P/s)$ for $s\in traces(P)$

$Ch(P)$ can be defined more explicitly in terms of a binary operator $Ch2(P,Q)$, where P is the current process and Q is the most recent checkpoint waiting to be reinstated. If catastrophe occurs before the first checkpoint, the system restarts, as described in the laws

L3 $Ch(P) = Ch2(P,P)$

L4 If $P = (x{:}B{\rightarrow}P(x))$

then $Ch2(P,Q) = (x{:}B{\rightarrow}Ch2(P(x),Q)\,|\,\nrightarrow{\rightarrow}Ch2(Q,Q)\,|\,$Ⓒ$\rightarrow Ch2(P,P))$

The law L4 is suggestive of a practical implementation method, in which the checkpointed state is stored on some cheap but durable medium such as magnetic disc or tape. When Ⓒ occurs, the current state is copied as the new checkpoint; when $\nrightarrow$ occurs, the checkpoint is copied back as the new current state. For reasons of economy, a system implementor ensures that as much data as possible is shared between the current and the checkpoint states. Such optimization is highly machine and application dependent; it is pleasing that the mathematics is so simple.

The checkpointing operator is useful not only for large-scale data base systems. When playing a difficult game, a human player may wish to explore a possible line of play without committing himself to it. So he presses the Ⓒ key to store the current position, and if his explorations are unsuccessful, use of the $\nrightarrow$ key will restore the status quo.

These ideas of checkpointing have been explored by Ian Hayes.

5.4.5 Multiple checkpoints

In using a checkpointable system $Ch(P)$ it may happen that a checkpoint is declared in error. In such cases, it may be desirable to cancel the most recent checkpoint, and go back to the one before. For this we require a system which retains two or more of the most recently checkpointed states. In principle, there is no reason why we should not define a system $Mch(P)$, which retains all checkpoints back to the beginning of time. Each occurrence of $\overleftarrow{q}$ returns to the state just *before* the most recent $\copyright$, rather than the state just after it. As always we insist

$$\alpha Mch(P) - \alpha P = \{\copyright, \overleftarrow{q}\}$$

A $\overleftarrow{q}$ before a $\copyright$ goes back to the beginning

L1 $Mch(P)/s^\wedge\langle \overleftarrow{q}\rangle = Mch(P)$ for $s \in traces(P)$

A $\overleftarrow{q}$ after a $\copyright$ cancels the effect of everything that has happened back to *and including* the most recent $\copyright$

L2 $Mch(P)/s^\wedge\langle\copyright\rangle^\wedge t^\wedge\langle \overleftarrow{q}\rangle = Mch(P/s)$ for $(s\!\restriction\!(\alpha P - \{\copyright\}))^\wedge t \in traces(P)$

A more explicit description of $Mch(P)$ can be given in terms of a binary operator $Mch2(P,Q)$, where P is the current process and Q is the stack of checkpoints waiting to be resumed if necessary. The initial content of the stack is an infinite sequence of copies of P

L3 $Mch(P) = \mu X.\ Mch2(P,X)$
         $= Mch2(P,Mch(P))$
         $= Mch2(P,Mch2(P,Mch2(P,...)))$

On occurrence of $\copyright$ the current state is pushed down; on occurrence of $\overleftarrow{q}$ the whole stack is reinstated

L4   If $P = (x:B \rightarrow P(x))$
    then $Mch2(P,Q) = (x:B \rightarrow Mch2(P(x),Q)$
                $\mid \copyright \rightarrow Mch2(P,Mch2(P,Q)))$
                $\mid \overleftarrow{q} \rightarrow Q)$

The pattern of recursions which appear in L4 is quite ingenious, but the multiple checkpoint facility could be very expensive to implement in practice when the number of checkpoints gets large.

5.4.6 Implementation

The implementation of the various versions of interrupt are based on the laws which show how the operators distribute through $\rightarrow$. Consider for example the alternation operator (5.4.3 L4)

$alternation(P,Q) =$
  $\lambda x.$ **if** $x =$ ⓧ **then** $alternation(Q,P)$
  else if $P(x) = "BLEEP$ **then** $"BLEEP$
                    else $alternation(P(x),Q)$

A more surprising implementation is that of *Mch* (5.4.5 L3, L4)

$Mch(P) = Mch2(P,Mch(P))$

where $Mch2(P,Q) =$
  $\lambda x.$ **if** $x =$ ⅂ **then** Q
  else if $x =$ ⓒ **then** $Mch2(P,Mch2(P,Q))$
  else if $P(x) = "BLEEP$ **then** $"BLEEP$
                    else $Mch2(P(x),Q)$

When this function is executed, the amount of store used grows in proportion to the number of checkpoints; and available storage is very rapidly exhausted. Of course, the storage can be reclaimed by the garbage collector on each occurrence of ⅂, but that is not really much consolation. As in the case of other recursions, constraints of practical implementation enforce a finite bound on the depth. In this case, the designer should impose a limit on the number of checkpoints retained, and discard the earlier ones. But such a design is not so elegantly expressible by recursion.

5.5   ASSIGNMENT

In this section we shall introduce the most important aspects of conventional sequential programming, namely assignments, conditionals, and loops. To simplify the formulation of useful laws, some unusual notations will be defined.

    The essential feature of conventional computer programming is assignment. If x is a program variable and e is an expression and P a process

$(x := e;\ P)$

is a process which behaves like P, except that the initial value of x is defined to be the initial value of the expression e. Initial values of all other variables are unchanged. Assignment by itself can be given a meaning by the definition

$(x := e) = (x := e;\ SKIP)$

Single assignment generalizes easily to multiple assignment. Let x stand for a list of distinct variables

$$x = x_0, x_1, \ldots, x_{n-1}$$

Let e stand for a list of expressions

$$e = e_0, e_1, \ldots, e_{n-1}$$

Provided that the lengths of the two lists are the same

$$x := e$$

assigns the initial value of e_i to x_i, for all i. Note that *all* the e_i are evaluated before *any* of the assignments are made, so that if y occurs in the expression g

$$y := f; \ z := g$$

is quite different from

$$y, z := f, g$$

Let b be an expression that evaluates to a Boolean truth value (either *true* or *false*). If P and Q are processes

$$P \triangleleft b \triangleright Q \qquad\qquad\qquad (P \text{ if } b \text{ else } Q)$$

is a process which behaves like P if the initial value of b is true, or like Q if the initial value of b is false. The notation is novel, but less cumbersome than the traditional

if b **then** P **else** Q

For similar reasons, the traditional loop

while b **do** Q

will be written

$$b * Q$$

This may be defined by recursion

D1 $\quad b * Q = \mu X.((Q;X) \triangleleft b \triangleright SKIP)$

Examples

X1 A process that behaves like CT_n (1.1.4 X2)

$$X1 = \mu X.(around \rightarrow X \,|\, up \rightarrow (n := 1; X))$$
$$\triangleleft n = 0 \triangleright$$
$$(up \rightarrow (n := n+1; X) \,|\, down \rightarrow (n := n-1; X))$$

The current value of the count is recorded in the variable n □

X2 A process that behaves like CT_0

$n:=0; \ X1$

The initial value of the count is set to zero. □

X3 A process that behaves like POS (5.1 X8)

$n:=1; \ (n>0)*(up \rightarrow n:=n+1 \,|\, down \rightarrow n:=n-1)$

Recursion has been replaced by a conventional loop. □

X4 A process which divides a natural number x by a positive number y, assigning the quotient to q and the remainder to r

$$QUOT = (q:=x \div y; \ r:=x-q \times y)$$ □

X5 A process with the same effect as X4, which computes the quotient by the slow method of repeated subtraction

$$LONGQUOT = (q:=0; \ r:=x; \ ((r \geq y)*(q:=q+1; \ r:=r-y)))$$ □

In a previous example (4.5 X3) we have shown how the behaviour of a variable can be modelled by a subordinate process which communicates its value with the process which uses it. In this chapter, we have deliberately rejected that technique, because it does not have the mathematical properties which we would like. For example, we want

$$(m:=1; \ m:=1) = (m:=1)$$

but unfortunately

$$(m.left!1 \rightarrow m.left!1 \rightarrow SKIP) \neq (m.left!1 \rightarrow SKIP)$$

5.5.1 Laws

In the laws for assignment, x and y stand for lists of distinct variables; $e, f(x), f(e)$ stand for lists of expressions, possibly containing occurrences of variables in x or y; and $f(e)$ contains e_i wherever $f(x)$ contains x_i for all indices i. For simplicity, in the following laws we shall assume that all expressions always give a result, for any values of the variables they contain.

L1 $(x:=x) = SKIP$

L2 $(x:=e; \ x:=f(x)) = (x:=f(e))$

L3 If x,y is a list of distinct variables $(x:=e) = (x,y:=e,y)$

L4 If x,y,z are of the same length as e,f,g respectively
$(x,y,z:=e,f,g) = (x,z,y:=e,g,f)$

Using these laws, it is possible to transform every sequence of assignments into a single assignment to a list of all the variables involved.

When $\lessdot b \gtrdot$ is considered as a binary infix operator, it possesses several familiar algebraic properties

L5–6 $\lessdot b \gtrdot$ is idempotent, associative, and distributes through $\lessdot c \gtrdot$

L7 $P \lessdot true \gtrdot Q = P$

L8 $P \lessdot false \gtrdot Q = Q$

L9 $P \lessdot \neg b \gtrdot Q = Q \lessdot b \gtrdot P$

L10 $P \lessdot b \gtrdot (Q \lessdot b \gtrdot R) = P \lessdot b \gtrdot R$

L11 $P \lessdot (a \lessdot b \gtrdot c) \gtrdot Q = (P \lessdot a \gtrdot Q) \lessdot b \gtrdot (P \lessdot c \gtrdot Q)$

L12 $x := e; \ (P \lessdot b(x) \gtrdot Q) = (x := e; \ P) \lessdot b(e) \gtrdot (x := e; \ Q)$

L13 $(P \lessdot b \gtrdot Q); \ R = (P; \ R) \lessdot b \gtrdot (Q; \ R)$

To deal effectively with assignment in concurrent processes, it is necessary to impose a restriction that no variable assigned in one concurrent process can ever be used in another. To enforce this restriction, we introduce two new categories of symbol into the alphabets of sequential processes

> $var(P)$ the set of variables that may be assigned within P
> $acc(P)$ the set of variables that may be accessed in expressions within P.

All variables which may be changed may also be accessed

$$var(P) \subseteq acc(P) \subseteq \alpha P$$

Similarly, we define $acc(e)$ as the set of variables appearing in e. Now if P and Q are to be joined by $\|$, we stipulate that

$$var(P) \cap acc(Q) = var(Q) \cap acc(P) = \{\}$$

Under this condition, it does not matter whether an assignment takes place before a parallel split, or within one of its components after they are running concurrently

L14 $((x := e; \ P) \| Q) = (x := e; \ (P \| Q))$

provided that $x \subseteq var(P) - acc(Q)$
   and $acc(e) \cap var(Q) = \{\}$

An immediate consequence of this is

$$(x := e; \ P) \| (y := f; \ Q) = (x, y := e, f; \ (P \| Q))$$

provided that $x \subseteq var(P) - acc(Q) - acc(f)$
   and $y \subseteq var(Q) - acc(P) - acc(e)$

This shows how the alphabet restriction ensures that assignments within one component process of a concurrent pair cannot interfere with assignments within the other. In an implementation, sequences of assignments may be carried out either together or in any interleaving, without making any difference to the externally observable actions of the process.

Finally, concurrent combination distributes through the conditional

L15 $\quad P \parallel (Q \lhd b \rhd R) = (P \parallel Q) \lhd b \rhd (P \parallel R)$

provided $acc(b) \cap var(P) = \{\}$.

This law again states that it does not matter whether b is evaluated before or after the parallel split.

We now deal with the problem which arises when expressions are undefined for certain values of the variables they contain. If e is a list of expressions, we define $\mathcal{D}e$ as a Boolean expression which is true just when all the operands of e are within the domains of their operators. For example, in natural number arithmetic,

$$\mathcal{D}(x \div y) = (y > 0)$$
$$\mathcal{D}(y+1, \, z+y) = true$$
$$\mathcal{D}(e+f) = \mathcal{D}e \wedge \mathcal{D}f$$
$$\mathcal{D}(r-y) = y \leq r$$

It is reasonable to insist that $\mathcal{D}e$ is always defined, i.e.,

$$\mathcal{D}(\mathcal{D}e) = true$$

We deliberately leave completely unspecified the result of an attempt to evaluate an undefined expression—anything whatsoever may happen. This is reflected by the use of *CHAOS* in the following laws.

L16' $\ (x := e) = (x := e \lhd \mathcal{D}e \rhd CHAOS)$

L17' $\ P \lhd b \rhd Q = ((P \lhd b \rhd Q) \lhd \mathcal{D}b \rhd CHAOS)$

Furthermore, the laws L2, L4, and L12 need slight modification

L2' $\quad (x := e; \, x := f(x)) = (x := f(e) \lhd \mathcal{D}e \rhd CHAOS)$

L4' $\quad (P \lhd b \rhd P) = (P \lhd \mathcal{D}b \rhd CHAOS)$

5.5.2 Specifications

A specification of a sequential process describes not only the traces of the events which occur, but also the relationship between these traces, the initial values of the program variables, and their final values. To denote the initial value of a program variable x, we simply use the variable name x by itself. To denote the final value, we decorate the name with a superscript $\sqrt{\ }$, as in $x^\sqrt{}$. The value of $x^\sqrt{}$ is not observable until the process is terminated, i.e., the last event of the trace is $\sqrt{}$. This fact is represented by not specifying anything about $x^\sqrt{}$ unless $\overline{tr}_0 = \sqrt{}$.

Examples

X1   A process which performs no action, but adds one to the value of x, and terminates successfully with the value of y unchanged

$$tr=\langle\rangle\vee(tr=\langle\sqrt{}\,\rangle\wedge x^\sqrt{}=x+1\wedge y^\sqrt{}=y)$$ □

X2   A process which performs an event whose symbol is the initial value of the variable x, and then terminates successfully, leaving the final values of x and y equal to their initial values

$$tr=\langle\rangle\vee tr=\langle x\rangle\vee(tr=\langle x,\sqrt{}\,\rangle\wedge x^\sqrt{}=x\wedge y^\sqrt{}=y)$$ □

X3   A process which stores the identity of its first event as the final value of x

$$\# tr\leq2\wedge(\# tr=2\Rightarrow(tr=\langle x^\sqrt{},\sqrt{}\,\rangle\wedge y^\sqrt{}=y))$$ □

The correct working of a process often depends on some precondition $S(x)$ on the initial values of the program variables x. This can be expressed by writing $S(x)$ as the antecedent of the specification.

X4   A process which divides a nonnegative x by a positive y, and assigns the quotient to q and the remainder to r

$$DIV=(y>0\Rightarrow tr=\langle\rangle\vee(tr=\langle\sqrt{}\,\rangle\wedge q^\sqrt{}=(x\div y)\wedge r^\sqrt{}=x-(q^\sqrt{}\times y)\wedge y^\sqrt{}=y\wedge x^\sqrt{}=x))$$

Without the precondition, this specification would be impossible to meet in its full generality.   □

X5   Here are some more complex specifications which will be used later

$$DIVLOOP=(tr=\langle\rangle\vee(tr=\langle\sqrt{}\,\rangle\wedge r=(q^\sqrt{}-q)\times y+r^\sqrt{}\wedge r^\sqrt{}<y$$
$$\wedge x^\sqrt{}=x\wedge y^\sqrt{}=y))$$

$$T(n)=r<n\times y$$ □

All variables in these and subsequent specifications are intended to denote natural numbers, so subtraction is undefined if the second operand is greater than the first.

We shall now formulate the laws which underlie proofs that a process satisfies its specification. Let $S(x, tr, x^\sqrt{})$ be a specification. In order to prove that *SKIP* satisfies this specification, clearly the specification must be true when the trace is empty; furthermore, it must be true when the trace is $\langle\sqrt{}\,\rangle$

and the final values of all variables $x^{\vee}$ are equal to their initial values. These two conditions are also sufficient, as stated in the following law

L1 If $S(x, \langle\rangle, x^{\vee})$
and $S(x, \langle\sqrt{}\rangle, x)$
then $SKIP$ **sat** $S(x, tr, x^{\vee})$.

X6 The strongest specification satisfied by $SKIP$ is

$$SKIP_A \text{ sat } (tr=\langle\rangle\vee(tr=\langle\sqrt{}\rangle\wedge x^{\vee}=x))$$

where x is a list of all variables in A and $x^{\vee}$ is a list of their ticked variants. X6 is an immediate consequence of L1 and vice versa. □

X7 $SKIP$ **sat** $(r<y\Rightarrow(T(n+1)\Rightarrow DIVLOOP))$
Proof
(1) Replacing tr by $\langle\rangle$ in the specification gives

$$r<y\wedge T(n+1)\Rightarrow\langle\rangle=\langle\rangle\vee\ ...$$

which is a tautology.
(2) Replacing tr by $\langle\sqrt{}\rangle$ and final values by initial values gives

$$r<y\wedge T(n+1)\Rightarrow((\langle\sqrt{}\rangle=\langle\rangle\vee(\langle\sqrt{}\rangle=\langle\sqrt{}\rangle\wedge x=x\wedge y=y$$
$$\wedge r=((q-q)\times y+r)\wedge r<y))$$

which is also a trivial theorem. This result will be used in X10. □

It is a precondition of successful assignment $x:=e$ that the expressions e on the right-hand side should be defined. In this case, if P satisfies a specification $S(x)$, $(x:=e; P)$ satisfies the same specification, after modification to reflect the fact that the initial value of x is e.

L2 If P **sat** $S(x)$
then $(x:=e; P)$ **sat** $(\mathcal{D}e\Rightarrow S(e))$

The law for simple assignment can be derived from L2 on replacing P by $SKIP$, and using X6 and 5.2 L1

L2A $x_0:=e$ **sat** $(\mathcal{D}e\wedge tr\neq\langle\rangle\Rightarrow tr=\langle\sqrt{}\rangle\wedge x_0^{\vee}=e\wedge x_1^{\vee}=x_1\wedge...)$

A consequence of L2 is that for any P, the strongest fact one can prove about $(x:=1/0; P)$ is

$$(x:=1/0; P) \text{ sat } true$$

Whatever non-vacuous goal you may wish to achieve, it cannot be achieved by starting with an illegal assignment.

Examples

X8 $SKIP$ **sat** $(tr \neq \langle\rangle \Rightarrow tr = \langle\,\surd\,\rangle \wedge q^{\surd} = q \wedge r^{\surd} = r \wedge y^{\surd} = y \wedge x^{\surd} = x)$

therefore $(r := x - q \times y; SKIP)$ **sat** $(x \geq q \times y \wedge tr \neq \langle\rangle \Rightarrow$
$$tr = \langle\,\surd\,\rangle \wedge q^{\surd} = q \wedge r^{\surd} = (x - q \times y) \wedge y^{\surd} = y \wedge x^{\surd} = x)$$

therefore $(q := x \div y; r := x - q \times y)$ **sat** $(y > 0 \wedge x \geq (x \div y) \times y \wedge tr \neq \langle\rangle \Rightarrow$
$$tr = \langle\,\surd\,\rangle \wedge q^{\surd} = (x \div y) \wedge r^{\surd} = (x - (x \div y) \times y) \wedge y^{\surd} = y \wedge x^{\surd} = x)$$

The specification on the last line is equivalent to DIV which was defined in
X4. □

X9   Assume X **sat** $(T(n) \Rightarrow DIVLOOP)$

therefore $(r := r - y; X)$ **sat** $(y \leq r \Rightarrow (r - y < n \times y \Rightarrow (tr = \langle\rangle \vee tr = \langle\,\surd\,\rangle \wedge (r - y) = ...)))$

therefore $(q := q + 1; r := r - y; X)$ **sat** $(y \leq r \Rightarrow (r < (n+1) \times y \Rightarrow DIVLOOP'))$

where $DIVLOOP' = (tr = \langle\rangle \vee (tr = \langle\,\surd\,\rangle \wedge (r - y) = (q^{\surd} - (q + 1)) \times y + r^{\surd}$
$$\wedge r^{\surd} < y \wedge x^{\surd} = x \wedge y^{\surd} = y))$$

By elementary algebra of natural numbers

$$y \leq r \Rightarrow (DIVLOOP' \equiv DIVLOOP)$$

therefore $(q := q + 1; r := r - y; X)$ **sat** $(y \leq r \Rightarrow (T(n+1) \Rightarrow DIVLOOP))$

This result will be used in X10. □

For general sequential composition, a much more complicated law is
required, in which the traces of the components are sequentially composed,
and the initial state of the second component is identical to the final state of
the first component. However, the values of the variables in this intermediate state are not observable; only the existence of such values is assured

L3 If P **sat** $S(x, tr, x^{\surd})$
   and Q **sat** $T(x, tr, x^{\surd})$
   and P does not diverge
   then $(P;Q)$ **sat** $(\exists y, s, t.\ tr = (s;t) \wedge S(x, s, y) \wedge T(y, t, x^{\surd}))$

In this law, x is a list of all variables in the alphabet of P and Q, $x^{\surd}$ is a list of
their superscripted variants, and y a list of the same number of fresh variables.

The specification of a conditional is the same as that of the first component if the condition is true, and the same as that of the second component if
false

L4 If P **sat** S and Q **sat** T
   then $(P \not\vdash b \not\vdash Q)$ **sat** $((b \wedge S) \vee (\neg b \wedge T))$

An alternative form of this law is sometimes more convenient

L4A   If P sat $(b \Rightarrow S)$ and Q sat $(\neg b \Rightarrow S)$
   then $(P \triangleleft b \triangleright Q)$ sat S

Example

X10   Let $COND = (q := q + 1; \ r := r - y; \ X) \triangleleft r \geq y \triangleright SKIP$
   and X sat $(T(n) \Rightarrow DIVLOOP)$.
   then $COND$ sat $(T(n+1) \Rightarrow DIVLOOP)$

The two sufficient conditions for this conclusion have been proved in X7 and
X9; the result follows by L4A.   □

The proof of a loop uses the recursive definition given in 5.5 D1, and the
law for unguarded recursion (3.7.1 L8). If R is the intended specification of
the loop, we must find a specification $S(n)$ such that $S(0)$ is always true, and
also

$$(\forall n. \ S(n)) \Rightarrow R.$$

A general method to construct $S(n)$ is to find a predicate $T(n,x)$, which
describes the conditions on the initial state x such that the loop is certain to
terminate in less than n repetitions. Then define

$$S(n) = (T(n,x) \Rightarrow R).$$

Clearly, no loop can terminate in less than no repetitions, so if $T(n,x)$ has
been correctly defined $T(0,x)$ will be false, and consequently $S(0)$ will be
true. The result of the proof of the loop will be $\forall n. \ S(n)$, i.e.,

$$\forall n. \ (T(n,x) \Rightarrow R)$$

Since n is chosen as a variable which does not occur in R, this is equivalent to

$$(\exists n. \ T(n,x)) \Rightarrow R.$$

No stronger specification can possibly be met, since $\exists n.T(n,x)$ is the precondition under which the loop terminates in some finite number of iterations.
   Finally, we must prove that the body of the loop meets its specification.
Since the recursive equation for a loop involves a conditional, this task splits
into two. Thus we derive the general law

L5   If $\neg T(0,x)$ and $T(n,x) \Rightarrow \mathscr{D}b$
   and $SKIP$ sat $(\neg b \Rightarrow (T(n,x) \Rightarrow R))$
   and $(X$ sat $(T(n,x) \Rightarrow R)) \Rightarrow ((Q;X)$ sat $(b \Rightarrow (T(n+1,x) \Rightarrow R)))$
   then $(b*Q)$ sat $((\exists n.T(n,x)) \Rightarrow R)$

Example

X11   We wish to prove that the program for long division by repeated
subtraction (5.5 X5) meets its specification DIV. The task splits naturally in

two. The second and more difficult part is to prove that the loop meets some suitably formulated specification, namely

$$(r \geq y) * (q := q + 1; \ r := r - y) \ \textbf{sat} \ (y > 0 \Rightarrow DIVLOOP)$$

First we need to formulate the condition under which the loop terminates in less than n iterations

$$T(n) = r < n \times y$$

Here $T(0)$ is obviously false; the clause

$$\exists n. \ T(n)$$

is equivalent to

$$y > 0$$

which is the precondition under which the loop terminates. The remaining steps of the proof of the loop have already been taken in X7 and X5. The rest of the proof is a simple exercise. $\square$

The laws given in this section are designed as a calculus of total correctness for purely sequential programs, which contain no input or output. If Q is such a program, then a proof that

$$Q \ \textbf{sat} \ (P(x) \wedge tr \neq \langle \rangle \Rightarrow tr = \langle \surd \rangle \wedge R(x, x^{\surd})) \tag{1}$$

establishes that if $P(x)$ is true of the initial values of the variables when Q is started, then Q will terminate and $R(x, x^{\surd})$ will describe the relationship between the initial values x and the final values $x^{\surd}$. Thus $(P(x), R(x,x^{\surd}))$ form a precondition/postcondition pair in the sense of Cliff Jones. If $R(x^{\surd})$ does not mention the initial values x, the assertion (1) is equivalent to

$$P(x) \Rightarrow wp(Q, R(x))$$

where wp is Dijkstra's weakest precondition.

Thus in the special case of noncommunicating programs, the proof methods are mathematically equivalent to ones that are already familiar, though the explicit mention of "$tr = \langle \rangle$" and "$tr = \langle \surd \rangle$" makes them notationally more clumsy. This extra burden is of course necessary, and therefore more acceptable, when the methods are extended to deal with communicating sequential processes.

5.5.3 Implementation

The initial and final states of a sequential process can be represented as a function which maps each variable name onto its value. A sequential process is defined as a function which maps its initial state onto its subsequent behaviour. Successful termination ($\checkmark$) is represented by the atom "SUCCESS. A process which is ready to terminate will accept this symbol, which it maps, not onto another process, but onto the final state of its variables.

Thus the process *SKIP* takes an initial state as a parameter, accepts "SUCCESS as its only action, and delivers its initial state as its final state

$$SKIP = \lambda s.\lambda y. \text{ if } y \neq \text{"}SUCCESS \text{ then "}BLEEP \text{ else } s$$

An assignment is similar, except that its final state is slightly changed

$$assign(x,e) = \lambda s. \ \lambda y. \text{ if } y \neq SUCCESS \text{ then "}BLEEP \text{ else } update(s,x,e)$$

where $update(s,x,e) = \lambda y.$ **if** $y = x$ **then** $eval(e,s)$ **else** $s(y)$
and $eval(e,s)$ is the result of evaluating the expression e in state s.

If e is undefined in state s, we do not care what happens. Here, for simplicity, we have implemented only the single assignment. Multiple assignment is a little more complicated.

To implement sequential composition, it is necessary first to test whether the first operand has successfully terminated. If so, its final state is passed on to the second operand. If not, the first action is that of the first operand

$$sequence(P,Q) =$$
$$\lambda s. \text{ if } P(s) \ (\text{"}SUCCESS) \neq \text{"}BLEEP \text{ then } Q(P(s)(\text{"}SUCCESS))$$
$$\text{else } \lambda y. \text{ if } P(s)(y) = \text{"}BLEEP \text{ then "}BLEEP$$
$$\text{else } sequence(P(s)(y), \ Q)$$

The implementation of the conditional is as a conditional

$$condition(P,b,Q) = \lambda s. \text{ if } eval(b,s) \text{ then } P(s) \text{ else } Q(s)$$

The implementation of the loop $(b*Q)$ is left as an exercise.

Note that the definition of *sequence* given above is more complicated than that given in Section 5.3.3, because it takes a state s as its first argument, and it has to supply the state as the first argument of its operands. Unfortunately, a similar complexity has to be introduced into the definitions of all the other operators given in earlier chapters. A simpler alternative would be to model variables as subordinate processes; but this would probably be a great deal less efficient than the use of conventional random access storage. When considerations of efficiency are added to those of mathematical convenience, there are adequate grounds for introducing the assignable program variable as a new primitive concept, rather than defining it in terms of previously introduced concepts.

6 SHARED RESOURCES

6.1 INTRODUCTION

In Section 4.5 we introduced the concept of a named subordinate process $(m{:}R)$, whose sole task is to meet the needs of a single main process S; and for this we have used the notation

$$(m{:}R//S)$$

Suppose now that S contains or consists of two concurrent processes $(P \parallel Q)$, and *both* P and Q require the services of the same subordinate process $(m{:}R)$. Unfortunately, it is not possible for P and Q both to communicate with $(m{:}R)$ along the same channels, because these channels would have to be in the alphabet of both P and Q; and then the definition of $\parallel$ would require that communications with $(m{:}R)$ take place only when both P and Q communicate the same message simultaneously—which (as explained in 4.5 X6) is far from the required effect. What is needed is some way of interleaving the communications between P and $(m{:}R)$ with those between Q and $(m{:}R)$. In this way $(m{:}R)$ serves as a resource shared between P and Q; each of them uses it independently, and their interactions with it are interleaved.

When the identity of all the sharing processes is known in advance, it is possible to arrange that each sharing process uses a different set of channels to communicate with the shared resource. This technique was used in the story of the dining philosophers (Section 2.5): each fork was shared between two neighbouring philosophers, and the footman was shared among all five. Another example was 4.5 X6, in which a buffer was shared between two processes, one of which used only the left channel and the other used only the right channel. A general method of sharing is provided by multiple

197

labelling (Section 2.6.4), which effectively creates enough separate channels for independent communication with each sharing process. Individual communications along these channels are arbitrarily interleaved. But this method requires that the names of all the sharing processes are known in advance; and so it is not adequate for a subordinate process intended to serve the needs of a main process which splits into an arbitrary number of concurrent subprocesses. This chapter introduces techniques for sharing a resource among many processes, even when their number and identities are not known in advance. It is illustrated by examples drawn from the design of an operating system.

6.2   SHARING BY INTERLEAVING

The problem described in Section 6.1 arises from the use of the combinator $\parallel$ to describe the concurrent behaviour of processes; and this problem can often be avoided by using instead the interleaving form of concurrency $(P \mathbin{|\!|\!|} Q)$. Here, P and Q have the same alphabet and their communications with external (shared) processes are arbitrarily interleaved. Of course, this prohibits direct communication between P and Q; but indirect communication can be re-established through the services of a shared subordinate process of appropriate design, as shown in 4.5 X6 and in X2 below.

Examples

X1   Shared subroutine

$doub{:}DOUBLE \mathbin{/\!/} (P \mathbin{|\!|\!|} Q)$

Here, both P and Q may contain calls on the subordinate process

$(doub.left!v{\rightarrow}doub.right?x{\rightarrow}SKIP)$

Even though these pairs of communications from P and Q are arbitrarily interleaved, there is no danger that one of the processes will accidentally obtain an answer which should have been received by the other. To ensure this, all subprocesses of the main process must observe a strict alternation of communications on the left channel with communications on the right channel of the shared subordinate. For this reason, it seems worthwhile to introduce a specialized notation, whose exclusive use will guarantee observance of the required discipline. The suggested notation is reminiscent of a traditional procedure call in a high-level language, except that the value parameters are preceded by ! and the result parameters by ?, thus

$doub!x?y = (doub.left!x{\rightarrow}doub.right?y{\rightarrow}SKIP)$ □

The intended effect of sharing by interleaving is illustrated by the following series of algebraic transformations. When two sharing processes both simultaneously attempt to use the shared subroutine, matched pairs of communications are taken in an arbitrary order, but the components of a pair of communications with one process are never separated by a communication with another. For convenience, we use the following abbreviations

$$
\begin{array}{lll}
d!v & \text{for} & d.left!v \\
d?x & \text{for} & d.right?x
\end{array} \Bigg\} \quad \text{within a main process}
$$

$$
\begin{array}{lll}
!v & \text{for} & right!v \\
?x & \text{for} & left?x
\end{array} \Bigg\} \quad \text{within a subordinate process}
$$

Let $D = ?x \to !(x+x) \to D$

and $P = d!3 \to d?y \to P(y)$

and $Q = d!4 \to d?z \to Q(z)$

and $R = (d:D \mathbin{/\!/} (P \| Q))$ (as in X1 above)

Then $P \| Q = (d!3 \to ((d?y \to P(y)) \| Q)$

           $[]d!4 \to (P \| (d?z \to Q(z))))$ by 3.6.1 L7

The sharing processes each start with an output to the shared process. It is the shared process that is offered the choice between them. But the shared process is willing to accept either, so after hiding the choice becomes non-deterministic

$$
\begin{aligned}
(d:D \mathbin{/\!/} (P \| Q)) &= ((d:(!3+3 \to D)) \mathbin{/\!/} ((d?y \to P(y)) \| Q)) & \left\{ \begin{array}{l} \text{4.5.1 L1} \\ \end{array} \right. \\
&\sqcap ((d:(!4+4 \to D)) \mathbin{/\!/} (P \| (d?z \to Q(z)))) & \text{3.5.1 L5} \\
&= (d:D \mathbin{/\!/} (P(6) \| Q)) \sqcap (d:D \mathbin{/\!/} (P \| Q(8))) & \left. \begin{array}{l} \text{etc.} \\ \end{array} \right.
\end{aligned}
$$

The shared process offers its result to whichever of the sharing processes is ready to take it. Since one of these processes is still waiting for output, it is the process which provided the argument that gets the result. That is why strict alternation of output and input is so important in calling a shared subroutine.

X2 Shared data structure
In an airline flight reservation system, bookings are made by many reservation clerks, whose actions are interleaved. Each reservation adds a passenger to the flight list, and returns an indication whether that passenger was already booked or not. For this oversimplified example, the set implemented in 4.5 X8 will serve as a shared subordinate process, named by the flight number

$$
AG109{:}SET \mathbin{/\!/} (\; \dots \; (CLERK \| CLERK \| \dots) \; \dots)
$$

Each *CLERK* books a passenger by the call

> *AG*109!*pass no*?*x*

which stands for

> (*AG*109.*left*!*pass no*→*AG*109.*right*?*x*→*SKIP*)   □

    In these two examples, each occasion of use of the shared resource involves exactly two communications, one to send the parameters and the other to receive the results; after each pair of communications, the subordinate process returns to a state in which it is ready to serve another process, or the same one again. But frequently we wish to ensure that a whole series of communications takes place between two processes, without danger of interference by a third process. For example, a single expensive output device may have to be shared among many concurrent processes. On each occasion of use, a number of lines constituting a file must be output consecutively, without any danger of interleaving of lines sent by another process. For this purpose, the output of each file must be preceded by an *acquire* which obtains exclusive use of the resource; and on completion, the resource must be made available again by a *release*.

X3 Shared line printer

> *LP* = *acquire*→μ*X*.(*left*?*s*→*h*!*s*→*X* | *release*→*LP*)

Here, *h* is the channel which connects *LP* to the hardware of the line printer. After acquisition, the process *LP* copies successive lines from its left channel to its hardware, until a release signal returns it to its original state, in which it is available for use by other processes. This process is used as a shared resource

> *lp*:*LP* // ... (*P* ‖ *Q*) ...

Inside *P* or *Q*, the output of the series of lines constituting a file is bracketed by an *lp.acquire* and *lp.release*

> *lp.acquire*→ ... *lp.left*!"*A.JONES*"→...
> *lp.left*!*nextline*→... *lp.release*→...   □

X4 An improvement on X3
When a line printer is shared between many users, the length of paper containing each file must be manually detached after output from the previous and the following files. For this purpose, the printing paper is usually divided into pages, which are separated by perforations; and the hardware of the printer allows an operation *throw*, which moves the paper rapidly to the end of the current page—or better, to the next outward-facing

fold in the paper stack. To assist in separation of output, files should begin and end on page boundaries, and a complete row of asterisks should be printed at the end of the last page of the file, and at the beginning of the first page. To prevent confusion, no complete line of asterisks is permitted to be printed in the middle of a file

$$LP = (h!throw \rightarrow h!asterisks \rightarrow acquire \rightarrow h!asterisks \rightarrow$$
$$\mu X.(left?s \rightarrow \textbf{if } s \neq asterisks \textbf{ then } (h!s \rightarrow X) \textbf{ else } X$$
$$| release \rightarrow LP)$$

This version of LP is used in exactly the same way as the previous one. $\square$

In the last two examples, the use of the signals *acquire* and *release* prevent aribtrary interleaving of lines from distinct files, and they do so without introducing the danger of deadlock. But if more than one resource is to be shared in this fashion, the risk of deadlock cannot be ignored.

X5 Deadlock

Ann and Mary are good friends and good cooks; they share a pot and a pan, which they acquire, use and release as they need them

$$UTENSIL = (acquire \rightarrow use \rightarrow use \rightarrow ... \rightarrow release \rightarrow UTENSIL)$$
$$pot:UTENSIL \; // \; pan:UTENSIL \; // \; (ANN \parallel MARY)$$

Ann cooks in accordance with a recipe which requires a pot first and then a pan, whereas Mary needs a pan first, then a pot

$$ANN \;\; = ... \; pot.acquire \rightarrow ... \; pan.acquire \rightarrow ...$$
$$MARY = ... \; pan.acquire \rightarrow ... \; pot.acquire \rightarrow ...$$

Unfortunately, they decide to prepare a meal at about the same time. Each of them acquires her first utensil; but when she needs her second utensil, she finds she cannot have it, because it is being used by the other.

The story of Ann and Mary can be visualized on a two-dimensional plot (Fig. 6.1), where the life of Ann is displayed along the vertical axis, and Mary's life on the horizontal. The system starts in the bottom left hand corner, at the beginning of both their lives. Each time Ann performs an action, the system moves one step upward. Each time Mary performs an action, the system moves one step right. The trajectory shown on the graph shows a typical interleaving of Ann's and Mary's actions. Fortunately, this trajectory reaches the top right hand corner of the graph where both cooks are enjoying their meal.

But this happy outcome is not certain. Because they cannot simultaneously use a shared utensil, there are certain rectangular regions in the state space through which the trajectory cannot pass. For example in the region

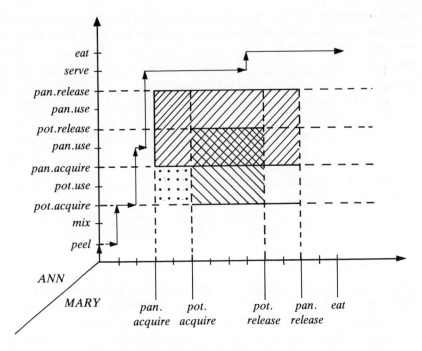

Figure 6.1

hatched ▨ both cooks would be using the pan, and this is not possible. Similarly, exclusion on the use of the pot prohibits entry into the region hatched ▧. Thus if the trajectory reaches the edge of one of these forbidden regions, it can only follow the edge upward (for a vertical edge) or rightward (for a horizontal edge). During this period, one of the cooks is waiting for release of a utensil by the other.

Now consider the zone marked with dots ▦. If ever the trajectory enters this zone, it will inevitably end in deadlock at the top right hand corner of the zone. The purpose of the picture is to show that the danger of deadlock arises solely as a result of a concavity in the forbidden region which faces towards the origin: other concavities are quite safe. The picture also shows that the *only* sure way of preventing deadlock is to extend the forbidden region to cover the danger zone, and so remove the concavity. One technique would be to introduce an additional artificial resource which must be acquired before either utensil, and must not be released until both utensils have been released. This solution is similar to the one imposed by the footman in the story of the dining philosophers (Section 2.5.3) where permission to sit down is a kind of resource, of which only four instances are

shared among five philosophers. An easier solution is to insist that any cook
who is going to want both utensils must acquire the pan first. This example is
due to E. W. Dijkstra.   □

The easier solution suggested for the previous example generalizes to
any number of users and any number of resources. Provided there is a fixed
order in which all users acquire the resources they want, there is no risk of
deadlock. Users should release their resources as soon as they have finished
with them; the order of release does not matter. Users may even acquire
resources out of order, provided that at the time of acquisition they have
already released all resources which are later in the standard ordering.
Observance of this discipline of resource acquisition and release can often be
checked by a visual scan of the text of the user processes.

6.3   SHARED STORAGE

The purpose of this section is to argue against the use of shared storage; the
section may be omitted by those who are already convinced.

The behaviour of systems of concurrent processes can readily be
implemented on a single conventional stored-program computer, by a
technique known as timesharing, in which a single processor executes each
of the processes in alternation, with process change on occurrence of interrupt from an external device or from a regular timer. In this implementation,
it is very easy to allow the concurrent processes to share locations of common
storage, which are accessed and assigned simply by means of the usual
machine instructions within the code for each of the processes.

A location of shared storage can be modelled in our theory as a shared
variable (4.2 X7) with the appropriate symbolic name, for example

$$(count{:}VAR \; /\!/ \; (count.left!0{\rightarrow}(P \parallel Q)))$$

Shared storage must be clearly distinguished from the local storage
described in 5.5. The simplicity of the laws for reasoning about sequential
processes derives solely from the fact that each variable is updated by at most
one process; and these laws do not deal with the many dangers that arise
from arbitrary interleaving of assignments from different processes.

These dangers are most clearly illustrated by the following example.

X1   Interference
The shared variable *count* is used to keep a count of the total number of
occurrences of some important event. On each occurrence of the event, the

relevant process *P* or *Q* attempts to update the count by the pair of communications

$$count.right?x;\ count.left!(x+1)$$

Unfortunately, these two communications may be interleaved by a similar pair of communications from the other process, resulting in the sequence

$$count.right?x \rightarrow count.right?y \rightarrow count.left!(y+1) \rightarrow count.left!(x+1) \rightarrow\ ...$$

As a consequence, the value of the count is incremented only by one instead of two. This kind of error is known as interference, and it is an easy mistake in the design of processes which share common storage. Further, the actual occurrence of the fault is highly nondeterministic; it is not reliably reproducible, and so it is almost impossible to diagnose the error by conventional testing techniques. As a result, I suspect there are several operating systems in common use which regularly produce slightly inaccurate summaries, statistics, and accounts.

A possible solution to this problem is to make sure that no change of process takes place during a sequence of actions which must be protected from interleaving. Such a sequence is known as a *critical region*. On an implementation by a single processor, the required exclusion is often achieved by inhibiting all interrupts for the duration of the critical region. This solution has an undesirable effect in delaying response to interrupts; and worse, it fails completely as soon as a second processing unit is added to the computer.

A better solution was suggested by E. W. Dijkstra in his introduction of the binary exclusion semaphore. A semaphore may be described as a process which engages alternately in actions named *P* and *V*

$$SEM = (P \rightarrow V \rightarrow SEM)$$

This is declared as a shared resource

$$(mutex\!:\!SEM\ /\!/\ ...)$$

Each process, on entry into a critical region, must send the signal

$$mutex.P$$

and on exit from the critical region must engage in the event

$$mutex.V$$

Thus the critical region in which the count is incremented should appear

$$mutex.P \rightarrow$$
$$count.right?x \rightarrow count.left!(x+1) \rightarrow$$
$$mutex.V \rightarrow\ ...$$

Provided that all processes observe this discipline, it is impossible for two processes to interfere with each other's updating of the count. But if any process omits a P or a V, or gets them in the wrong order, the effect will be chaotic, and will risk a disastrous or (perhaps worse) a subtle error.

A much more robust way to prevent interference is to build the required protection into the very design of the shared storage, taking advantage of knowledge of its intended pattern of usage. For example, if a variable is to be used only for counting, then the operation which increments it should be a single atomic operation

$$count.up$$

and the shared resource should be designed like CT_0 (1.1.4 X2)

$$count{:}CT_0 \; /\!/ \; (\dots \; P \,\|\, Q \; \dots)$$

In fact there are good reasons for recommending that each shared resource be specially designed for its purpose, and that pure storage should not be shared in the design of a system using concurrency. This not only avoids the grave dangers of accidental interference; it also produces a design that can be implemented efficiently on networks of distributed processing elements as well as single-processor and multiprocessor computers with physically shared store.

6.4 MULTIPLE RESOURCES

In Section 6.2, we described how a number of concurrent processes with different behaviour could share a single subordinate process. Each sharing process observes a discipline of alternating output and input, or alternating acquire and release signals, to ensure that at any given time the resource is used by at most one of the potentially sharing processes. Such resources are known as *serially reusable*. In this section we introduce arrays of processes to represent multiple resources with identical behaviour; and indices in the array ensure that each element communicates safely with the process that has acquired it.

We shall therefore make substantial use of indices and indexed operators, with obvious meaning. For example

$$\mathop{\|}_{i<12} P_i = (P_0 \,\|\, P_1 \,\|\, \dots \,\|\, P_{11})$$

$$\mathop{\|\!\|\!\|}_{i<4} P = (P \,\|\!\|\!\| \, P \,\|\!\|\!\| \, P \,\|\!\|\!\| \, P)$$

$$\mathop{\|}_{i\geq 0} P_i = (P_0 \,\|\, P_1 \,\|\, \dots)$$

$$\mathop{[]}_{i\geq 0} (f(i)\!\rightarrow\!P_i) = (f(0)\!\rightarrow\!P_0 \,|\, f(1)\!\rightarrow\!P_1 \,|\; \dots)$$

In the last example, we insist that f is a one–one function, so that the choice between the alternatives is made solely by the environment.

Examples

X1   Re-entrant subroutine
A shared subroutine that is serially reusable can be used by only one calling process at a time. If the execution of the subroutine requires a considerable calculation, there could be corresponding delays to the calling processes. If several processors are available to perform the calculations, there is good reason to allow several instances of the subroutine to proceed concurrently on different processors. A subroutine capable of several concurrent instances is known as *re-entrant*, and it is defined as an array of concurrent processes

$$doub{:}(\;\|_{i<27}\;(i{:}DOUBLE))\;/\!/\;...$$

A typical call of this subroutine could be

$$(doub.3.left!30{\rightarrow}doub.3.right?y{\rightarrow}SKIP)$$

The use of the index 3 ensures that the result of the call is obtained from the same instance of *doub* to which the arguments were sent, even though some other concurrent process may at the same time call another instance of the array, resulting in an interleaving of the messages

$$doub.3.left.30, ... doub.2.left.20, ... doub.3.right.60, ... doub.2.right.40, ...$$

When a process calls a re-entrant subroutine, it really does not matter which element of the array responds to the call; any one that happens to be free will be equally good. So rather than specifying a particular index 2 or 3, a calling process should leave the selection arbitrary, by using the construct

$$\underset{i\geq0}{[]}\;(doub.i.left!30{\rightarrow}doub.i.right?y{\rightarrow}SKIP)$$

This still observes the essential discipline that the same index is used for sending the arguments and (immediately after) for receiving the result. □

In the example shown above, there is an arbitrary limit of 27 simultaneous activations of the subroutine. Since it is fairly easy to arrange that a single processor divides its attention among a much larger number of processes, such arbitrary limits can be avoided by introducing an infinite array of concurrent processes

$$doub{:}(\;\|_{i\geq0}\;i{:}D)$$

where D can now be designed to serve only a single call and then stop

$$D = left?x \rightarrow right!(x+x) \rightarrow STOP$$

A subroutine with no bound on its re-entrancy is known as a *procedure*. The intention in using a procedure is that the effect of each call

$$\underset{i \geq 0}{[]} \ (doub.i.left!x \rightarrow doub.i.right?y \rightarrow SKIP)$$

should be identical to the call of a subordinate process D declared immediately adjacent to the call

$$(doub: D \ // \ (doub.left!x \rightarrow doub.right?y \rightarrow SKIP))$$

This latter is known as a *local* procedure call, since it suggests execution of the procedure on the same processor as the calling process; whereas the call of a shared procedure is known as a *remote* call, since it suggests execution on a separate possibly distant processor. Since the effect of remote and local calls is intended to be the same, the reasons for using the remote call can only be political or economic—e.g., to keep the code of the procedure secret, or to run it on a machine with special facilities which are too expensive to provide on the machine on which the using processes run.

A typical example of an expensive facility is a high-volume backing store, such as a disc or bubble memory.

X2 Shared backing storage

A storage medium is split into B sectors which can be read and written independently. Each sector can store one block of information, which it inputs on the left and outputs on the right. Unfortunately the storage medium is implemented in a technology with destructive read-out, so that each block written can be read only once. Thus each sector behaves like $COPY$ (4.2 X1) rather than VAR (4.2 X7). The whole backing store is an array of such sectors, indexed by numbers less than B

$$BSTORE = \underset{i<B}{\|} \ i:COPY$$

This store is intended for use as a subordinate process

$$(back:BSTORE \ // \ ...)$$

Within its main process, the store may be used by the communications

$$back.i.left!bl \rightarrow \ ... \ back.i.right?y \rightarrow \ ...$$

The backing store may also be shared by concurrent processes. In this case, the action

$$\underset{i<B}{[]} \ (back.i.left!bl \rightarrow \ ...)$$

will simultaneously acquire an arbitrary free sector with number i, and write the value of bl into it. Similarly, $back.i.right?x$ will in a single action both read the content of sector i into x and release this sector for use on another occasion, very possibly by another process. It is this simplification that is the real motive for using $COPY$ to model the behaviour of each sector: the story of destructive read-out is just a story.   □

Of course, successful sharing of this backing store requires the utmost discipline on the part of the sharing processes. A process may input from a sector only if the same process has most recently output to that very sector; and each output must eventually be followed by such an input. Failure to observe such disciplines will lead to deadlock, or even worse confusion. Methods of enforcing this discipline painlessly will be introduced after the next example, and will be extensively illustrated in the subsequent design of modules of an operating system (Section 6.5).

X3   Two line printers
Two identical line printers are available to serve the demands of a collection of using processes. They both need the kind of protection from interleaving that was provided by LP (6.2 X4). We therefore declare an array of two instances of LP, each of which is indexed by a natural number indicating its position in the array

$$LP2 = (0:LP\|1:LP)$$

This array may itself be given a name for use as a shared resource

$$(lp:LP2 \ // \ ...)$$

Each instance of LP is now prefixed twice, once by a name and once by an index; thus communications with the using process have three or four components, e.g.,

$$lp.0.acquire, \ lp.1.left."A. \ JONES", \ ...$$

As in the case of a re-entrant procedure, when a process needs to acquire one of an array of identical resources, it really cannot matter which element of the array is selected on a given occasion. Any element which is ready to respond to the acquire signal will be acceptable. A general choice construction will make the required arbitrary choice

$$\underset{i\geq0}{[]} \ (lp.i.acquire\rightarrow \ ... \ lp.i.left!x\rightarrow \ ... \ lp.i.release\rightarrow SKIP)$$

Here, the initial $lp.i.acquire$ will acquire whichever of the two LP processes is ready for this event. If neither is ready, the acquiring process will wait; if both are ready, the choice between them is nondeterministic. After the initial acquisition, the bound variable i takes as its value the index of the selected resource, and all subsequent communications will be correctly directed to that same resource.   □

When a shared resource has been acquired for temporary use within another process, the resource is intended to behave exactly like a locally ·declared subordinate process, communicating only with its using subprocess. Let us therefore adapt the familiar notation for subordination, and write

$\qquad (myfile::lp \; // \; ... \; myfile.left!x \; ...)$

instead of the much more cumbersome construction

$\qquad \underset{i \geq 0}{[]} \; (lp.i.acquire \rightarrow \; ... \; lp.i.left!x \; ...; \; lp.i.release \rightarrow SKIP)$

Here, the local name $myfile$ has been introduced to stand for the indexed name $lp.i$, and the technicalities of acquisition and release have been conveniently suppressed. The new "::" notation is called *remote subordination*; it is distinguished from the familiar ":" notation in that it takes on its right, not a complete process, but the name of a remotely positioned array of processes.

X4   Two output files
A using process requires simultaneous use of two line printers to output two files, $f1$ and $f2$

$\qquad (f1::lp \; // \; (f2::lp \; // \; ... \; f1.left!s1 \rightarrow f2.left!s2 \rightarrow \; ...))$

Here, the using process interleaves output of lines to the two different files; but each line is printed on the appropriate printer. Of course, deadlock will be the certain result of any attempt to declare *three* printers simultaneously; it is also a likely result of declaring two printers simultaneously in each of two concurrent processes, as shown in the history of Ann and Mary (6.2 X5).   □

X5   Scratch file
A scratch file is used for output of a sequence of blocks. When the output is complete, the file is rewound, and the entire sequence of blocks is read back from the beginning. When all the blocks have been read, the scratch file will then give only *empty* signals; no further reading or writing is possible. Thus a scratch file behaves like a file output to magnetic tape, which must be rewound before being read. The *empty* signal serves as an end-of-file marker

$\qquad SCRATCH = WRITE_{\langle\rangle}$
$\qquad WRITE_s \quad = (left?x \rightarrow WRITE_{s ^\frown \langle x \rangle}$
$\qquad\qquad\qquad\quad | \; rewind \rightarrow READ_s)$
$\qquad READ_{\langle x \rangle ^\frown s} = (right!x \rightarrow READ_s)$
$\qquad READ_{\langle\rangle} \quad = (empty \rightarrow READ_{\langle\rangle})$

This may conveniently be used as a simple unshared subordinate process

$$(myfile:SCRATCH \ // \ ... \ myfile.left!v \ ... \ myfile.rewind \ ...$$
$$... \ (myfile.right?x\rightarrow \ ...$$
$$| \ myfile.empty\rightarrow \ ...) \ ...)$$

It will serve later as a model for a shared process.   □

X6 Scratch files on backing store
The scratch file described in X5 can be readily implemented by holding the stored sequence of blocks in the main store of a computer. But if the blocks are large and the sequence is long, this could be an uneconomic use of main store, and it would be better to store the blocks on a backing store. Since each block in a scratch file is read and written only once, a backing store (X2) with destructive read-out will suffice. An ordinary scratch file (held in main store) is used to hold the sequence of indices of the sectors of backing store on which the corresponding actual blocks of information are held; this ensures that the correct blocks are read back, and in the correct sequence

$$BSCRATCH = (pagetable:SCRATCH \ //$$
$$\mu X.(left?x\rightarrow(\ \underset{i<B}{[]} \ back.i.left!x\rightarrow pagetable.left!i\rightarrow X)$$
$$| \ rewind\rightarrow pagetable.rewind\rightarrow$$
$$\mu Y.(pagetable.right?i\rightarrow back.i.right?x\rightarrow right!x\rightarrow Y$$
$$| \ pagetable.empty\rightarrow empty\rightarrow Y)))$$

BSCRATCH uses the name *back* to address a backing store (X2) as a subordinate process. This should be supplied

$$SCRATCHB = (back:BSTORE \ // \ BSCRATCH)$$

SCRATCHB can be used as a simple unshared subordinate process in exactly the same way as the scratch file of X5

$$(myfile:SCRATCHB \ // \ ... \ myfile.left!v \ ... \ )$$

The effect is exactly the same as use of *SCRATCH*, except that the maximum length of the scratch file is limited to *B* blocks.   □

X7 Serially reused scratch files
Suppose we want to share the scratch file on backing store among a number of interleaved users, who will acquire, use, and release it one at a time in the manner of a shared line printer (6.2 X3). For this purpose, we must adapt *BSCRATCH* to accept *acquire* and *release* signals. If a user releases his scratch file before reading to the end, there is a danger that the unread blocks on backing store will never be reclaimed. This danger can be averted by a

loop that reads back these blocks and discards them

$$SCAN = \mu X.(pagetable.right?i{\rightarrow}back.i.right?x{\rightarrow}X$$
$$| \, pagetable.empty{\rightarrow}SKIP)$$

A shared scratch file first acquires its user, and then behaves like **BSCRATCH**. The release signal causes an interrupt (Section 5.4) to the **SCAN** process

$$SHBSCR=acquire{\rightarrow}(BSCRATCH^{\wedge}(release{\rightarrow}SCAN))$$

The serially reusable scratchfile is provided by the simple loop

$$*SHBSCR$$

which uses **BSTORE** as a subordinate process

$back$: $BSTORE$ $//$ $*SHBSCR$ □

X8   Multiplexed scratch files
In the previous two examples only one scratch file is in use at a time. A backing store is usually sufficiently large to allow many scratch files to exist simultaneously, each occupying a disjoint subset of the available sectors. The backing store can therefore be shared among an unbounded array of scratch files. Each scratch file acquires a sector when needed by outputting to it, and releases it automatically on inputting that block again. The backing store is shared by the technique of multiple labelling (Section 2.6.4), using as labels the same indices (natural numbers) which are used in constructing the array of sharing processes

$$FILESYS=\mathbb{N}:(back:BSTORE) \; // \; (\underset{i\geq0}{\parallel} \; i:SHBSCR)$$

where $\mathbb{N}=\{i\,|\,i\geq0\}$

This filing system is intended to be used as a subordinate process, shared by interleaving among any number of users

$$filesys:FILESYS \; // \; ... \; (USER1 \parallel\!\parallel USER2 \parallel\!\parallel ...)$$

Inside each user, a fresh scratch file can be acquired, used, and released by remote subordination

$$myfile::filesys \; // \; (... \, myfile.left!v \, ... \, myfile.rewind \, ... \, myfile.right?x \, ...)$$

which is intended (apart from resource limitations) to have exactly the same effect as the simple subordination of a private scratch file (X5)

$$(myfile:SCRATCH \; // \; ... \, myfile.left!v \, ... \, myfile.rewind \, ... \, myfile.right?x \, ...)$$
□

The structure of the filing system (X8) and its mode of use is a paradigm solution of the problem of sharing a limited number of actual resources (sectors on backing store) among an unknown number of users. The users do not communicate directly with the resources; there is an intermediary *virtual resource* (the *SHBSCR*) which they declare and use as though it were a private subordinate process. The function of the virtual resource is twofold

(1)   it provides a nice clean interface to the user; in this example, *SHBSCR* glues together into a single contiguous scratch file a set of sectors scattered on backing store.

(2)   It guarantees a proper disciplined access to the actual resources; for example, *SHBSCR* ensures that each user reads only from sectors allocated to that user, and cannot forget to release sectors on finishing with a scratch file.

Point (1) ensures that the discipline of point (2) is painless.

The paradigm of actual and virtual resources is very important in the design of resource-sharing systems. The mathematical definition of the paradigm is quite complicated, since it uses an unbounded set of natural numbers to implement the necessary dynamic creation of new virtual processes, and of new channels through which to communicate with them. In a practical implementation on a computer, these would be represented by control blocks, pointers to activation records, etc. To use the paradigm effectively, it is certainly advisable to forget the implementation method. But for those who wish to understand it more fully before forgetting it, the following further explanation of X8 may be helpful.

Inside a user processor a scratch file is created by remote subordination

$$myfile::filesys \;//\; (\ldots myfile.left!v \ldots myfile.rewind \ldots myfile.right?x \ldots)$$

By definition of remote subordination this is equivalent to

$$(\underset{i \geq 0}{[\,]} \; filesys.i.acquire \rightarrow$$
$$filesys.i.left!v \ldots filesys.i.rewind \ldots filesys.i.right?x \ldots$$
$$filesys.i.release \rightarrow SKIP)$$

Thus all communications between *filesys* and its users begin with *filesys.i* ..., where *i* is the index of the particular instance of *SHBSCR* which has been acquired by a particular user on a particular occasion. Furthermore, each occasion of its use is surrounded by a matching pair of signals

$$(filesys.i.acquire \rightarrow \ldots filesys.i.release)$$

On the side of the subordinate process, each virtual scratchfile begins by acquiring its user, and continues according to the pattern specified in X6 and X7

$$(acquire \rightarrow \ldots left?x \ldots rewind \ldots right!v \ldots release \ldots)$$

All other communications of the virtual scratch file are with the subordinate
BSTORE process, and are concealed from the user. Each instance of the
virtual scratch file is indexed by a different index i, and then named by the
name *filesys*. So the externally visible behaviour of each instance is

$(filesys.i.acquire \rightarrow$
$\qquad filesys.i.left?x \ ... \ filesys.i.rewind \ ... \ filesys.i.right!v \ ...$
$filesys.i.release)$

This exactly matches the user's pattern of communication as described in the
previous paragraph. The matching pairs of *acquire* and *release* signals ensure
that no user can interfere with a scratch file that has been acquired by
another user.

We turn now to the communications within *FILESYS* between the
array of virtual scratch files and the backing store. These are concealed from
the user, and do not even have the name *filesys* attached to them. The
relevant events are

$i.back.j.left.v$	denotes communication of block v from the ith element of the array of scratch files to the jth sector of backing store
$i.back.j.right.v$	denotes a communication in the reverse direction.

Each sector of the backing store behaves like *COPY*. After indexing with a
sector number j and naming by *back*, the jth sector behaves like

$$\mu X.(back.j.left?x \rightarrow back.j.right!x \rightarrow X)$$

After multiple labelling by natural numbers it behaves like

$$\mu X.(\underset{i\geq0}{[]} \ i.back.j.left?x \rightarrow (\underset{k\geq0}{[]} \ k.back.j.right!x \rightarrow X))$$

This is now ready to communicate on any occasion with any element of the
array of virtual scratch files. Each individual scratch file observes the discipline of reading only from those sectors which the scratch file itself has
most recently written to.

In the above description the role of the natural numbers i and j is merely
to permit any scratch file to communicate with any sector on disc, and to
communicate safely with the user that has acquired it. The indices therefore
serve as a mathematical description of a kind of crossbar switch which is used
in a telephone exchange to allow any subscriber to communicate with any
other subscriber. A crude picture of this can be drawn as in Fig. 6.2.

If the number of sectors in the backing store is infinite, *FILESYS*
behaves exactly like a similarly constructed array of simple scratch files

$$\underset{i\geq0}{\|} \ i:(acquire \rightarrow (SCRATCH^{\wedge}(release \rightarrow STOP)))$$

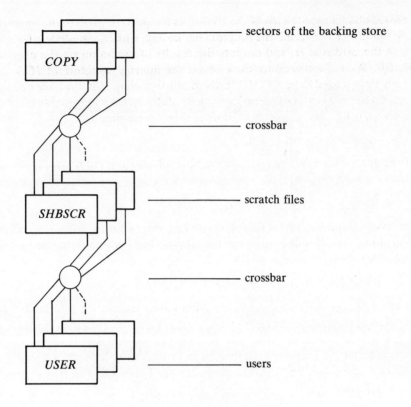

Figure 6.2

With a backing store of finite size, there is a danger of deadlock if the backing store gets full at a time when all users are still writing to their scratch files. In practice, this risk is usually reduced to insignificance by delaying acquisition of new files when the backing store is nearly full.

6.5 OPERATING SYSTEMS

The human users of a single large computer submit programs on decks of cards for execution. The data for each program immediately follows it. The task of a batch processing operating system is to share the resources of the computer efficiently among these jobs. For this we postulate that each user's program is executed by a process *JOB*, which inputs the cards of the program on channel *cr.right*, runs the program on the data which immediately follows it in the card reader, and outputs the results of execution on the channel *lp.left*. We do not need to know about the internal structure of *JOB*—in early days it used to be a FORTRAN monitor system. However, we need to rely on the fact that it will terminate successfully within a reasonable interval after starting. The alphabet of *JOB* is therefore defined

$$\alpha JOB = \{cr.right, \ lp.left, \ \surd\}$$

If *LPH* represents the hardware of the line printer and *CRH* represents the hardware of the card reader, a single job for a single user will be executed by

$$JOB1 = (cr{:}CRH \ /\!/ \ lp{:}LPH \ /\!/ \ JOB)$$

An operating system that runs just one job and then terminates is not much use. The simplest method of sharing a single computer among many users is to run their jobs serially, one after the other

$$BATCH0 = (cr{:}CRH \ /\!/ \ lp{:}LPH \ /\!/ \ [JOB)$$

But this design ignores some important administrative details, such as separation of files output by each job, and separation of card decks containing each job from the previous job, so that one job cannot read the cards containing its successor. To solve these problems we use the *LP* process defined in 6.2 X4, and a *CR* process defined below (X1)

$$
\begin{aligned}
JOBS \quad &= {}^{*}((cr.acquire{\rightarrow}lp.acquire{\rightarrow}JOB); \\
&\quad (cr.release{\rightarrow}lp.release{\rightarrow}SKIP)) \\
BATCH1 = \quad &(cr{:}CR \ /\!/ \ lp{:}LP \ /\!/ \ JOBS).
\end{aligned}
$$

BATCH1 is an abstract description of the simplest viable operating system, sharing a computer among many users whose jobs are executed one at a time in succession. The operating system expedites the transition between successive jobs, and protects each job from possible interference by its predecessors.

Examples

X1 A shared card reader
A special separator card is inserted at the front of each jobfile loaded into the card reader. The card reader is acquired to read all cards of a single jobfile and is then released. If the user attempts to read beyond a separator card, further copies of the separator card are supplied, without further input from the card reader. If the user fails to read up to the separator card, the left-over cards are flushed out. Superfluous separators are ignored. Input from the hardware is achieved by *h?x*.

The shared card reader needs to read one card ahead, so the value of the buffered card is used as an index

$$CR = h?x \rightarrow \textbf{if } x = separator \textbf{ then } CR \textbf{ else } (acquire \rightarrow CR_x)$$

where $CR_x = (right!x \rightarrow h?y \rightarrow$
$\qquad\qquad \textbf{if } y \neq separator \textbf{ then } CR_y$
$\qquad\qquad \textbf{else } \mu X.(right!separator \rightarrow X \mid release \rightarrow CR)$
$\qquad\quad \mid release \rightarrow$
$\qquad\qquad \mu X.(h?y \rightarrow \textbf{if } y = separator \textbf{ then } CR \textbf{ else } X))$

After ignoring an initial subsequence of separators, this process acquires its user and copies on its right channel the sequence of nonseparator cards which it reads from the hardware. On detecting a separator card, its value is replicated as necessary until the user releases the resource. But if the user releases the reader before the separator card is reached, the remaining cards of the deck up to the next separator card must be flushed out by reading and ignoring them.   □

The *BATCH1* operating system is logically complete. However, as the hardware of the central processor gets faster, it outstrips the capacity of readers and printers to supply input and transmit the output of the jobs. In order to establish a match between input, output, and processing speeds, it is necessary to use two or more readers and printers. Since only one job at a time is being processed, the extra readers should be occupied in reading ahead the card file for the following job or jobs, and the extra printers should be occupied in printing the output file for the previous job or jobs. Each input file must therefore be held temporarily in a scratch file during the period between actual input on a card reader and its consumption by *JOB*; and each output file must be similarly buffered during the period between production of the lines by *JOB* and its actual output on the line printer. This technique is known as *spooling*.

The overall structure of a spooled operating system is

$$OPSYS1 = insys:INSPOOL \ \| \ outsys:OUTSPOOL \ \| \ BATCH$$

Here *BATCH* is like *BATCH1*, except that it uses remote subordination to acquire any one of the waiting input files, and also to acquire an output file which is destined for subsequent printing

$$BATCH = {}^*(cr::insys \ \| \ lp::outsys \ \| \ JOB)$$

The spoolers are defined in the next two examples.

X2 Spooled output
A single virtual printer uses a temporary scratch file (6.4 X5) to store blocks that have been output by its using process. When the using process signals

release of the virtual printer, then an actual printer (6.4 X3) is acquired to output the content of the temporary file

$$VLP = (temp:SCRATCH \;//$$
$$\mu X.left?x{\rightarrow}temp.left!x{\rightarrow}X$$
$$| \; release{\rightarrow}temp.rewind{\rightarrow}$$
$$(actual::lp \;//$$
$$\mu Y.(temp.right?y{\rightarrow}actual.left!y{\rightarrow}Y$$
$$| \; temp.empty{\rightarrow}SKIP)))$$

The requisite unbounded array of virtual line printers is defined

$$VLPS = \underset{i \geq 0}{\|} \; i:(acquire{\rightarrow}VLP)$$

Since we want the actual line printers (6.4 X3) to be used only in spooling mode, we can declare them local to the spooling system using multiple labelling to share them among all elements of the array *VLPS* as in 6.4 X8

$$OUTSPOOL = (\mathbb{N}:(lp:LP2) \;//\; VLPS) \qquad\qquad \square$$

X3 Spooled input
Input spooling is very similar to output spooling, except that a real card reader is acquired first, and is released at the end of the input for a single job; a user process is then acquired to execute the job, and the contents of the cards are output to it

$$VCR = temp:SCRATCH \;//$$
$$(actual::cr \;//$$
$$(\mu X.actual.right?x{\rightarrow}\text{if } x=separator \text{ then } SKIP$$
$$\qquad\qquad\qquad \text{else } temp.left!x{\rightarrow}X));$$
$$(temp.rewind{\rightarrow}acquire{\rightarrow}$$
$$(\mu Y.(temp.right?x{\rightarrow}right!x{\rightarrow}Y$$
$$| \; temp.empty{\rightarrow}right!separator{\rightarrow}Y))^{\wedge}(release{\rightarrow}SKIP))$$

$$INSPOOL = (\mathbb{N}:cr:(0:CR \| 1:CR)) \;//\; (\underset{i \geq 0}{\|} \; i:VCR) \qquad \square$$

The input and output spoolers now supply an unbounded number of virtual card readers and virtual line printers for use of the *JOB* process. As a result, it is possible for two or more *JOB* processes to run concurrently, sharing these virtual resources. Since no communication is required between the jobs, simple interleaving is the appropriate sharing method. This technique is known as *multiprogramming*; or if more than one actual hardware processor is used, it is known as *multiprocessing*. However, the logical effects of multiprogramming and multiprocessing are the same. Indeed, the operating system defined below has the same logical specification as $OPSYS1$ defined above

$$OPSYS = insys:INSPOOL \ // \ outsys:OUTSPOOL \ // \ BATCH4$$

where $BATCH4 = (\underset{i<4}{\|||} \ BATCH)$

In mathematics, the change to multiprogramming has been remarkably simple: historically it caused much greater agony.

In the design of the VLP process within $OUTSPOOL$ (X2) the subordinate process $SCRATCH$ was used to store the lines produced by each JOB until they are output on an actual printer. In general the output files are too large to be held in the main store of a computer, and should be held on a backing store as illustrated in 6.4 X8. All the temporary files should share the same backing store, so we need to replace the subordinate process

$$temp:SCRATCH \ // \ ...$$

within VLP by a declaration of a remote subordinate process

$$temp::filesys \ // \ ...$$

and then declare the filing system (6.4 X8) as a subordinate process of the output spooler

$$(filesys:FILESYS \ // \ OUTSPOOL)$$

If the volume of card input is significant, a similar change must be made to $INSPOOL$. If a separate backing store is available for this purpose, the change is easy. If not, we will need to share a single backing store between the temporary files of both the input and the output spoolers. This means that $FILESYS$ must be declared as a subordinate process, shared by multiple labelling between both spoolers; and this involves a change in the structure of the system. We will do this redesign in a top-down fashion, trying to re-use as many of the previously defined modules as possible.

The operating system is composed from a batched multiprogramming system $BATCH4$, and an input-output system, serving as a subordinate process

$$OP = IOSYSTEM \ // \ BATCH4$$

The input-output system shares a filing system between an input spooler and an output spooler

$$IOSYSTEM = SH:(filesys:FILESYS)$$
$$// \ (lp:OUTSPOOL' \ \| \ cr:INSPOOL')$$

and $SH = \{lp.i | i \geq 0\} \cup \{cr.i | i \geq 0\}$

and *OUTSPOOL'* and *INSPOOL'* are the same as X2 and X3, except that

> *temp*:*SCRATCH*

is replaced by the equivalent remote subordination

> *temp*::*filesys*

In the design of the four operating systems described in this chapter (*BATCH*1, *OPSYS*1, *OPSYS*, and *OP*) we have emphasized above all else the virtue of modularity. This means that we have been able to re-use large parts of the earlier systems within the later systems. Even more important, every decision of detail is isolated within one or two modules of the system. Consequently, if a detail must be changed, it is very easy to identify which module must be altered, and the alteration can be confined to that single module. Among the easy changes are

> the number of line printers

> the number of card readers

> the number of concurrent batches

But not all changes will be so easy: a change to the value of the separator card will affect three modules, *CR* (X1), *INSPOOL* (X3) and *JOB*.

There are also a number of valuable improvements to the system which would require very significant changes in its structure

(1) The user jobs should also have access to the filing system, and to multiple virtual input and output devices.

(2) Users' files should be stored permanently between the jobs they submit.

(3) A method of checkpointing for rapid recovery from breakdown may be needed.

(4) If there is a backlog of jobs input but not yet executed, some method is needed to control the order in which waiting jobs are started. This point is taken up more fully in the next section.

One of the problems encountered in making these improvements is the impossibility of sharing resources between a subordinate and its main process, in those cases where the technique of multiple labelling is not appropriate. It seems that a new definition of subordination is required, in which the alphabet of the subordinate is not a subset of the alphabet of the main process. But this is a topic which is left for future research.

6.6   SCHEDULING

When a limited number of resources is shared among a greater number of potential users, there will always be the possibility that some aspiring users will have to wait to acquire a resource until some other process has released it. If at the time of release there are two or more processes waiting to acquire it, the choice of which waiting process will acquire the resource has been nondeterministic in all examples given so far. In itself, this is of little concern; but suppose, by the time a resource is released again, yet another process has joined the set of waiting processes. Since the choice between waiting processes is again nondeterministic, the newly joined process may be the lucky one chosen. If the resource is heavily loaded, this may happen again and again. As a result, some of the processes may happen to be delayed forever, or at least for a wholly unpredictable and unacceptable period of time. This is known as the problem of infinite overtaking (Section 2.5.5).

One solution to the problem is to ensure that all resources are lightly used. This may be achieved either by providing more resources, or by rationing their use, or by charging a heavy price for the services provided. In fact, these are the only solutions in the case of a resource which is consistently under heavy load. Unfortunately, even a resource which is on average lightly loaded will quite often be heavily used for long periods (rush hours or peaks). The problem can sometimes be mitigated by differential charging to try to smooth the demand, but this is not always successful or even possible. During the peaks, it is inevitable that, on the average, using processes will be subject to delay. It is important to ensure that these delays are reasonably consistent and predictable—you would much prefer to know that you will be served within the hour than to wonder whether you will have to wait one minute or one day.

The task of deciding how to allocate a resource among waiting users is known as *scheduling*. In order to schedule successfully, it is necessary to know which processes are currently waiting for allocation of the resource. For this reason, the acquisition of a resource cannot any longer be regarded as a single atomic event. It must be split into two events

> *please*, which requests the allocation
> *thankyou*, which accompanies the actual allocation of the resource.

For each process, the period between the *please* and the *thankyou* is the period during which the process has to wait for the resource. In order to identify the requesting process, we will index each occurrence of *please*, *thankyou* and *release* by a different natural number. The requesting process acquires its number on each occasion by the same construction as remote subordination (6.4 X3)

$$\underset{i\geq0}{[]} (res.i.please; \; res.i.thankyou; \; ...; \; res.i.release \rightarrow SKIP)$$

A simple and effective method of scheduling a resource is to allocate it to the process which has been waiting longest for it. This policy is known as *first come first served* (FCFS) or *first in first out* (FIFO). It is the queuing discipline observed by passengers who form themselves into a line at a bus stop.

In a place such as a bakery, where customers are unable or unwilling to form a line, there is an alternative mechanism to achieve the same effect. A machine is installed which issues tickets with strictly ascending serial numbers. On entry to the bakery, a customer takes a ticket. When a server is ready, he calls out the lowest ticket number of a customer who has taken a ticket but not yet been served. This is known as the bakery algorithm, and is described more formally below. We assume that up to R customers can be served simultaneously.

Example

X1 The bakery algorithm
We need to keep the following counts

> p customers who have said *please*
> t customers who have said *thankyou*
> r customers who have released their resources.

Clearly, at all times $r \leq t \leq p$. Also, at all times, p is the number that will be given to the next customer who enters the bakery, and t is the number of the next customer to be served; futhermore, $p-t$ is the number of waiting customers, and $R+r-t$ is the number of waiting servers. All counts are initially zero, and can revert to zero again whenever they are all equal—say at night after the last customer has left.

One of the main tasks of the algorithm is to ensure that there is never simultaneously a free resource and a waiting customer; whenever such a situation arises, the very next event must be the *thankyou* of a customer obtaining the resource

$$BAKERY = B_{0,0,0}$$
$$B_{p,t,r} = \textbf{if } 0<r=t=p \textbf{ then } BAKERY$$
$$\textbf{else if } R+r-t>0 \wedge p-t>0$$
$$\textbf{then } t.thankyou \rightarrow B_{p,t+1,r}$$
$$\textbf{else } (p.please \rightarrow B_{p+1,t,r}$$
$$| \, (\underset{i<t}{[]} \; i.release \rightarrow B_{p,t,r+1}))$$

The bakery algorithm is due to Leslie Lamport. ◻

7 DISCUSSION

7.1 INTRODUCTION

The main objective of my research into communicating processes has been to find the simplest possible mathematical theory with the following desirable properties

(1) It should describe a wide range of interesting computer applications, from vending machines, through process control and discrete event simulation, to shared-resource operating systems.

(2) It should be capable of efficient implementation on a variety of conventional and novel computer architectures, from time-sharing computers through multiprocessors to networks of communicating microprocessors.

(3) It should provide clear assistance to the programmer in his tasks of specification, design, implementation, verification and validation of complex computer systems.

It is not possible to claim that all these objectives have been achieved in an optimal fashion. There is always hope that a radically different approach, or some significant change to the detailed definitions, would lead to greater success in one or more of the objectives listed above. This chapter initiates a discussion of some of the alternatives which I and others have explored, and an explanation of why I have not adopted them. It also gives me an opportunity to acknowledge the influence of the original research of other workers in the field. Finally, I hope to encourage further research both into the foundations of the subject and into its wider practical application.

7.2 SHARED STORAGE

The earliest proposals in the 1960s for the programming of concurrent operations within a single computer arose naturally from contemporaneous developments in computer architecture and operating systems. At that time processing power was scarce and expensive, and it was considered very wasteful that a processor should have to wait while communicating with slow peripheral equipment, or even slower human beings. Consequently, cheaper special-purpose processors (channels) were provided to engage independently in input–output, thereby freeing the central processor to engage in other tasks. To keep the valuable central processor busy, a timesharing operating system would ensure that there were several complete programs in the main store of the computer; and at any time several of the programs could be using the input–output processors, while another program used the central processor. At the termination of an input–output operation, an interrupt would enable the operating system to reconsider which program should be receiving the attention of the central processor.

The scheme described above suggests that the central processor and all the channels should be connected to all the main storage of the computer; and accesses from each processor to each word of store were interleaved with those from the other processors. Nevertheless, each program under execution was usually a complete job submitted by a different user, and wholly independent of all the other jobs.

For this reason, great care was expended in the design of hardware and software to divide the store into disjoint segments, one for each program, and to ensure that no program could interfere with the store of another. When it became possible to attach several independent central processors to the same computer, the effect was to increase the throughput of jobs; and if the original operating system were well structured this could be achieved with little effect on the code of the operating system, and even less on the programs for the jobs which it executed.

The disadvantages of sharing a computer among several distinct jobs were

(1)   The amount of storage required goes up linearly with the number of jobs executed.

(2)   The amount of time that each user has to wait for the result of his job is also increased, except for the highest priority jobs.

It therefore seems tempting to allow a single job to take advantage of the parallelism provided by the hardware of the computer, by initiating several concurrent processes within the same area of storage allocated to a single program.

7.2.1 Multithreading

The first proposal of this kind was based on a jump (**go to** command). If L is a label of some place in the program, the command

fork L

transfers control to the label L, and *also* allows control to pass to the next command in sequence. From then on, the effect is that two processors execute the same program at the same time; each maintains its own locus of control threading its way through the commands. Since each locus of control can fork again, this programming technique is known as *multithreading*.

Having provided a method for a process to split in two, some method is also required for two processes to merge into one. A very simple proposal is to provide a command

join

which can be executed only when *two* processes execute it simultaneously. The first process to reach the command must wait until another one also reaches it. Then only one process goes ahead to execute the following command.

In its full generality, multithreading is an incredibly complex and error-prone technique, not to be recommended in any but the smallest programs. In excuse, we may plead that it was invented before the days of structured programming, when even FORTRAN was still considered to be a high-level programming language!

A variation of the fork command is still used in the UNIX™ operating system. The fork does not mention a label. Its effect is to take a completely fresh copy of the whole of storage allocated to the program, and to allocate the copy to a new process. Both the original and the new process resume execution at the command following the fork. A facility is provided for each process to discover whether it is the *parent* or the *offspring*. The allocation of disjoint storage areas to the processes removes the main difficulties and dangers of multithreading, but it can be inefficient both in time and in space. This means that concurrency can be afforded only at the outermost (most global) level of a job, and its use on a small scale is discouraged.

7.2.2 cobegin ... coend

A solution to the problems of multithreading was proposed by E. W. Dijkstra: make sure that after a fork the two processors execute completely different blocks of program, with no possibility of jumping between them. If

CSP–O

P and Q are such blocks, the compound command

    cobegin P; Q **coend**

causes P and Q to start simultaneously, and proceed concurrently until they have both ended. After that, only a single processor goes on to execute the following commands. This structured command can be implemented by the unstructured fork and join commands, using labels L and J

    fork L; P; **go to** J; L:Q; J:**join**

The generalization to more than two component processes is immediate and obvious

    cobegin P; Q; ... ; R **coend**

    One great advantage of this structured notation is that it is much easier to understand what is likely to happen, especially if the variables used in each of the blocks are distinct from the variables used in the other (a restriction that can be checked or enforced by a compiler for a high-level language). In this case, the processes are said to be *disjoint*, and (in the absence of communication) the concurrent execution of P and Q has exactly the same effect as their sequential execution in either order

    begin P; Q **end** = **begin** Q; P **end** = **cobegin** P; Q **coend**

Furthermore, the proof methods for establishing correctness of the parallel composition can be even simpler than the sequential case. That is why Dijkstra's proposal forms the basis for the parallel construct in this book. The main change is notational; to avoid confusion with sequential composition, I have introduced the $\|$ operator to separate the processes; and this permits the use of simple brackets to surround the command instead of the more cumbersome **cobegin** ... **coend**.

7.2.3 Conditional critical regions

The restriction that concurrent processes should not share variables has the consequence that they cannot communicate or interact with each other in any way, a restriction which seriously reduces the potential value of concurrency.

    After reading this book, the introduction of (simulated) input and output channels may seem the obvious solution; but in earlier days, an obvious technique (suggested by the hardware of the computers) was to communicate by sharing main storage among concurrent processes. Dijkstra showed how this could be safely achieved by critical regions (Section 6.3) protected by mutual exclusion semaphores. I later proposed that this method should be formalized in the notations of a high-level programming language. A group of variables which is to be updated in critical regions within several sharing processes should be declared as a shared resource, for example

shared *n* : *integer*;
shared *position* : **record** *x*, *y* : *real* **end**

Each critical region which updates this variable is preceded by a **with** clause, quoting the variable name

with *n* **do** *n* := *n*+1;
with *position* **do begin** *x* := *x*+*deltax*; *y* := *y*+*deltay* **end**

The advantage of this notation is that a compiler automatically introduces the necessary semaphores, and surrounds each critical region by the necessary *P* and *V* operations. Furthermore, it can check at compile time that no shared variable is ever accessed or updated except from within a critical region protected by the relevant semaphore.

Cooperation between processes which share store sometimes requires another form of synchronization. For example, suppose one process updates a variable with the objective that other processes should read the new value. The other processes must not read the variable until the updating has taken place. Similarly, the first process must not update the variable again until all the other processes have read the earlier updating.

To solve this problem, a convenient facility is offered by the conditional critical region. This takes the form

with *sharedvar* **when** *condition* **do** *critical region*

On entry to the critical region, the value of the condition is tested. If it is true, the critical region is executed normally. But if the condition is false, this entry into the critical region is postponed, so that other processes are permitted to enter their critical regions and update the shared variable. On completion of each such update, the condition is retested. If it has become true, the delayed process is permitted to proceed with its critical region; otherwise that process is suspended again. If more than one delayed process can proceed, the choice between them is arbitrary.

To solve the problem of updating and reading a message by many processes, declare as part of the resource an integer variable to count the number of processes that must read the message before it is updated again

shared *message* : **record** *count* : *integer* ; *content* : ... **end**;
message.count:=0;

The updating process contains a critical region

> **with** *message* **when** *count*=0 **do**
>   **begin** *content*: = ... ;
>   ... ;
>   *count* : = *number of readers*
> **end**

Each reading process contains a critical region

> **with** *message* **when** *count*>0 **do**
>   **begin** *my copy* : = *content*; *count* : = *count*−1 **end**

Conditional critical regions may be implemented by means of semaphores. Compared with direct use of synchronization semaphores by the programmer, the overhead of conditional critical regions may be quite high, since the conditions of all processes waiting to enter the region must be retested on every exit from the region. Fortunately, the conditions do not have to be retested more frequently than that, because restrictions on access to shared variables ensure that the condition tested by a waiting process can change value only when the shared variable itself changes value. All other variables in the condition must be private to the waiting process, which obviously cannot change them while it is waiting.

7.2.4 Monitors

The development of monitors was inspired by the **class** of SIMULA 67, which was itself a generalization of the procedure concept of ALGOL 60. The basic insight is that all meaningful operations on data (including its initialization and also perhaps its finalization) should be collected together with the declaration of the structure and type of the data itself; and these operations should be invoked by procedure calls whenever required by the processes which share the data. The important characteristic of a monitor is that only one of its procedure bodies can be active at one time; even when two processes call a procedure simultaneously (either the same procedure or two different ones), one of the calls is delayed until the other is completed. Thus the procedure bodies act like critical regions protected by the same semaphore.

For example a very simple monitor acts like a count variable. In notations based on PASCAL PLUS it takes the form

```
1   monitor count;
2   var n : integer;
3   procedure *up; begin n:=n+1 end;
4   procedure *down; when n>0 do begin n:=n−1 end;
5   function *grounded: Boolean; begin grounded := (n=0) end;
```

```
6  begin n:=0;
7    •••;
8    if n≠0 then print(n)
9  end
```

Line 1   declares the monitor and gives it the name *count*.
2   declares the shared variable n local to the monitor.
It is inaccessible except within the monitor itself.
3⎫ ⎧declare three procedures with their bodies.
4⎬ ⎨The asterisks ensure they can be called from the
5⎭ ⎩program which uses the monitor.
6   The monitor starts execution here.
7   The three fat dots are an *inner* statement, which stands
for the block that is going to use this monitor.
8   The final value of n (if non-zero) is printed on exit
from the user block.

A new instance of this monitor can be declared local to a block P

instance *rocket:count*; P

Within the block P, the starred procedures may be called by commands

rocket.up; ... *rocket.down*; ... ; **if** *rocket.grounded* **then** ...

However an unstarred procedure or variable such as n cannot be accessed
from within P and observance of this restriction is enforced by a compiler.
The mutual exclusion inherent in the monitor ensures that the procedure of
the monitor can be safely called by any number of processes within P, and
there is no danger of interference in updating n. Note that an attempt to call
rocket.down when $n=0$ will be delayed until some other process within P
calls *rocket.up*. This ensures that the value of n can never go negative.

The effect of the declaration of an instance of a monitor is explained by
a variation of the copy rule for procedure calls in ALGOL 60. Firstly, a copy
is taken of the text of the monitor; the using block P is copied in place of the
three dots inside the monitor, and all local names of the monitor are prefixed
by the name of the instance, as shown below

> *rocket.n* : *integer*;
> **procedure** *rocket.up*; **begin** *rocket.n*:=*rocket.n*+1 **end**;
> **procedure** *rocket.down*;
>   **when** *rocket.n*>0 **do begin** *rocket.n*:=*rocket.n*−1 **end**;
> **function** *rocket.grounded:Boolean*;
>   **begin** *rocket.grounded*:=(*rocket.n*=0) **end**
> **begin** *rocket.n*:=0;
> P;
>   **if** *rocket.n*≠0 **then** *print*(*rocket.n*)
> **end**

Note how the copy rule has made it impossible for the user process to forget to initialize the value of *n*, or to forget to print its final value when necessary.

The inefficiency of repeated testing of entry conditions has led to the design of monitors with a more elaborate scheme of explicit waiting and explicit signalling for resumption of waiting processes. These schemes even allow a procedure call to suspend itself in the middle of its execution, after automatically releasing exclusion so that some later call of a procedure by another process can signal resumption of the suspended process. In this way, a number of ingenious scheduling techniques can be efficiently implemented; but I now think that the extra complexity is hardly worthwhile.

7.2.5   Nested monitors

A monitor instance can be used like a semaphore to protect a single resource such as a line printer which must not be used by more than one process at a time. Such a monitor could be declared

> **monitor** *singleresource*;
> **var** *free*:*Boolean*;
> **procedure** **acquire*; **when** *free* **do** *free*:=*false*;
> **procedure** **release*; **begin** *free*:=*true* **end**;
> **begin** *free*:=*true*; ··· **end**

However, the protection afforded by this monitor can be evaded by a process which uses the resource without acquiring it, or frustrated by one which forgets to release it afterwards. Both of these dangers can be averted by a construction similar to that of the virtual resource (6.4 X4). This takes the form of a monitor declared locally within the actual resource monitor shown above. The name of the virtual resource is starred to make it accessible for declaration by user processes. However, the stars are removed from **acquire* and **release*, so that these can be used only within the virtual resource monitor, and cannot be misused by other processes.

> **monitor** *singleresource*;
>   *free*: *Boolean*;
>   **procedure** *acquire*;
>   **when** *free* **do** *free*:=*false*;
>   **procedure** *release*;
>   **begin** *free*:=*true*; **end**
>   **monitor** **virtual*;
>   **procedure** **use*(*l*: *line*); **begin** ... **end**;
>   **begin** *acquire*; ··· ; *release* **end**
>   **begin** *free*:=*true*; ··· ; **end**

An instance of this monitor is declared

instance *lpsystem: singleresource*; *P*

A block within *P* which requires to output a file to a line printer is written

instance *mine: lpsystem.virtual*;
    begin ... *mine.use(l1)*; ... *mine.use(l2)*; ... **end**

The necessary acquisition and release of the line printer are automatically inserted by the virtual monitor before and after this user block, in a manner which prevents antisocial use of the line printer. In principle, it would be possible for the using block to split into parallel processes, all of which use the instance *mine* of the virtual monitor, but this is probably not the intention here. A monitor which is to be used only by a single process is known in PASCAL PLUS as an *envelope*, and it can be implemented more efficiently without exclusion or synchronization; and the compiler checks that it is not inadvertently shared.

    The meaning of these instance declarations can be calculated by repeated application of the copy rule, with the result shown below

```
var lpsystem.free: Boolean;
procedure lpsystem.acquire;
    when lpsystem.free do lpsystem.free:=false;
procedure lpsystem.release; begin lpsystem.free:=true end;
begin lpsystem.free:=true
    ⋮
  begin
  procedure mine.lpsystem.use (l: line); begin ... end;
    lpsystem.acquire;
    ... mine.lpsystem.use(l1);
    ... mine.lpsystem.use(l2);
    lpsystem.release;
  end;
    ⋮
end
```

The explicit copying shown here is only for initial explanation; a more experienced programmer would never wish to see the expanded version, or even think about it.

    These notations were used in 1975 for the description of an operating system similar to that of Section 6.5; and they were later implemented in PASCAL PLUS. Extremely ingenious effects can be obtained by a mixture of starring and nesting; but the PASCAL- and SIMULA-based notations seem rather clumsy, and explanations in terms of substitution and renaming are rather difficult to follow. It was Edsger W. Dijkstra's criticisms of these aspects that first impelled me towards the design of communicating sequential processes.

However, it is now clear from the constructions of Section 6.5 that the control of sharing requires complication, whether it is expressed within the conceptual framework of communicating processes or within the copy-rule and procedure-call semantics of PASCAL PLUS. The choice between the languages seems partly a matter of taste, or perhaps efficiency. For implementation of an operating system on a computer with shared main storage, PASCAL PLUS probably has the advantage.

7.2.6   Ada™

Facilities offered for concurrent programming in Ada are an amalgam of the remote procedure call of PASCAL PLUS, with the less structured form of communication by input and output. Processes are called tasks, and they communicate by *call* statements (which are like procedure calls with output and input parameters), and *accept* statements (which are like procedure declarations in their syntactic form and in their effect). A typical accept statement might be

> **accept** *put*(V: **in** *integer*; *PREV*: **out** *integer*) **do**
> $PREV$:$=K$; K:$=V$ **end**

A corresponding call might be

> *put*(37, X)

The identifier *put* is known as an *entry* name.

An accept and a call statement with the same name in different tasks are executed when both processes are ready to execute them together. The effect is as follows

(1)   Input parameters are copied from the call to the accepting process.
(2)   The body of the accept statement is executed.
(3)   The values of the output parameters are copied back to the call.
(4)   Then both tasks continue execution at their next statements.

The execution of the body of an accept is known as a *rendezvous*, since the calling and accepting task may be thought to be executing it together. The rendezvous is an attractive feature of Ada, since it simplifies the very common practice of alternating output and input, without much complicating the case when only input or only output is required.

The Ada analogue of [] is the select statement which takes the form

select
    accept *get* (*v*:**out** *integer*) **do** *v*: = *B*[*i*] **end**; *i*: = *i* + 1; ...
    or accept *put* (*v*:**in** *integer*) **do** *B*[*j*]: = *v* **end**; *j*: = *j* + 1; ...
    or ...
end select

Exactly one of the alternatives separated by **or** will be selected for execution, depending on the choice made by the calling task(s). The remaining statements of the selected alternative after the **end** of the **accept** are executed on completion of the rendezvous, concurrently with continuation of the calling task. Selection of an alternative can be inhibited by falsity of a preceding **when** condition, for example

    when not *full* ⇒ **accept** ...

This achieves the effect of a conditional critical region.

One of the alternatives in a select statement may begin with a **delay** instead of an **accept**. This alternative may be selected if no other alternative is selected during elapse of a period greater than the specified number of seconds' delay. The purpose of this is to guard against the danger that hardware or software error might cause the select statement to wait forever. Since our mathematical model deliberately abstracts from time, a delay cannot be faithfully represented, except by allowing wholly nondeterministic selection of the alternative beginning with the delay.

One of the alternatives in a select statement may be the statement **terminate**. This alternative is selected when all tasks which might call the given task have terminated; and then the given task terminates too. This is not as convenient as the inner statement of PASCAL PLUS, which allows the monitor to tidy up on termination.

A select statement may have an **else** clause, which is selected if none of the other alternatives can be selected immediately, either because all the **when** conditions are false, or because there is no corresponding call already waiting in some other task. This would seem to be equivalent to an alternative with zero delay.

A call statement may also be protected against arbitrary delay by a **delay** statement or an **else** clause. This may lead to some inefficiencies in implementation on a distributed network of processors.

Tasks in Ada are declared in much the same way as subordinate processes (Section 4.5); but like monitors in PASCAL PLUS, each one may serve any number of calling processes. Furthermore, the programmer must arrange for the task to terminate properly. The definition of a task is split into two parts, its specification and its body. The specification gives the task name and the names and parameter types of all entries through which the task may be called. This is the information required by the writer of the program which uses the task, and by the compiler of that program. The body of the task defines its behaviour, and may be compiled separately from the using program.

Each task in Ada may be given a fixed *priority*. If several tasks are capable of making progress, but only a lesser number of processors are available, the tasks with lower priority will be neglected. The priority of execution of a rendezvous is the higher of the priorities of the calling and of the accepting tasks. The indication of priority is called a *pragma*; it is intended to improve critical response times compared with non-critical ones, and it is not intended to affect the logical behaviour of the program. This is an excellent idea, since it separates concern for abstract logical correctness from problems of real time response, which can often be more easily solved by experiment or by judicious selection of hardware.

Ada offers a number of additional facilities. It is possible to test how many calls are waiting on an entry. One task may abruptly terminate (*abort*) another task, and all tasks dependent upon it. Tasks may access and update shared variables. The effect of this is made even more unpredictable by the fact that compilers are allowed to delay, reorder, or amalgamate such updating just as if the variable were not shared. There are some additional complexities and interaction effects with other features which I have not mentioned.

Apart from the complexities listed in the preceding paragraph, tasking in Ada seems to be quite well designed for implementation and use on a multiprocessor with shared storage.

7.3   COMMUNICATION

The exploration of the possibility of structuring a program as a network of communicating processes was also motivated by spectacular progress in the development of computer hardware. The advent of the microprocessor rapidly reduced the cost of processing power by several orders of magnitude. However, the power of each individual microprocessor was still rather less than that of a typical computer of the traditional and still expensive kind. So it would seem to be most economical to obtain greater power by use of several microprocessors cooperating on a single task. These microprocessors would be cheaply connected by wires, along which they could communicate with each other. Each microprocessor would have its own local main store, which it could access at high speed, thus avoiding the expensive bottleneck that tends to result from allowing only one processor at a time to access a shared store.

7.3.1 Pipes

The simplest pattern of communication between processing elements is just single-directional message passing between each process and its neighbour in a linear pipe, as described in Section 4.4. The idea was first propounded by Conway who illustrated it by examples similar to 4.4 X2 and X3, except that all components of a pipe were expected to terminate successfully instead of running forever. He proposed that the pipe structure should be used for writing a multiple-pass compiler for a programming language. On a computer with adequate main storage, all the passes are simultaneously active, and control transfers between the passes together with the messages, thus simulating parallel execution. On a computer with less main storage, only one pass at a time is active, and sends its output to a file in backing store. On completion of each pass, the next pass starts, taking its input from the file produced by its predecessor. However, the final result of the compiler is exactly the same, in spite of the radical differences in the manner of execution. It is characteristic of a successful abstraction in programming that it permits several different implementation methods which are efficient in differing circumstances. In this case, Conway's suggestion could have been very valuable for software implementation on a computer range offering widely varying options of store size.

The pipe is also the standard method of communication in the UNIX™ operating system, where the notation '|' is used instead of '≫'.

7.3.2 Multiple buffered channels

The pipe construction allows a linear chain of processes to communicate in a single direction only, and it does not matter whether the message sequence is buffered or not. The natural generalization of the pipe is to permit any process to communicate with any other process in either direction; and at first sight it seems equally natural to provide buffering on all the communication channels. In the design of the RC4000 operating system, a facility for buffered communication was implemented in the kernel; and was used for communication between modules providing services at a higher level. On a grander scale, a store-and-forward packet switching network, like ARPAnet in the United States, inevitably interposes buffering between the source and destination of messages.

When the pattern of communication between processes is generalized from a linear chain to a network that may be cyclic, the presence or absence of buffering can make a vital difference to the logical behaviour of the system. The presence of buffering is not always favourable: for example, it is possible to write a program that can deadlock if the length of the buffer is allowed to grow greater than five, as well as a different program that will deadlock unless the buffer length is allowed to exceed five. To avoid such irregularities, the length of all buffers should be unbounded. Unfortunately this leads to grave problems of implementation efficiency when main storage is filled with buffered messages. The mathematical treatment is also complicated by the fact that every network is an infinite-state machine, even when the component processes are finite. Finally, for rapid and controllable interaction between humans and computers, buffers only stand in the way, since they can interpose delay between a stimulus and a response. If something goes wrong in processing a buffered stimulus, it is much more difficult to trace the fault and recover from it. Buffering is a batch-processing technique, and should be avoided wherever fast interactions are more important than heavy processor utilization.

7.3.3 Functional multiprocessing

A deterministic process may be defined in terms of a mathematical function from its input channels to its output channels. Each channel is identified with the indefinitely extensible sequence of messages which pass along it. Such functions are defined in the usual way by recursion on the structure of the input sequences, except that the case of an empty input sequence is not considered. For example, a process which outputs the result of multiplying each number input by n is defined

$$prod_n(left) = \langle n \times left_0 \rangle ^\wedge prod_n(left')$$

A function which takes two sorted streams (without duplicates) as parameters and outputs their sorted merge (suppressing duplicates) is defined

$merge2(left1, left2) =$
    if $left1_0 < left2_0$ **then** $\langle left1_0 \rangle ^\wedge merge2(left1', left2)$
    else if $left2_0 < left1_0$ **then** $\langle left2_0 \rangle ^\wedge merge2(left1, left2')$
                else $\langle left2_0 \rangle ^\wedge merge2(left1', left2')$

An acyclic network can be represented by a composition of such functions. For example, a function which merges three sorted input streams can be defined

$$merge3(left1, left2, left3) = merge2(left1, merge2(left2, left3))$$

Figure 7.1 shows a connection diagram of this function.

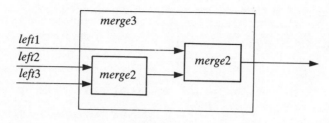

Figure 7.1

A cyclic network can be constructed by a set of mutually recursive equations. For example, consider the problem attributed by Dijkstra to Hamming, namely to define a function which outputs in ascending sequence all numbers which have only 2, 3, and 5 as non-trivial factors. The first such number is 1; and if x is any such number, so are $2 \times x$, $3 \times x$, and $5 \times x$. We therefore use three processes $prod_2$, $prod_3$, and $prod_5$ to generate these products, and feed them back into the process $merge3$, which ensures they are eventually output in ascending order (Fig. 7.2).

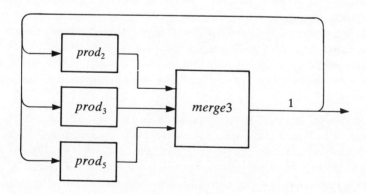

Figure 7.2

The function which outputs the desired result has no inputs; it is simply defined

$Hamming =$
$\quad \langle 1 \rangle ^\wedge merge3(prod_2(Hamming), prod_3(Hamming), prod_5(Hamming))$

The functional approach to multiprocessor networks is very different from that taken in this book in the following respects

(1)   A general implementation requires unbounded buffering on all channels.

(2)   Each value output into the buffer must be retained in the buffer until all the inputting processes have taken it, which they may do at different times.

(3)   There is no possibility for a process to wait for one of two inputs, whichever one arrives first.

(4)   The processes are all deterministic.

Recent research has been directed towards reducing the inefficiency of (1) and (2), and towards relaxing the restrictions (3) and (4).

7.3.4   Unbuffered communication

For many years now, I have chosen to take unbuffered (synchronized) communication as basic. My reasons have been

(1)   It matches closely a physical realization on wires which connect processing agents. Such wires cannot store messages.

(2)   It matches closely the effect of calling and returning from subroutines within a single processor, copying the values of the parameters and the results.

(3)   When buffering is wanted, it can be implemented simply as a process; and the degree of buffering can be precisely controlled by the programmer.

(4)   Other disadvantages of buffers have been mentioned at the end of Section 7.3.2.

Of course, none of these arguments carry absolute conviction. For example, if buffered communication were taken as primitive, this would make no logical difference in the common case of alternation of subroutine call and return; and synchronization can be achieved in all other cases by following every output by input of an acknowledgement, and every input by output of an acknowledgement.

7.3.5   Communicating sequential processes

This was the title of my first complete exposition of a programming language based on concurrency and communication. That early proposal differs from this book in two significant respects.

(1)   Parallel composition

Channels are not named. Instead, the component processes of a parallel construction have unique names, prefixed to them by a pair of colons

$$[a::P \parallel b::Q \parallel ... \parallel c::R]$$

Within process P, the command $b!v$ outputs the value v to the process named b. This value is input by a command $a?x$ occurring within the process Q. The process names are local to the parallel command in which they are introduced, and communications between the component processes are hidden.

The advantage of this scheme is that there is no need to introduce into the language any concept of channel or channel declaration. Furthermore, it is logically impossible to violate the restriction that a channel is between two processes only, and one of them uses it for input and the other for output. But there are some disadvantages, both in practice and in theory.

(1)   A serious practical disadvantage is that a subordinate process needs to know the name of its using process; this complicates construction of libraries of subordinate processes.

(2)   A disadvantage in the underlying mathematics is that parallel composition is an operation with a variable number of parameters and cannot be reduced to a binary associative operator like $\parallel$.

(2)   Automatic termination

In the early version, all processes of a parallel command were expected to terminate. The reason for this was the hope that the correctness of a process could be specified in the same way as for a conventional program by a *post-condition*, i.e., a predicate intended to be true on successful termination. (That hope was never fulfilled, and other proof methods (Section 1.10) now seem more satisfactory). The obligation that a subordinate process should terminate imposes an awkward obligation on the using process to signal its termination to all subordinates. An *ad hoc* convention was therefore introduced. A loop of the form

$$*[a?x{\rightarrow}P \; [] \; b?x{\rightarrow}Q \; [] \; ... \;]$$

terminates automatically on termination of all the processes $a, b, ...$ from which input is requested. This enables the subordinate process to complete any necessary finalization code before termination—a feature which had proved useful in SIMULA and PASCAL PLUS.

The trouble with this convention is that it is complicated to define and implement; and methods of proving program correctness seem no simpler with it than without. Now it seems to me better (as in Section 4.5) to relax the restriction that simple subordinate processes must terminate; and take other measures (Section 6.4) in the more complicated cases.

7.3.6   Occam

In contrast to Ada, occam is a very simple programming language, and very closely follows the principles expounded in this book. The most immediately striking differences are notational; occam syntax is designed to be composed at a screen with the aid of a syntax checking editor; it uses prefix operators instead of infix, and it uses indentation instead of brackets.

$$
\begin{array}{ll}
SEQ & \text{for } (P;\ Q;\ R) \\
\quad P & \\
\quad Q & \\
\quad R & \\
\end{array}
$$

$$
\begin{array}{ll}
PAR & \text{for } (P \parallel Q \parallel R) \\
\quad P & \\
\quad Q & \\
\quad R & \\
\end{array}
$$

$$
\begin{array}{ll}
ALT & \text{for } (c?x \rightarrow P\ [\,]\ d?y \rightarrow Q) \\
\quad c?x & \\
\qquad P & \\
\quad d?y & \\
\qquad Q & \\
\end{array}
$$

$$
\begin{array}{ll}
IF & \text{for } (P \triangleleft B \triangleright Q) \\
\quad B & \\
\qquad P & \\
\quad NOT\ B & \\
\qquad Q & \\
\end{array}
$$

$$
\begin{array}{ll}
WHILE\ B & \text{for } (B*P) \\
\quad P & \\
\end{array}
$$

The *ALT* construct corresponds to the Ada select statement, and offers a similar range of options. Selection of an alternative may be inhibited by falsity of a Boolean condition *B*

$$
\begin{array}{l}
B\ \&\ c?x \\
\quad P \\
\end{array}
$$

The input may be replaced by a *SKIP,* in which case the alternative may be selected whenever the Boolean guard is true; or it may be replaced by a wait, which allows the alternative to be selected after elapse of a specified interval.

The occam language does not have any distinct notations for pipes (Section 4.4), subordinate processes (Section 4.5), or shared processes (Section 6.4). All the required patterns of communication must be achieved by explicit identity of channel names. To help in this, procedures may be declared with channels as parameters. For example, the simple copying process may be declared

```
PROC copy(CHAN left, right)=
   WHILE TRUE
      VAR x:
         SEQ
            left?x
            right!x:
```

The double buffer *COPY*≫*COPY* can now be constructed

```
CHAN mid:
   PAR
      copy(left, mid)
      copy(mid, right)
```

A chain of n buffers may be constructed using an array of n channels and an iterative form of the parallel construct, which constructs $n-1$ processes, one for each value of i between 0 and $n-2$ inclusive

```
CHAN mid[n-1]:
   PAR
      copy(left, mid[0])
      PAR i=[0 FOR n-2]
         copy(mid[i], mid[i+1])
      copy(mid[n-2], right)
```

Because occam is intended to be implemented with static storage allocation on a fixed number of processors, the value n in the above example must be a constant. For the same reason, recursive procedures are not allowed.

A similar construction may be used to achieve the effect of subordinate processes, for example

```
PROC double(left, right)=
  WHILE TRUE
    VAR x:
      SEQ
        left?x
        right!(x+x):
```

This may be declared subordinate to a single using process *P*

```
CHAN doub.left, doub.right:
  PAR
    double(doub.left, doub.right)
    P
```

Inside *P* a number is doubled by

```
doub.left!4; doub.right?y; ...
```

Processes may be shared using arrays of channels (with one element per using process) and an iterative form of the *ALT* construction. For example, take an integrator, which after each new input outputs the sum of all numbers it has input so far

```
CHAN add, integral[n−1]:
  PAR
    VAR sum, x:
      SEQ
        sum:=0
        ALT i=[0 FOR n]
          add[i]?x
            SEQ
              sum:=sum+x
              integral[i]! sum
    PAR i=[0 FOR n]
      ... user processes ...
```

Like Ada, occam allows a programmer to assign relative priorities to processes combined in parallel. This is done by using *PRI PAR* instead of *PAR*; and the earlier processes in the list have higher priority. The screen-editing facilities provided with the language facilitate reordering of processes when necessary. A similar option is offered for the *ALT* construction, namely *PRI ALT*. This ensures that if more than one alternative is ready for immediate selection, the textually earliest will be chosen—otherwise the effect is the same as the simple *ALT*. Of course, the programmer is urged to ensure that his programs are logically correct, independent of the assignment of priorities.

There are also facilities for distributing processes among distinct processors, and for specifying which physical pins on each processor are to be used for each relevant channel of the occam program, and which pin is to be used for loading the code of the program itself.

7.4   MATHEMATICAL MODELS

Recognition of the idea that a programming language should have a precise mathematical meaning or semantics dates from the early 1960s. The mathematics provides a secure, unambiguous, precise and stable specification of the language to serve as an agreed interface between its users and its implementors. Furthermore, it gives the only reliable grounds for a claim that different implementations are implementations of the same language. So mathematical semantics are as essential to the objective of language standardization as measurement and counting are to the standardization of nuts and bolts.

In the later 1960s an even more important role for mathematical semantics was recognized, that of assisting a programmer to discharge his obligation of establishing correctness of his program. Indeed R. W. Floyd suggested that the semantics be conveniently formulated as a set of valid proof rules, rather than as an explicit mathematical model. This suggestion has been adopted in the specification of PASCAL and Euclid and Gypsy.

The early design of Communicating Sequential Processes (Section 7.3.5) had no mathematical semantics, and it left open a number of important design questions, for example

(1)   Is it permissible to nest one parallel command inside another?

(2)   If so, is it possible to write a recursive procedure which calls itself in parallel?

(3)   Is it theoretically possible to use output commands in guards?

The mathematical model given in this book answers "yes" to all these questions.

7.4.1 A calculus of communicating systems

The major breakthrough in the mathematical modelling of concurrency was made by Robin Milner. The objective of his investigation was to provide a framework for constructing and comparing different models, at different levels of abstraction. So he starts with the basic syntax of expressions intended to denote processes, and he defines a series of equivalences between the expressions, of which the most important are

strong equivalence
observational equivalence
observational congruence

Each equivalence defines a different model of concurrency. The initials CCS usually refer to the model obtained by adopting observational congruence as the definition of equality between processes.

The basic notations of CCS are illustrated by the following correspondences

$a.P$ corresponds to $a{\to}P$

$(a.P)+(b.Q)$ corresponds to $(a{\to}P\,|\,b{\to}Q)$

NIL corresponds to $STOP$

More important than these notational distinctions are differences in the treatment of hiding. In CCS, there is a special symbol τ which stands for the occurrence of a hidden event or an internal transition. The advantage of retaining this vestigial record of a hidden event is that it can be freely used to guard recursive equations and so ensure that they have unique solutions, as described in Section 2.8.3. A second (but perhaps less significant) advantage is that processes which can engage in an unbounded sequence of τs do not all reduce to $CHAOS$; so possibly useful distinctions can be drawn between divergent processes. However, CCS fails to distinguish a possibly divergent process from one that is similar in behaviour but nondivergent. I expect this would make efficient implementation of the full CCS language impossible.

CCS does not include $\sqcap$ as a primitive operator. However, nondeterminism can be modelled by use of τ, for example

$(\tau.P)+(\tau.Q)$ corresponds to $P \sqcap Q$

$(\tau.P)+(a.Q)$ corresponds to $P \sqcap (P \,[]\, (a{\to}Q))$

But these correspondences are not exact, because in CCS nondeterminism defined by τ would not be associative, as shown by the fact that the trees in Fig. 7.3 are distinct

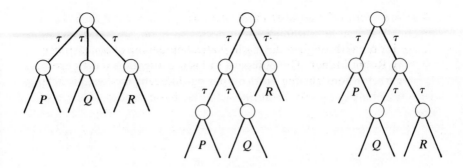

Figure 7.3

Furthermore, prefixing does not distribute through nondeterminism, because the trees in Fig. 7.4 are distinct when $P \neq Q$

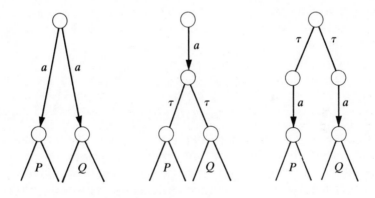

Figure 7.4

These examples show that CCS makes many distinctions between processes which would be regarded as identical in this book. The reason for this is that CCS is intended to serve as a framework for a family of models, each of which may make more identifications than CCS but cannot make less. To avoid restricting the range of models, CCS makes only those identifications which seem absolutely essential. In the mathematical model of this book we have pursued exactly the opposite goal—we have made as many identifications as possible, preserving only the most essential distinctions. We have therefore a far richer set of algebraic laws. It is hoped that these laws will be practically useful in reasoning about designs and implementations; in particular, they permit more transformations and optimizations than CCS.

The basic concurrent combinator of CCS is denoted by the single bar $|$. It is rather more complicated than the $\parallel$ combinator, in that it includes aspects of hiding, nondeterminism and interleaving as well as synchronization.

Each event in CCS has two forms, either simple (a) or overbarred $(\bar{a})$. When two processes are put together to run concurrently, synchronization occurs only when one process engages in a barred event and the other process engages in the corresponding simple event. Their joint participation in such an event is hidden by immediate conversion to τ. However, synchronization is not compulsory; each of the two events can also occur visibly and independently as an interaction with the outer environment. Thus in CCS

$$(a.P)\,|\,(b.Q) = a.(P\,|\,(b.Q))+b.((a.P)\,|\,Q)$$
$$(a.P)\,|\,(a.Q) = a.(P\,|\,(a.Q))+a.((a.P)\,|\,Q)$$
$$(a.P)\,|\,(\bar{a}.Q) = \tau.(P\,|\,Q)+a.(P\,|\,(\bar{a}.Q))+\bar{a}.((a.P)\,|\,Q)$$

Consequently, only two processes can engage in a synchronization event; if more than two processes are ready, the choice of which pair succeeds is nondeterministic

$$\begin{aligned}(a.P)\,|\,(a.Q)\,|\,(\bar{a}.R) = {}&\tau.(P\,|\,(a.Q)\,|\,R)+\tau.((a.P)\,|\,Q\,|\,R)\\
&+a.(P\,|\,(a.Q)\,|\,(\bar{a}.R))\\
&+a.((a.P)\,|\,Q\,|\,(\bar{a}.R))\\
&+\bar{a}.((a.P)\,|\,(a.Q)\,|\,R)\end{aligned}$$

Because of the extra complexity of the parallel operator, there is no need for a concealment operator. Instead there is a *restriction* operator $\backslash$, which simply prevents all occurrence of the relevant events, and removes them from the alphabet of the process, together with their overbarred variant. The effect is illustrated by the following laws of CCS

$$\begin{aligned}(a.P)\backslash\{a\} \qquad &= (\bar{a}.P)\backslash\{a\} \qquad\qquad = NIL\\
(P+Q)\backslash\{a\} \qquad &= (P\backslash\{a\})+(Q\backslash\{a\})\\
((a.P)\,|\,(\bar{a}.Q))\backslash\{a\} \quad &= \tau.((P\,|\,Q)\backslash\{a\})\\
((a.P)\,|\,(a.Q)\,|\,(\bar{a}.R))\backslash\{a\} &= \tau.((P\,|\,(a.Q)\,|\,R)\backslash\{a\})\\
&\quad+\tau.(((a.P)\,|\,Q\,|\,R)\backslash\{a\})\end{aligned}$$

The last law above illustrates the power of the CCS parallel combinator in achieving the effect of sharing the process $(\bar{a}.R)$ among two using processes $(a.P)$ and $(a.Q)$. It was an objective of CCS to achieve the maximum expressive power with as few distinct primitive operators as possible. This is the source of the elegance and power of CCS, and greatly simplifies the investigation of families of models defined by different equivalence relations.

In this book, I have taken a complementary approach. Simplicity is sought through design of a single simple model, in terms of which it is easy to define as many operators as seem appropriate to investigate a range of distinct concepts. For example, the nondeterministic choice $\sqcap$ introduces nondeterminism in its purest form, and is quite independent of environmental choice represented by $(x:B{\rightarrow}P(x))$. Similarly, $\parallel$ introduces concurrency and synchronization, quite independent of nondeterminism or hiding, each of which is represented by a distinct operator. The fact that the corresponding concepts are distinct is perhaps indicated by the simplicity of the algebraic laws. A reasonably wide range of operators seems to be needed in practical application of useful mathematical theories. Minimization of operator sets is also useful, more especially in theoretical investigations.

Milner has introduced a form of modal logic to specify the observable behaviour of a process. The modality

 S

describes a process which may do a and then behave as described by S, and the dual

$\boxed{a}\ S$

describes a process that if it starts with a must behave like S afterwards. A calculus of correctness is defined which permits a proof that a process P meets specification S, a fact which is expressed in the traditional logical notation

$P \models S$

The calculus is very different from that governing the **sat** relation, because it is based on the structure of the specification rather than the structure of the programs. For example, the rule for negation is

If it is *not* true that $P \models F$
then $P \models \neg F$

This means that the whole process P must be written before the proof of its correctness starts. In contrast, the use of **sat** permits proof of the correctness of a compound process to be constructed from a proof of correctness of its parts. Furthermore, there is never a need to prove that a process does *not* satisfy its specification. Modal logic is a subject of great theoretical interest, but in the context of communicating processes it does not yet show much promise for useful application.

In general, equality in CCS is a strong relation, since equal processes must resemble each other both in their observable behaviour and in the structure of their hidden behaviour. CCS is therefore a good model for formulating and exploring various weaker definitions of equivalence, which ignore more aspects of the hidden behaviour. Milner accomplished this by introducing the concept of observational equivalence. This involves definition of the set of observations or experiments that may be made on a process; then two processes are equivalent if there is no observation that can be made of one of them but not the other—a nice application of the philosophical principle of the identity of indiscernibles. The principle was taken as the basis of the mathematical theory in this book, which equates a process with the set of observations that can be made of its behaviour. A sign of the success of the principle is that two processes P and Q are equivalent if and only if they satisfy the same specifications

$$\forall S. \ P \models S \equiv Q \models S$$

Unfortunately, it doesn't always work as simply as this. If two processes are to be regarded as equal, the result of transforming them by the same function should also be equal, i.e.,

$$(P \equiv Q) \Rightarrow (F(P) \equiv F(Q))$$

Since τ is supposed to be hidden, a natural definition of an observation would lead to the equivalence

$$(\tau.P) \equiv P$$

However $(\tau.P + \tau.NIL)$ should not be equivalent to $(P + NIL)$, which equals P, since the former can make a nondeterministic choice to deadlock instead of behaving like P.

Milner's solution to this problem is to use the concept of *congruence* in place of equivalence. Among the experiments which can be performed on the process P is to place it in an environment $F(P)$ (where F is composed of other processes by means of operators of the language), and then to observe the behaviour of this assembly. Processes P and Q are (observationally) congruent if for every F expressible in the language the process $F(P)$ is observationally equivalent to $F(Q)$. According to this definition $\tau.P$ is not congruent to P. The discovery of a full set of laws of congruence is a significant mathematical achievement.

The need for the extra complexity of observational congruence is due to the inability to make sufficiently penetrating observations of the behaviour of P, without placing it in an environment $F(P)$. That is why we have had to introduce the concept of a refusal *set*, rather than just a refusal of a single event. The refusal set seems to be the weakest kind of observation that efficiently represents the possibility of nondeterministic deadlock; and it therefore leads to a much weaker equivalence, and to a more powerful set of algebraic laws than CCS.

The description given above has overemphasized the differences of CCS, and has overstated the case for practical application of the approach taken in this book. The two approaches share their most important characteristic, namely a sound mathematical basis for reasoning about specifications, designs and implementations; and either of them can be used for both theoretical investigations and for practical applications.

SELECT BIBLIOGRAPHY

Conway, M.E.   'Design of a Separable Transition-Diagram Compiler,'
                Comm. ACM **6** (7), 8–15 (1983)
                The classical paper on coroutines.

Hoare, C.A.R.   'Monitors: An Operating System Structuring Con-
                cept,' *Comm. ACM* **17** (10), 549–557 (1974)
                A programming language feature to aid in construction
                of operating systems.

Hoare, C.A.R.   'Communicating Sequential Processes,' *Comm. ACM*
                21 (8), 666–677 (1978)
                A programming language design—an early version of
                the design propounded in this book.

Milner, R.   *A Calculus of Communicating Systems*, Lecture Notes
                in Computer Science 92, Springer Verlag, New York
                (1980)
                A clear mathematical treatment of the general theory
                of concurrency and synchronization.

Kahn, G.   'The Semantics of a simple language for Parallel Pro-
                gramming,' in *Information Processing*, 74, North Hol-
                land, Amsterdam pp.471–475 (1974)
                An elegant treatment of functional multiprogramming.

Welsh, J. and   *Structured System Programming*, Prentice-Hall,
McKeag, R.M.   London, pp. 324 (1980)
                       An account of PASCAL PLUS and its use in structur-
                       ing an operating system and compiler.

Filman, R.E. and   *Coordinated Computing, Tools and Techniques for
Friedman, D.P.   Distributed Software*, McGraw-Hill pp.370 (1984)
                       A useful survey and further bibliography.

Dahl, O-J.   'Hierarchical Program Structures,' in *Structured Pro-
                       gramming*, Academic Press, London pp.175–220
                       (1982)
                       An introduction to the influential ideas of SIMULA
                       67.

(INMOS Ltd.)   *occam*^{TM} *Programming Manual* Prentice-Hall Inter-
                       national, pp.100 (1984).

(ANSI/MIL-STD   *Ada*^{TM} *Reference Manual*
1815A)   Chapter 9 describes the tasking feature.

Brookes, S.D.,   'A Theory of Communicating Sequential Processes,'
Hoare, C.A.R.   *Journal ACM* **31** (7), 560–599 (1984)
and Roscoe, A.W.   An account of the mathematics of nondeterministic
                       processes, but excluding divergences.

Brookes, S.D. and   'An Improved Failures Model for Communicating
Roscoe, A.W.   Sequential Processes,' in *Proceedings NSF-SERC
                       Seminar on Concurrency*, Springer Verlag, New York,
                       Lecture Notes in Computer Science (1985)
                       The improvement is the addition of divergences.

INDEX